D0046649

WORKING SEX

I wrote this book. It's about sex. You bought this book. You had a pretty good idea what it was about, judging from the title. We just had a transaction based on sex and money. Let's get that straight right from the beginning.

This will be important later on.

WORKING SEX

SEX

An Odyssey Into
Our Cultural Underworld

Marianne Macy

Carroll & Graf Publishers, Inc.
New York

Copyright © 1996 by Marianne Macy

All rights reserved

First edition 1996

Second printing, October 1996

Carroll & Graf Publishers, Inc.
260 Fifth Avenue
New York, NY 10001

ISBN 0-7867-0249-4

Library of Congress Cataloguing-in-Publication Data is available

Manufactured in the United States of America

Acknowledgments

It would have been impossible to do this book without the support of the following people. Thanks to:

All the Macys and extended family;

Stefan Kanfer, Tom Bentkowski, Gary Fossieck, Larry Levine and Beldock, Levine & Hoffman, Naomi Wallace, Eddie Gorodetski, Penn Jillette and Teller, Rob Pike, Colin Summers, Joe Lagani, Stephen J. Dubner, Julie Perez, James Hamilton, Sam Brylawski, Jim Abrahamson, Tessa Jarrett, Jerri Nunn, Steve Savage, David Kerr and Leslie Mason, Guy Spencer, Adam Turtletaub, Isaac Thorp, Peter Gethers, and Ed Kosner;

My publishers, Kent Carroll, Herman Graf, and their fine staff;

Everybody in the book.

Contents

Introduction   *ix*

1. *Sex and Escorts: The Beginning*   *3*

2. *Sex and the Person You Love Most*   *13*

3. *Working Sex: A Porn of Her Own*   *31*

4. *Sex and Strippers*   *91*

5. *Sex and D&S*   *143*

6. *Sex and Transsexualism: Sexual Dysphoria and Societal Dysphoria*   *201*

7. *Sex and Escorts: The End*   *241*

Afterword   *275*

Suggested Reading   *277*

Index   *281*

Introduction

In 1990, I was freelancing as a magazine writer in New York. What became this book started as a story on escort services for *New York* magazine. My assignment was to work undercover posing as a woman who wanted to become an escort. Did the job merely involve dining and dancing, as the advertisements said, or was there more to it? For a period of weeks I would dress up, fix my hair and makeup, and go to the different apartments and office buildings in New York City from which young women were dispatched to men who called for them. In between sending out the escorts, the people who booked the calls—"Alright, Mr.——. You would like a blond? Measurements? Type? How about . . ." would look me over to see if I was pretty or sexy enough to hire. As much as possible, I talked to the escorts or bookers and managers running each place.

It was an incredible experience. Even now, five years later, a close friend reminded me how shocked she was when someone in her office put on her desk the issue of *New York* magazine with a cover that read: *Escort: What I Learned Job-Hunting in the World of Sex For Sale.* The person who gave her the magazine had recognized my name from phone messages, and asked if she knew I was working on this story. "My own family didn't know," I told her. It was eye-opening, those secret weeks of stepping into a new world. It gave me a sense of kinship with the escorts, who had to hide their work from society. But that world was their day-to-day reality. It was their work.

Many people have asked me questions about my experiences. What was it like working as an escort? Were some escort services better than others? Should prostitution be legalized? Did *women* ever hire *men* for sex?

This book gave me an an opportunity to investigate the questions and assumptions that continue to come up about sex workers: Are they on drugs, depressed, from broken homes or sexually abused as children, self-destructive if not downright suicidal? Was their work a job? Was it an adventure? What about economics? There are many theories about people who work in sex. It's a subject that elicits passionately opinionated responses. But this book is about the people who actually *do* the work, not just talk about it. I spent five years documenting, talking to, and following around people who make their living from sex.

The escort story made me reexamine my ideas about people who sold sex. It's odd to do something that by most people's standards is a success—a bestselling national magazine cover story, TV movie deal, television job offers—and then find out that the people you wrote about thought you screwed up.

I tried to fill in the gaps to present a bigger picture, talking to other people whose work involved sex. Exotic dancers. A masturbation teacher. A transsexual who did role-play sessions for clients with gender ambivalence. People who made pornography, erotic films, and sexually explicit instructional videos, and the people who sold them. Professional practitioners of domination and submission. Ph.Ds. and other people who worked in the medical, psychological, and sexological sciences.

While I worked on this book, many of the working sex people began to meet those in social science organizations. In the early 1990s, sex workers were going to conferences and making presentations, answering questions. These first tentative meetings of academics (including therapists and medical doctors) and practitioners revealed the gap between people who dealt with theories about sex more often than they dealt with people who actually had sex.

I was amazed at how many doctors and therapists had never met a dominatrix, a transsexual, or talked with someone who made porn. These were the people who advertised themselves to the general public as experts on the human psyche, especially sexuality. How could they counsel and explain without firsthand experience? Many sexological and psychological organizations realized this dichotomy, and invited professional sex practitioners whom you'll meet in these pages to speak at their meetings. It was a start. Watching professional sex workers educating academically credentialed social and medical scientists was a fascinating process to observe.

The sex industry is a multibillion dollar business that is a ubiquitous part of our society. Perversely, it's also a disavowed part of our society.

Because of the barrier that insulates sex workers from academics, if the laity fears them and the public mistrusts them, a leap into their world may be the only way to discover some truth about these people.

I found that no blanket statement was appropriate. Everyone in this book challenged my preconceptions. The questions raised by their lives and work are complex. The decisions they make are highly individual. Their work has a great deal to teach us about sexual "norms," misunderstanding and ignorance about sexuality, even how conventional wisdom can ruin sex between people. The people in this book offered up their lives and work for documentation because they wanted the public to better understand what they do. This is a collective portrait; who they are, what they actually do, what they're really like, what they want us to know. That's what drew me to this subject and kept me involved. The people in this book all had a remarkable openness. All of them used this openness to relate to the most sensitive area of other people's lives. Working sex involves hope and fantasy as well as any physical requirements.

In these pages you'll accompany me on a journey. You will hear about the danger faced and social stigmas battled. But you will also hear about *why* people choose to make a living through sex, and what they like as well as abhor about it.

Sex industry people want to avoid "protection" from "exploitation" on one flank—"Please don't make any laws to 'protect' us," porn star Veronica Vera implored a congressional commission on pornography. "Leave us our precious right to choose!" On another flank, they face condemnation from much of society.

Why was it that some people who sold sex, the mainstream media, for example, were considered respectable, while others (sex workers who appeared in mainstream magazines' articles about them, usually under coverlines guaranteed to pull in readers due to the sensational! sexual! nature of the story) weren't? Subject and medium were as directly connected as if they were on opposite sides of a mirror, but one was sanctioned and the other wasn't. How did that split work? Why did the split occur?

The literary critic Leslie Fiedler wrote a book called *Freaks: Myths and Images of the Secret Self*, in which he pointed out that society has always designated a section of the population to stand for what people were most fascinated by, attracted to, and afraid of in themselves. As an influential alternative rock group, The Residents, put it, "Everyone laughs when they come to the freak show, but nobody laughs when they leave."

We wouldn't have a sex industry if there wasn't a market for it, but what fascinated me was how disavowed that connection was. Why? It was as if there were things we weren't supposed to see.

> *"The true Freak stirs both supernatural terror and natural sympathy, since, unlike the fabulous monsters, he is one of us, the human child of human parents, however altered by forces we do not quite understand into something mythic and mysterious. . . . Only the true Freak challenges the conventional boundaries between male and female, sexed and sexless, self and other, and consequently between reality and illusion, experience and fantasy, fact and myth."*
> —Leslie Fiedler, *Freaks: Myths and Images of the Secret Self*

In *Working Sex*, we'll look at how these ideas color professional sex, and how the people who do this work recognize this and try to get beyond mythological, limited versions of what men, women, and sex are.

The people profiled in this book generally trusted their own perceptions. "If I was feeling this, I was sure other people had felt it too," was a statement I heard again and again. They wouldn't accept their assigned status as freaks, or if they did, they used those archetypes and myths for their own purposes.

In "Sex and Strippers," a couple demonstrate the personas they'd employ to garner responses from their audiences. Those roles change for different audiences, different sexes, different sexual orientations. Dianah and Kirk were two young strippers who met and fell in love. Their story reveals the pressures of the business, and how those pressures worked against their relationship. Stripping is a business with disparate rewards for men and women, and following their story can help us see why. What works in sex work? These are the people to ask.

In "Sex and the Person You Love Most," you'll meet Betty Dodson, who since the 1970s has helped women to explore their orgasmic potential by conducting workshops in which she teaches masturbation. When I first heard of Dodson's work, I couldn't believe it. This woman taught *what* to paying customers? This was the one area in which I had some experience. What I didn't realize was how much she had to teach me, not just about sexual response but how it was conditioned. I saw why Betty Dodson had made a living teaching women basic concepts about their own sexuality.

"Working Sex: A Porn of Her Own" follows Candida Royalle, who from the mid 1970s through the early '80s starred in porn films made by men and for men. She wondered why women's eroticism wasn't represented in pornography, and set out to create her own company, Femme, which makes erotic films for women and couples. What was it like being a porn star in a business that was defined by men? What was it about the work she believed needed to be challenged? What do her films, then and now, have to teach us about our evolving understanding of sex, sex roles, and how they are depicted and communicated? Is the anticensorship, sex-positive work of Royalle and a broad spectrum of women, not just in the porn industry but in broadcasting, publishing, business, and science, a better alternative than that proposed by antipornography activists such as Catharine MacKinnon and Andrea Dworkin?

Other chapters visit other territories. "Sex and Transsexualism" looks at the very nature of sex roles through the eyes of people who wish to change their sex. It explores whether sexual identity and genitals are necessarily the same thing. Is the most important sexual organ the brain?

The people in this book offer sex services for a variety of needs. That's the common factor in all the jobs depicted here. People whose work involves sex have to think about sex on complex levels. It's a business about people, and people are not simple. If you're hesitant to identify with the feelings expressed by people in this book, well, keep an open mind. Appreciating these people helps us reconsider not just our attitudes about their work, but about sex in our society and our own lives.

WORKING SEX

1

Sex and Escorts: The Beginning

"What size are your breasts?" Dave asks.

"Excuse me?"

"Your breasts. Bra size. I gotta have your measurements. I need measurements and a physical description of you: weight, height, are you pretty/okay looking/not bad? Anything other than that I don't want to hear about. Don't waste my time; don't waste yours. I don't need to know your age so much as what age you could pass for."

—from "What I Learned Job-Hunting in
   The World of Sex For Sale"
   New York Magazine, June 18, 1990

The idea for the article was simple. Take a young woman, preferably attractive. Have her do undercover reporting by approaching escort services in the big city for a job. But she's not sure what the job entails, so she has to ask each place what's required. "Your Yellow Pages ad says, 'Dining and Dancing.' How much dining and dancing is there?"

Not much, it turned out. I went from place to place, where I was strip-searched and checked for unmarketable birthmarks or needle tracks. I would sit in living rooms in apartment buildings all over Manhattan with good-looking women who looked like young women I might meet anywhere. In a side room, bookers worked the calls flooding in. The reader got to follow along, to places like the Crown Club, Lt.d, where Susan, the hyper-energetic, attractive madam, told me about her place.

> "We charge by the hour, not the act, Marianne. Of course, if you please the clients, you'll be requested more and we'll send you out more." This makes her think of something and she swings her small foot determinedly. "One thing you cannot do is give the client your phone number and arrange to meet him privately. It'll happen all the time: They like you, they decide they want you. Don't even *think* about it. That's stealing, Marianne. It's as if I went into your purse right now and took your wallet out." I assure her the security they provide is too important to me; can she tell me more about that?
>
> She says she doesn't send girls outside Manhattan, and most clients are regulars. She checks out the men's addresses and phone numbers and uses beepers for time warnings. The girl calls her at the beginning and end of the session. Susan tells me that although closing time is 4 A.M, most nights she's there until 6 or 7 A.M., until all her brood are present and accounted for. "I'm Jewish; working for me is like having a Jewish mother. It'll drive you crazy, but I'm there caring about you. When I got into this business, I swore one thing: Nobody who works for me would ever be hurt."

"We need pull quotes for the captions. Any ideas?" asked my editor when we were closing the story above the din of computers, phones, and people rushing up and down the hall at *New York* magazine.

"Why don't you take this one from Susan at the Crown Club?" I suggested.

> "Sometimes I just can't satisfy them—everything's wrong," she sighs, lighting a cigarette. "Like, what do I do if somebody calls for a pair of big, luxurious gazongas and you're the only one here? God knows I'm not going to send you on that call, Marianne."

"Wow! You're a good sport! Let me run this by Ed." She hurried down the hall, and returned, shaking her head. "He said it's too much."

"How come it's not too much in the text?" I asked, curious. She didn't answer, busy extracting a quote about escort dates without sex being just "occasional gravy."

Was I scared? People asked. How could I not be? I didn't know where I was going, whom I'd meet, what was going on. I'd entered a world where you called on the phone to apply for a job and the first question you had to answer was about your bra size. But once I was in that world, it became a normal question. In the hidden world, things weren't hidden. They had to adapt their language and deportment to accommodate the "polite" society where they got their work . . .

". . . We are a social service, furnishing social exchange between adults," she says coolly. "This is our function, and we do it well. Of course, we are not so naive as to think that sex does not occur between our clients and escorts, but what can we do about that? These things happen between people. If I send a beautiful woman to a man for social reasons, well, he's a man, he'll respond as such. We have no control over such things. But we are strictly a social service, furnishing social companionship. What happens after that is beyond our control."

—Interviewer, at International Escorts

When I turned the first draft in, Ed Kosner, who was then editor-in-chief of the magazine, saw me in his office. He said I'd done a very good job. It was fast-paced and well-written and reported. He was sorry, but they couldn't run it. My editor, Deborah Harkins, who'd worked on the article intensely, could hardly look at me.

"Everything is from the point of view of the escorts and the women running the business," Ed said. "All your reporting casts it in a favorable light. The money's great, the hours are flexible, no mention of danger or what's bad about it. Woman are going to want to run out and do it."

"What if I interviewed a working escort outside the services?" I asked.

"How would you do that?" he asked.

"I'll take a hotel room, go there with a guy, have him request an escort, and then interview her. She'll be anonymous, safe, and away from the services."

Ed Kosner seemed surprised, but intrigued by the suggestion. He agreed.

*   *   *

I've said I was afraid, but I felt many things. I was fascinated by the people, how the industry worked, how the outside world reacted and judged. The assignment was a secret. I consider myself good at secrets, while not many people are.

My family didn't know. My friends didn't know. I remember speaking on the phone while putting on a garter belt, which I'd never worn before. Fastening the stocking involves twisting at the waist, keeping hold of a gossamer piece of silk on the back of your thigh while closing an eyehole catch over it, none of which you can see. "I sound funny? Really? No, not much is new. How are you doing?"

I became someone who lived at night, coming home at three A.M., and writing until dawn. A strange thing happened as a result of all this. No one knew where I was or what I was doing, and I had entered a world where the same was true of the people I was reporting on. I felt a kinship with them. It was as if I'd walked through the other side of a mirror. Image and reality were so closely connected. The clients were mainstream people. The services were operating out of middle-class apartment buildings, places I passed every day in New York.

And it was exciting. I feel uneasy saying this when I think of the real danger and economics involved for actual escorts compared to voyeuristic reporters, but I'd be lying if I denied it. Seeing their work was fascinating, and it was fiercely, hotly erotic. I've talked to escorts who say it's a job, you get sick of it. I've talked to escorts who find it continually stimulating and rewarding. Finally, I realized, it was surprisingly familiar.

I was not the only one who understood this. For weeks and months later, I was contacted or stopped by dozens of women, who told me they identified with the escorts.

There was much about the world of sex for sale that was like "the world." "I've been on more job interviews than not where I felt that the size of my breasts or my looks determined whether or not I got the job," confided one of the Hollywood producers who called to option the story. Recognitions reverberated: such as women being more valuable if they were younger (or could fake it), being evaluated on their body shape or hair color. These attitudes in the world of sex for sale were just more concentrated, easier to see there. Maybe that's why we tried to put so much distance between "us" and "them". It was easier than making those connections.

*   *   *

The escort, a blond woman in her twenties, froze, poised to scream, when she saw me in the corner of the room. She looked so shocked and frightened I felt terrible. I started talking like mad.

"You don't have to be afraid. You can leave right away if you want. We're reporters who are working on a story about escorts. We'll pay you for your time, the same as you'd make on a call. It's just talking, and it's your choice."

Recovering, she looked at me and the man I was with, a photographer I'd only recently met. I'd watched him open the door and seen her face register pleasure when she saw him. He was both handsome and sexy, and her hello was enthusiastic. We'd only been together for a few weeks, but in that moment a queer, quick feeling in my chest surprised me. Then she turned to enter the room. . . .

She walked over to the phone and picked it up. He and I looked at each other. It was our turn to be anxious.

"Hello? Yes, I'm here. Yes, everything's fine. Okay." She hung up. "We call in at the start of the hour, and they call at the end. I want a *really* good tip for this."

"She relies on pure instinct to help her decide, the minute the door is opened, if a call is okay. If she doesn't like what she sees, she makes an excuse and leaves. 'I guess you could say I'm snooty. I summarize people in one look.'

Kate likes late-night calls: 'More times than not, the guy is too drunk or drugged to have sex.' Party calls are very profitable, sometimes they go on from nine P.M. until noon the next day. . . .

. . . 'This guy who was freebasing cocaine flipped out on me. Started running around the room, thinking the Columbian government was out to get him. Things like that scare you. What if he takes out a gun and starts firing at the imaginary Colombian government and kills you by accident?' "

She told us about how important it was for the escort to be vigilant and know the business. Know the financial split when going out with a driver, because he's the one you hand the money to, she said, and you can get cheated. The booker was an important person to have on your side, "without her, you'll starve."

She kept her work life and her private life separate, with two sets of clothes in her closet. She thought an independent support system was essential. "I know my mother and my fiancé are in my life. The ones who don't have that think the people in this business are their people. It's like a self-destruction mechanism." It wasn't a Cinderella business, she cautioned. Forget about the fantasy of meeting a rich man who would take care of you "like some *Pretty Woman* bullshit."

The phone call came. She didn't have time to eat the sandwiches we got, but declined taking any with her. When the door closed we sagged back on the bed.

"She was great," he said. "I think you got what you were looking for."

I nodded weakly. The little vein in my eyelid that twitches when I'm stressed tossed like an ocean. "I think so. She was."

*   *   *

The magazine wanted to have numerous people commenting on escorts. Isaac Thorp was leaving the sex crimes division of the Brooklyn DA's office to escape from New York and move to North Carolina. Years of dealing with rape and abuse cases had done it for him. He told *New York* magazine readers that the city was so overwhelmed with violence that struggling to alleviate it had to be the priority, not wiping out consensual sex between adults. "You'd *laugh* if someone said, 'I'm trying so-and-so for prostitution.'"

A psychiatrist and professor from the University of California named Harold Greenwald, who had written a book on call girls, said he thought they felt inadequate, getting paid for lovemaking made up for parental rejection. He thought the clients saw them as depreciated women, someone they could feel superior to, and that the majority of escorts he'd treated were suicidal.

Lieutenant Willam Bayer, the senior officer on the famous Mayflower Madame case, the only escort service ever busted for prostitution, claimed that this had only happened because Sydney Biddle Barrow's business had drawn complaints from the neighbors. Bayer pointed out that the escort services business was a victimless crime and the public didn't want their tax dollars wasted on pursuing it.

When the reporting was finished and the copy was in hand, the story needed to be packaged. When they asked if I'd pose for the cover of the magazine, I didn't know what to think. I wanted to do more undercover pieces, and being on the cover of *New York* magazine might have made that impossible. I suggested using the Yellow Page ads as the illustration and asked why they needed me.

"People are going to read this and want to know who the person was who did this," answered Ed Kosner.

"Why must it take five hours to shoot a cover photograph?" I asked my art director friend Tom when I staggered back from Soho. "Just the makeup took nearly an hour. I looked as if I'd had eight hours of sleep every night for the past decade. I didn't look like a freelance writer."

"That's nothing," Tom trumped. "We had to do a Priscilla Presley spread last month. Four hours makeup, six hours studio. Image is a serious affair."

Indeed it was. They did more than a cover photograph, I discovered the day "Escort: What I Learned Job-Hunting In the World of Sex For Sale," hit the stands. They used the reporter-in-black-cocktail-dress-motif, a takeoff on Sydney Biddle Barrow's "Mayflower Madame" image, on five pages, not including the cover. Fortunately I'd prepared my family twenty-four hours before.

"You did what?" my mother asked.

"What did you think they'd put on the cover of that magazine," my father tried to console her. "How I Learned to Sew from Aunt Tilly?"

It had taken four years of temp jobs and odd jobs to support my freelance writing aspirations. This article changed everything. I was suddenly fielding network news job offers, movie producers, and a phone that never seemed to stop ringing. My favorite was when women I'd done temp jobs with sent me photocopies of their bosses' expense accounts with the cover companies of the escort services circled.

The Hollywood producers started calling at nine A.M. Monday morning, the day the magazine hit the newsstands, which was six A.M. California time. I figured out that East Coast magazines inform their producer friends ahead of time that something notable is coming down the pike. The television shows called, everyone from *Good Morning America* through *Joan Rivers*. After the first few days when my phone exploded either with everyone I ever knew or everyone who suddenly wanted to know me, *New York* was kind enough to let me out of the clause in my contract that said I'd do media appearances. We didn't need to. The magazine sold more copies than any other magazine that year. I wasn't prepared to handle the reaction.

Fortunately I had friends who gave me perspective. There was Eddie, who'd headed the comedy channel when it started, and had written for every late night show that featured funny people and rock bands, but whose true pride in life came from being a great kisser.

"Producers are like Mynah birds," Eddie cautioned. "They see something bright and shiny. They fly over and pick it up with their beaks and then drop it for the next shiny thing. Don't get bent out of shape."

My friend Gregory, who had cowritten a script for the hit movie *FX*, wanted to write the screenplay for *Escort*. He suggested a few changes. "It's about this escort, and she wants to see what writing for magazines is like. She goes to all the magazines, runs the gamut, *People* to *Atlantic Monthly*, the *New Yorker*, you name it. But in the end . . . she doesn't write anything!"

My sister, who worked on Wall Street, gave me a stack of business cards that senior executives of firms she dealt with had given her, instructing, "Tell Marianne how much money I make." Famous people called to ask me out. People stopped me on the street. Every day it got more . . . bizarre.

There was one group of people who didn't like me. Escorts.

*   *   *

The calls started coming in the first night. "You uptight bitch! We consider this a profitable way to make a living! Fuck you!"

"Hi, Marianne. I'm Cathy, escort for eight years. I liked your story, but I don't believe you thought enough about why someone would choose to do this. I'd like to talk to you about it. Here's my number. . . ."

"Marianne, I'm looking at your picture with that nice strapless dress crossing your shoulders. I keep reading the part where your naked body is examined under the lamp. I have my pants off and I'm uhhhhhh, uhhhhhhhh. . . ."

"My name is Charles. I'm a businessman who travels so much it trashes every relationship I get into. I appreciate and treat call girls well. If it wasn't for them, I'd never get laid. Well, I mean, I would, but let's face it, my lifestyle isn't fair to girlfriends. This works for me. I don't look down on escorts. I just wanted you to know."

I had to get an unlisted phone number. Meanwhile, I was getting an education in how to view sex for sale by the conflicting reactions that were coming in. The testimonies I was getting challenged pat psychological and moral answers. Were call girls suicidal or did they just have an ability to compartmentalize? What about the economic questions about jobs that were available to women and how lousy the money was compared to escorting? What about societal stigmas and individual choice? I realized I needed to do more work.

*   *   *

"A group called PONY (Prostitutes of New York) wrote, saying we didn't represent their point of view. They're upset we ran the comments of the psychiatrist claiming that escorts were suicidal. They say their organization exists to fight such stereotypes and push for legalization of prostitution. They want us to interview them."

"I think we should," I said to my editor Deborah, back in her computer-crammed cranny at *New York.* "I've been deluged with calls like that from people in the business. They may have something worth listening to."

I'd come to pick up mail and had just heard the thing had outsold every issue of any magazine that year. If the subject was so fascinating to people, why didn't we do more? Why didn't we do it from the point of view of people in the business, I asked now.

"People who want to legalize prostitution! PONY! Oh, come on, Marianne! Now you want to support sex for sale?"

I looked at a stack of magazines with my own image under a blazing sexy coverline. What did they think we were selling?

* * *

"And what we want is for you to re-create your undercover story, only this time, for television," said the network newsmagazine producer. "We'll follow you with hidden cameras. We'll capture the whole thing. The danger you faced. . . ."

"The people in the escort services themselves aren't dangerous. They weren't a threat," I said, knowing by now I might as well be speaking Swahili. What a bizarre turnaround. Instead of focusing on humanizing the women in the business, thinking about the economic context of their choices, many of the shows reacted as if I was intrepid for going undercover with these scary people. They were just women like me who had a different job. I tried to tell him, "The biggest danger I faced was potential electrocution from loyal *New York* readers masturbating on their phones."

The guy didn't miss a beat. "Do you look like that in real life? Was that really you in those pictures?"

Three weeks after the "Escort" story ran, I cut my hair off, which had the immediate effect of stopping people from recognizing me. It was an emotional reaction. I wanted to go undercover again, in my own life, undisturbed. But the one thing I couldn't do was to stop thinking, or continuing to talk to people about sex for sale. And then the conversation expanded into my entire life. It just kept going.

2

Sex and the Person You Love Most

Betty Dodson teaches masturbation. She's internationally known, and since 1973 has conducted her Bodysex Workshops, where women pay to join a group of other women, get naked, and follow Dodson's instructions on onanism.

When I first heard of her, I had trouble understanding the nature of her work. Secretly, my attitude was, I suppose this is a good thing for repressed women, but for me personally. . . . Well, I may not know much, but this is one thing I *do* know how to do. Still, I was impressed by the intensity with which people urged me to meet Dodson. If I was writing a book about people whose work was sex, she was one person I should not miss. Betty is more than a one-woman institution, they said. She's . . . her *own concept*. You know she's doing something right if she's been able to make a living and be acclaimed as a visionary for a quarter of a century, via . . . masturbation.

If they ever publish a "Great People In Sex" coffee table book, Betty Dodson will be in it. She's been documented by many different journalists, among them, Gay Talese in *Thy Neighbor's Wife*, who wrote about her work, her erotic art shows in the 1960s and 70s, and her presence at the Sandstone sexual utopian community in California.

In *Vogue* magazine in 1980, Amy Gross, now editor-in-chief of *Mirabella*, writing about Talese writing about Dodson, described Betty

Dodson as "a woman who has appalled me for years." Gross was also
appalled that Talese devoted nine pages to Dodson and her

> "seminars for women in which everyone lies about scrutinizing one
> another's genitals (I'll spare you, and me, the details). I have never
> been in such a rush to get out of a chapter! Betty Dodson as the voice
> of feminist sexuality! Betty Dodson, the only woman who puts as
> much stock in her physical genitalia as the typical American teenage
> boy!"

It is unclear as to whether Ms. Gross was saying that the assembled
company lay about the floor scrutinizing each other's genitals, or if she
meant to suggest they dissembled, told untruths related to actual scrutinizing of the genitals. Her meaning thus obfuscated, it is difficult to
comprehend what appalls her. As for her last comment about Betty
Dodson putting stock in her genitalia, that was exactly what the workshops were about.

Then there was Germaine Greer on Betty Dodson, writing for *Marie
Claire* in 1990. Germaine Greer, of the sexually assertive school of
feminist writing, proved to be less than generous where sexual soul
sister Dodson was concerned. In the *Marie Claire* article, Greer wrote
historically about masturbation, finding references to midwives in the
1500s helping massage "womb-furie," dildos that date to the Romans,
and a 1686 vogue in England's royal court for an Italian import, "Signor
Dildo." Greer said this sort of thing was cyclical: "The truth about
masturbation is that it rapidly becomes boring." Well, speak for yourself, Germaine.

Still, Greer thinks there's a middle ground between one point: "It's
absurd to be deeply ashamed of masturbation" and another: "It is no
less absurd to be proud of masturbating."

"To become a career masturbator, like Betty Dodson, is to spend
your intellectual and spiritual powers on vacancy," wrote Greer. "Masturbation is like housework; doing it once only leads to doing it again.
It is an exercise in futility, unless, like Betty Dodson, you invest it with
displaced significance, by calling it liberation and praising the masturbating woman as truly independent."

And Germaine Greer, the 1970s author of "Lady, Love Your Cunt,"
concluded by asking, "Whatever became of dignity? And passion, what
of it?"

While I researched this story, interviewed Dodson and people who'd attended her workshops, the one constant was the strong reaction Dodson invoked. It helped me understand *my* reactions to her.

Betty Dodson, responding to Greer's article by letter, proposed a duel between "two post-menopausal feminists who have fought the good fight for the last twenty years. One attacks the other's concept of the importance of liberating masturbation. She says it's boring like housework. The accused whips out her electric vibrator and throws a switch, saying it's thrilling and creative. With broad humor, it might make a great movie, but a thoughtful magazine article, never."

Dodson went on to point out that many things were repetitious but not necessarily futile, including getting out of bed in the morning. Who appointed Greer Supreme Judge of what qualifies as "significant" in women's lives? Dodson inquired. She also pointed out that Greer's article had declared that vibrator sales had peaked in the 1970s, whereas at Eve's Garden sexual boutique in New York, sales had increased 300 percent in the past twenty years. Even Dr. Ruth had introduced her own model, the Eroscolator.

In spite of Greer's vicious attack, Dodson had added, she'd never forget the inspiration Germaine Greer's early writing had given her, especially *The Female Eunuch.*

"Feminists who hate sex as they grow older alienate younger women who want to understand their sexuality," Betty Dodson concluded. "And attacking another feminist's lifework is to end a dialogue before it begins. We women must learn to disagree and support one another as we continue to search for equality, especially in the areas of our sexuality."

AVOIDING BLINDNESS

"They thought I was a joke, Marianne, the best dirty joke on the planet," Betty Dodson sighed. It was a Saturday afternoon, and we sat talking in the comfort of her New York living room where she hosts her workshops. The room is devoid of furniture, is carpeted wall to wall, and offers lots of mirrors and pillows. It's a snowy white space that looks out high over Manhattan. The design is to help people relax. I'd been here before, for meetings and earlier interviews with Betty. I'd seen her movie, *Sex For One.* This room has housed years of meditation, masturbation, groups seeking to discover another part of themselves, and private clients, men and women alike. If you believe places can be repositories for the energy that's passed through them, you might say there's a lot of good sex karma here. At the very least, you'd allow it's peaceful.

Betty imitated, "Didja hear that there's this woman who gets a bunch of other women together and they all masturbate in the nude— WAAAAAAAAHHHHHHH!"

She retraced some of the rocky road that she'd trod during thirty years as an expert on masturbation. Her press files show her to have established herself as a serious presence in the '60s sexual revolution. A 1969 *Time* magazine article mentions her during a tour of the current zeitgeist, citing such films such as *I Am Curious Yellow,* Andy Warhol's *Blue Movie* and Russ Meyer's *Vixen,* as well as theater pieces like *Hair, Oh, Calcutta,* and *Sweet Eros,* during the latter, *Time* observed, "Sally Kirkland, the latter day Isadora Duncan of nudothespianism, was tied naked to a chair." Betty Dodson made the grade as a "gifted, Paris-trained Manhattan artist," who used models "for her large-scale canvases of multiple coupling."

Speaking of those large-scale canvases, 8,000 people turned out for Dodson's 1968 exhibit at the Wickersham Gallery. To celebrate what they deemed the return of the Nude In Art, the gallery hired the models who had posed for Dodson to mingle with the guests.

The show was a raging success. One thing that struck Dodson was the amount of personal response her art sparked. "After hearing so many stories," she wrote later, "I discovered that nearly everyone was affected by socially imposed negative attitudes toward sex. Many of these sex histories dealt with unnecessary pain and suffering, often from simple lack of information."

At the same time, Betty Dodson was going through her own personal sexual reevaluation. At thirty-five, she was divorced, her marriage and sex life having died a painful death from lack of communication and outmoded sex roles. If she and her husband could have talked about it and worked on it, she would later observe, the marriage might have succeeded. But the pressure of who they thought they should be kept each of them locked in rigid behavior. Things fell apart. She would explore this theme in her work for years to come. Decades later, she ran into her ex-husband, who was still having performance problems. Betty offered to treat him professionally, as a client, but he refused.

After the divorce, she experimented with new lovers and getting to know her own body. She believed people had to know themselves sexually first, and that women especially needed to know they could please themselves rather than be dependent upon men. After her successful Wickersham show, she decided to incorporate this belief in her paintings.

Betty's next show depicted four nudes masturbating to orgasm. This time, instead of being hailed, people were horrified. Art showing couples having sex was groovy, a happening, fine, wild, the Age of Aquarius Incarnate. Art with people having sex with themselves was . . . weird! Worse, it was downright embarrassing. Betty Dodson had created art that provided a mirror of people's ambivalence about masturbation.

The Wickersham would no longer show her work. The media lost interest. Betty appreciated the significance of her rise and fall. She felt more adamant about her beliefs because of the reaction caused by her new work. "If you can inhibit a child from touching itself, that's control," she concluded. She felt that this control over sexuality was something women too easily handed over. She'd change that. It was her mission.

In 1971, the *Evergreen Review* published an article entitled, "The Fine Art of Lovemaking: An Interview With Betty Dodson." In the introduction, interviewer Mary Phillips wrote, "Betty Dodson has grounded her feminism in sexual terms that many women in the movement have not yet come to grips with. But she arrived at her insights through the same personal experiences, conflicts, and pain that all women have known at some level just by living their lives." The text was beautifully laid out between prints of Dodson's erotic art, which framed her complex discussion of politics, sexuality, and self-exploration.

Ms. magazine had held on to an original draft of Dodson's first major exploration of her subject, entitled, "Liberating Masturbation" for *two and a half years* before running it in August 1974. *Ms.* feared losing subscribers, but readers felt differently. "I got an enormous response from women through the magazine, which seemed to make the editors even angrier," she recalled. "I was never invited back for anything again." But she was thrown into the spotlight of the women's community. Betty Dodson found her work developing as more and more women came to her.

In the 1970s, she responded to the thousands of letters she received from women begging for information about masturbation by mailing out photocopies of the *Ms.* piece. *Evergreen Review* was published by Barney Rosset, who ran the successful publishing house Grove Press. I asked Betty why she didn't try to publish her work through them, rather than sending out thousands of photocopies. "You could have been wealthy," I said.

"I didn't think in those terms then," she responded. "It was a time of great political commitment and inspiration and my thought was just to get the information out there for women. It was years before I conceived of what I was doing as a business."

Also in the early 1970s she was invited to speak to the New York Psychiatric Association. "I talked about women not knowing what their genitals looked like. They thought they were nasty and ugly and smelly. I drew a cunt on the blackboard and ten psychiatrists got up and walked out, they were so offended. I was radical, brazen, and did not couch my language at all. Dr. Ruth told me that she was there when I showed my cunt slides to this organization and the doctor who was sitting next to her nearly fell off his seat."

"Did you speak with Dr. Ruth again?" I asked.

"She asked if she could use my drawings on her show," Betty answered. "I asked why didn't she have *me* on. She said she needed someone with credentials!"

Dodson exhibited her erotic art on the West Coast, and its popularity led to her running sexuality workshops there. What Georgia O'Keefe had suggested with her flowers, Dodson blatantly celebrated. It's a complimentary difference to contemplate. To look at an O'Keefe painting, the viewer thinks, how beautiful . . . that flower looks like a woman's genitals. And Dodson's? Why, that painting of a woman's genitals looks like a flower.

In Betty Dodson's *Sex For One, The Joy of Selfloving*, an informative book on masturbation that relates her own sexual evolution, she wrote about how, for most of her life, she'd believed her genitals were malformed, ugly. After she was divorced, she'd carried this belief with her until a lover discovered how she felt and was shocked. He showed her a stack of soft-core porn magazines with "split beaver" shots (where women held their genitals open to be photographed). Years of body loathing ended in the half hour she looked at the photographs and realized she was "normal." Far from the idea that "porn degrades women" Dodson's experience was that it could have an educational, positive function.

Until I'd seen Dodson's drawings, it had never really occurred to me that I hadn't seen many representations of women's genitals in art or media. Nudes, sure. Bodies wall to wall. The phallus? All over art museums. Women's genitals? Well, there was O'Keefe. And . . . I couldn't think of any others. The idea of female genitals being the subject of a painting, being viewed as a beautiful thing? Unusual in our culture.

Twenty women posed for intimate photos of their genitals in the 1970s as Dodson prepared a slide show and more paintings. None of them had ever had the experience of seeing themselves in such a range of colors, shapes, and styles. Dodson described them in her book: "A Baroque style with complex folds and drapery, a Gothic cunt with archways, and many Valentine Cunts. . . ." For the clitoris, "the variations were astounding—ranging from tiny little seed pearls to rather large protruding jewels." Colors of the folds of the vagina were different too. "Our colors ranged from pale pink to dark brown, and one woman had a two-tone cunt. Her inner lips were dark brown surrounded by a delicate peach. Another woman who had very dark brown genitals and black pubic hair said her lover called her 'The Black Orchid.' "

Betty Dodson showed her slides to 1,000 women at the 1973 National Organization of Women's Conference on Women's Sexuality, and when the lights came back on, there was a standing ovation. From that day to today, women still react with wonder when they attend her workshops, view her art, and see recent video projects.

In the 1980s, Dodson published the first version of her book *Liberating Masturbation*. It became a cult favorite, selling 150,000 copies, many of which she self-published and sent out by mail. Since 1986, *Sex For One: The Joy of Selfloving*, as the revised edition is now called, has become a bestselling title, with nearly a quarter of a million copies sold. Dodson produced a videotape of her workshops in 1990, which has sold 50,000 copies all over the world. The number of people who have seen it is probably much higher because she gets letters from people saying that a friend or family member sent them a copy. Dodson is producing a sequel with more information. "I was sixty years old when I did the first video," she explained. "Grey hair, little tubby body."

The first time I saw it, I thought, *she has guts*. The sight of a nude woman in her sixties who looks good and is demonstrably comfortable in her sexuality was something I'd never seen before. I began to understand why women gravitated to her and paid $200 to $300 for her workshops.

"People think that once you've broken through sexual repression and you are not longer restricted or limited by what people think, you're home free," Dodson said. "Unfortunately, it's not so." She described an incident at a business conference where people exhorted her to screen her video. She found it difficult, even agonizing, to sit and watch with them. Just because she'd spent thirty years being a sexual revolutionary didn't mean she wasn't susceptible to shyness or embarrassment. Her regret over showing the video was alleviated when a couple of days afterward members of the group called to express their appreciation.

"I deal with it constantly, the whole process," Dodson confessed to me. "Before every workshop I have sweat running down my arms." She thought about it for a minute, then shrugged. "I hope my life continues this way because if I don't challenge myself I'm not really living. When I leave this planet I want every part of me to be so used up that my clit is ready to drop off."

ON ONANISM

Some scattered facts about masturbation:

Masters and Johnson, in *Human Sexual Response*, tell us that not only is masturbation the most probable way for men and women to achieve an orgasm, it produces the most intense orgasm. Also that orgasm increases vascularity, which increases the potential of future orgasms.

In 1952, a doctor named Kegel discovered that his female patients who strengthened the Pobococcygens (pc for short) muscles by doing his exercises experienced an increase in their frequency of orgasm.

In *The New York Times* in 1987, Jane Brody reported that "the late Dr. Rene A. Spitz, a Denver psychoanalyst who studied young children, observed in 1962 that emotionally healthy infants whose mothers were close and caring were more likely to masturbate than those who had rejecting mothers or were orphaned. Dr. Spitz reasoned that the latter groups had failed to learn from their care-givers the pleasures of touch."

Helen Singer Kaplan, pioneering sex therapist, observed in her clinical experience that those who masturbate during adolescence seem less likely to develop sexual problems as adults.

My favorite paper on masturbation was sexologist John Money's "Food, Fitness, and Vital Fluids: Sexual Pleasure from Graham Crackers to Kellogg's Cornflakes," from the *British Journal of Sexual Medicine*.

Here, Money reported on the rise to fame of Reverend Sylvester Graham, a health reformer and cracker-inventer (yes, that Graham) who believed that in addition to crackers made of whole wheat flour, sexual abstinence was the key to good health.

Graham's "A Lecture to Young Men," expounded the theories of

Swiss doctor Samuel August Tissot, the title of whose paper, "Onania, or the Heinous Sin of Self-Pollution," gives a clue to his bias.

Graham's career as a reformer, Money writes, "spanned less than ten years. By his late forties he was burned out." He found a disciple in John Harvey Kellogg, who advocated Graham's ideas of diet, exercise, and sexual abstinence. "Practicing what he preached, he did not consummate his marriage." At least he had hobbies. He spent his honeymoon writing what Money called "probably the most extreme statement of Victorian antisexualism ever published."

In 1898, Kellogg developed the cornflake, which he hoped would prevent sexual degeneracy. "Cornflakes were invented as an antimasturbation food and extinguisher of sexual desire," Money continued, "but only provided they were not contaminated by sugar. John Harvey's younger brother, William Keith Kellogg, added the sugar, and won the legal right to use the family name on the product. The rift between the two brothers made William Keith a multimillionaire. John Harvey Kellogg remained a hedonic pauper, devoid of sexual pleasure, advocating erotic renunciation, until he died at the age of ninety-one in 1943." There's a message there.

Robert T. Francoeur is another major figure in the sexological community, a minister as well as a Ph.D., who believes sexuality is an integral part of spirituality. (He also shows up in Gay Talese's *Thy Neighbor's Wife* at the utopian Sandstone retreat in the 1960s.) In his book, *Becoming a Sexual Person*, Francoeur traced masturbation as viewed throughout publications of the Boy Scout Handbook. In 1934 the *Handbook* cautioned against any "habit" that might cause a boy to lose "fluid" from his body, which would weaken him and make him less resistant to disease. In 1968, the *Boy Scout Handbook* warned that masturbation may cause sexual guilt and worries, and should be avoided. By 1987, Francoeur observed, the manual merely suggested that boy scouts with questions should talk to parents, ministers, or physicians about any sexual concerns they may have.

Historian Thomas Laqueur's book *Making Sex* explores the amazing contortions that ostensibly objective scientists and medical practicners put themselves through when discussing sexual behavior. Laqueur makes it clear that social convention affected what they saw. It's scary to read the historical record tracing attitudes toward masturbation, because it makes you see that it was a sexual practice that was individual, outside the social order, and therefore a target of science and medicine. We still see traces of that history.

Laquer demonstrates how history was rewritten to fit social mores. When Masters and Johnson "revealed" that female orgasm was almost entirely clitoral, he points out, this bit of news "would have been commonplace to every seventeenth-century midwife and had been documented in considerable detail by nineteenth-century investigators. A great wave of amnesia descended on scientific circles around 1900, and hoary truths were hailed as earth-shattering in the second half of the twentieth century." In a world where science was cyclically rewritten, Betty Dodson would always have work.

ATTENDING THE WORKSHOP

I thought she was admirable. I'd talked to scores of women who swore by Betty Dodson, and I could see why. Now I had only one area left to research before I could write about her. In 1994, a year after I'd started interviewing Dodson, I registered for her workshop and found I was terrified to attend.

My reluctance was a surprise to me. It was another instance in which I would discover that theory is one thing, practice another. In theory, I was an avid supporter of Betty Dodson. In practice, sex for one meant sex for one. Not in a room with forty other people.

I was disconcerted at my reaction even as I was helpless before it. I'd registered months before. Two weeks prior I couldn't think about the date without feeling as if I would have heart palpitations. Why? I asked myself. What's wrong with going into a room with a couple of dozen strangers, taking your clothes off, and masturbating? For three days, I thought obsessively about it. The more I fought my distress, the worse it got.

The day before the workshop, I called my friend Tom Bentkowski, who is the art director of *Life* magazine. I called him because of all the people I know, he was the one person whose advice I couldn't predict. He is a curious mix of traits. In some ways, he is one of the most conservative, pragmatic, methodological, and deliberate people I know. He is also one of the most artistic, unpredictable, and open-minded people I know. He once dreamed he was commissioned to paint Prince Charles's portrait. He dreamed he painted Charles as Marlon Brando, in the *Streetcar Named Desire* T-shirt look. At the unveiling, Prince Charles considered and said, "You know . . . I like it."

"You have to go," Tom said instantly when he heard my story.

"Why?"

"Well," said Tom, "masturbation is the one activity, unlike your other subjects, where you can't violate the journalistic objectivity code with anyone besides yourself."

As I was silent, considering, he added, "Do you see what I mean? For the story on escort services you reported by going to job interviews and seeing what they said. If you interview a stripper and he flirts with you, and you sleep with him, that's a violation of objective reporting. But reporting on masturbation? It's the one thing in your whole sex book where the only person involved in the sexual activity is you. In fact, because of the nature of it, if you don't do the seminar, you haven't done the reporting. You have to go."

I did what I always do when stress descends: I got sick. I had a murderous cold, which did not enhance the idea of group stripping and diddling, but I went. I showed up at the Open Center in Soho to find a group of women ranging in age from twenty to seventy. Dodson began the workshop by announcing that New York laws prohibited group nudity in public spaces, so the workshop would be held clothed. While immediately relieved, I realized within a few minutes that with the atmosphere of trust Betty Dodson created, I would have been able to do it nude and felt fine.

I found the openness of the women in the group moving. A number of them declared how much they needed help, and how eager they were to get it. Three of the women said they'd never had an orgasm. Several said they wanted to see if they could have orgasms more easily, learn new techniques. It hadn't even occured to me there might be variations to try.

And that is the key. Betty Dodson offered a way for women to find out what else they could do for themselves. Masturbation is the first step—basic, primary identity, the idea that first our bodies must be for ourselves. Years before, an editor named Lee Eisenberg had given me a backhanded compliment about one of my projects, saying: "Your idea is only brilliant because it's so obvious that no one else would bother thinking of it." I guess that makes it *not* so obvious, then, right? I told Lee I was a master of the obvious. As sex went, Betty Dodson had not only mastered the obvious, but made it valuable. Sex for one is important. Although most of us don't give it the significance it merits. Betty Dodson did.

*   *   *

"You're not allowed to touch your patients. That's one of the funda-mental tenets of the professional psychological and sexological organi-zations," Dodson had reminded me.

Maybe those guidelines have a good purpose, to maintain a respect-able boundary. But maybe touch is an arbitrary and metaphorical limit. I'm sure plenty of "professionals" do just as much damage never laying a finger on you.

"Okay, breathe. Don't hold your breath when the feelings start. The tendency is to stop breathing, but instead, breathe *into* it. The other way cuts it off, this extends your pleasure. Now, rock the pelvis and feel how you can change the tension in your lower body by movement. Don't stop with the tension, just hold it, expect to go anywhere with it . . . that's good."

She moved from woman to woman lying down on the floor, putting her hands on their stomach, hips, repositioning them. She came to me, and showed me how to breathe in such a way that I was more con-nected to the flow of energy. She nodded, satisfied, and moved on. I saw her redirect most of the women in the room, and later, over lunch, all said it had made a difference.

The use of surrogates, sex counselors who touch and have sex with patients, is controversial. I found myself considering this while watch-ing Betty conduct her workshop. She'd related an incident where a therapist became incensed because his patient deserted him after a few sessions with a surrogate. The patient decided he was learning all he needed to know about sex from the surrogate.

"Once you get the hands-on practical information, sitting around talking becomes moot," Betty said. As she worked with the women, and they experimented in the relaxed atmosphere she provided, I could literally see them learn. She taught them ways of moving into and enhancing orgasm. "We're taught to behave, not experience," she said to one.

At different times throughout the day, the women exchanged experi-ences. One revealed that she couldn't watch as she gave birth to her child because she'd been taught never to look at her genitals. I thought this was amazing until no less than four women gave similar examples of constraint. A pretty blond in her twenties told how her boyfriend had encouraged her to come to the workshop, because she never had masturbated, didn't even "know how to do it." She felt happy and inspired to have his support.

There was a discussion of vibrators, the various shapes and models, how to use them. "They were originally advertised for facial massage,"

Dodson said. "Now, if you have any brains *at all*. . . ." Some of the women discussed how they viewed vibrators as machines, inhuman, that it was not the "real thing." Anything that gives you pleasure is real, she pointed out.

"The instructions say never to use it over thirty minutes," one mature woman noted.

"Question authority!" Betty snorted. "Go right ahead! See what happens!" She talked about being a good lover to yourself. "Don't just put the thing on high for two minutes and Boom! Sense the feeling, experiment with pace. Take time. Try to find as many different levels of sensitivity as you can. You're not racing to catch the subway."

Did a lot of it seem a little strange? Sure. It was territory we were unaccustomed to exploring. Betty Dodson's work was subversive. It was saying to women, who put other people's needs before their own, that it's alright, you can do this. Take the time to try things that please just yourself. For some it was a new idea, explorations of your own sensuality just for yourself.

I thought of the people who'd so vociferously mocked Dodson's work. They missed the point. It wasn't just about imbuing masturbation with significance. What she was about was simple, so obvious that almost no one would think of it. She was urging people to explore their own sexuality by themselves, and in doing so, opening the door to caring for themselves in other ways. To learn. To really consider what was important. When I saw how foreign a concept this was to otherwise smart, capable women, I understood why, for thirty years, women have loved her work.

* * *

The masturbation workshoppers blinked, a bit disoriented, and walked to a nearby Soho restaurant to order lunch.

One woman, unlike most of the group, had spent many years attending workshops and lectures related to sexuality. She told a story of a workshop Shere Hite had conducted back in the 1970s, where not a single woman recognized a projected slide of a uterus.

The senior member of the group was in her seventies. She'd decided to take the workshop because, what the hell, before she died, she wanted to experience something she never had before.

My table neighbor introduced herself to me as an artist. She was in her fifties. Her husband had died eight years ago. There was no sex in her life. "It felt as if I was dead, too, I finally realized," she told me, "I haven't met anyone I'd be interested in. It's hard at my age." She'd finally decided to add some form of sexuality to her life. She'd never masturbated, but she'd read about Betty Dodson, so after many years of nearly registering for a workshop, here she was. "I was afraid to tell my friends," she said, looking around nervously as if afraid one would appear. "They'd think this is," she lowered her voice, "too much like being a lesbian."

What fear had done to our sexuality! These women were bravely working to take charge of their own bodies. Betty Dodson later told me, "I'm not trying to sell my lifestyle to anyone. Everyone has to do what's right for themselves. I just want them to know they deserve more pleasure."

When I started work on this book, a question I was frequently asked was, "Why do you want to spend that much time with *those* people?" *Those* people who had made sex their work turned out to be sensitive and flexible, much more so than the ones who would ask me that question. My working sex friends understood that sex involved consent, communication, and trust. They understood that everyone had to go on their own journey. All Betty Dodson offered was a tour. You could travel as far as you wanted, getting off whenever you were ready.

The afternoon included more exercises, one of which was about fantasy. By talking about their sexual fantasies, people got to share, compare, and learn. Some of the shyest, most inexperienced women came out with the wildest stuff.

"I love doing the groups," Betty told me. "I love the energy, but I've never felt an overt sexual desire in a teaching context. It's as if I make love to everyone, whatever problem they're having I absorb it and diffuse it. A lot of time there's crying. Suffering is familiar and pleasure is scary."

She spoke that afternoon of images of stimulation, beginning with what she called the "typical male model," a simple fast build up to orgasm. Then there was a "sleeping beauty orgasm," prolonged stimulation, play, fondling, looking, and utter relaxation. She described a "rock and roll orgasm," tension alternating with relaxation, that lead to expanded pleasure over an extended period of time.

She demonstrated ways of controlling response with breath and body muscle exercises. She spoke of altered states of orgasm, that if she maintained stimulation for hours at a time, she could enter a yoga-like trance, "beyond orgasm into ecstacy." She'd been enlisted by a medical school researching brain waves, who hooked her up to electroencephalograph machines and found she'd slipped into the deepest meditative state, theta waves, in this process.

Betty expressed time and time again that she wants people in her workshops to have available new ideas, try out different techniques. "It would be a complete contradiction for me to set myself up as the person with the answers. I want everyone to find their own answers for their own body," she qualified.

Leonore Tiefer is a sexologist who questioned Masters and Johnson's "human sexual response cycle," which charted the phases of physical response: excitement, plateau, orgasm, and resolution. Tiefer asked a good question. Why did Masters and Johnson set up a model that resembled clockwork with a set sequence? Maybe things worked in a different order, maybe it wasn't so set, maybe the danger of such a model was that it invalidated individual experience.

It seems any convincing presentation of "this is the way sex is" carries more pressure than liberation. I realized that in her workshops, Betty Dodson offered women tools for combating their own vulnerability. It was why for a quarter of a century she'd drawn such appreciative groups.

Her sessions were meant to be like dance or painting workshops, the chance to try out new methods. She thought that sex was like art. Everyone should make their own.

"If I spend four hours at the computer the society pats me on the back. If I spend four hours beating off the society thinks I'm a nut. I know four hours beating off beats the computer," Betty declared.

By the end of the day, we'd absorbed so much mental and physical information, and so expanded our sense of our orgasmic potential, we were exhausted, exhilarated, and a lot more knowledgeable and self-aware than when we'd walked in.

WORKSHOPS FOR MEN AND COUPLES

Although rarely, Dodson had also conducted sessions for men. In her book, she wrote about a male group of different sexual orientations, straight, gay, bisexual. It had been a great experience for them to compare their preconceptions in discussions with each other. It had been great for her, too.

Most men believe sex begins with erection and ends with ejaculation. Betty discovered men were amazed to find they could have an orgasm without an erection. "I tell them, 'Keep breathing, rock your hips, squeeze your pelvic muscles, and fantasize.' Usually I can see the minute they let go of their resistance, get into the good sensations, and finally come all over the vibrator with a 'soft-on.' "

They'll say it felt great, she said, but how could they have sex without an erection with a woman? "I'll list ways, massage, playing with manual masturbation, oral sex, use a dildo for manual or anal play, sex toys for penetration, and share masturbation with a vibrator, to name a few." She doesn't know if her clients will dare trying something sexual with a woman that doesn't fit into their gender conditioning.

When Betty discussed the few times she tried couples workshops, it raised questions about how the sexes repeat familiar patterns rather than learning something new. When put together in a workshop the sexes re-enforced their traditional roles.

She related a recent experience of a masturbation workshop for couples. "I don't want to do it again," she said grimly.

Couples who were already married or together, she felt, did benefit from it. But the single people arrived . . . "looking for love in all the wrong places!"

The unattached people paired off. As Betty described them: "four pussy hounds and four bottomless pits! The women had passive, sweet little voices . . ." her voice imitates, "big eyes, and aaavaaaaill-able, that was the message."

She observed the dynamics of her own workshop with interest. "They're all cruisin' and lookin' and checkin'. . . . The guys picked the women they sat next to."

The first day of the workshop, the singles "staked out territory. They did this mindless rubbing thing, a sort of hanging on, not really touching. And when there was a break they all kneaded each other's shoulders, another phony contact. So they paired off, and afterward they must have fucked and sucked all night, because the next day in the masturbation ritual, two women slept through it. Three of the guys couldn't get a hard-on."

She sighs and rolls her eyes. "Why did they pay $300 for a masturbation workshop?" She adds that people are so conditioned that even if they want the information, they can't be in a sexual situation that requires new behavior. "Two of the men couldn't handle their own cocks the second day," she said. "They need a woman to do it for them, just as some women can't get off themselves, they need a man to do it for them. It's the 'do me, do me,' syndrome."

The men-only groups had open discussions, although Dodson noticed that unlike women who enjoyed the process of discovering their more mysterious genitals, men seemed fairly well acquainted with theirs. But the couples workshop?

"The men did this macho casual thing of not looking at their genitals when women were around. Not one man could get into the genital exploration with a woman around, no attitude of, 'My cock is my best friend!' With women around, it's, 'Well, it's okay . . . ' They weren't adept at masturbation. They're in a rut, doing it the same old way, no anal eroticism, no exploring the pelvic muscles, thinking an ejaculation is the same thing as an orgasm. In short," Betty concluded, "the result of the mixed sex workshop was to have people revert to sex roles and stay there."

"I guess it's a great study in conditioning," I suggested.

"A microcosm of our culture," Betty Dodson said in disgust.

3

Working Sex:
A Porn of
Her Own

WORKING FOR YOU: YOUR TAX DOLLARS

The two dark blue hardcover books containing the Meese Commission Report are kept in the library of the Sexuality Information and Education Council of the United States. Inside the first volume is a handwritten note by Mary Calderone, who headed up the organization for years.

"Disorganized, without index, nothing alphabetized, I am afraid this is for laughing *and* regret at the effort and money spent." Also handwritten is her signature and clarification: "Mary S. Calderone (who testified)."

The 1970 Presidential Commission on Obscenity and Pornography, after spending two million dollars, could support no links between pornography, sex crimes, or antisocial behavior, and in fact, when pressed at least for the answer to what pornography was, concluded, "definition is simply futile." In the mid-1980s the Meese Commission decided to take another crack at it, this time for a more reasonable half a million dollars.

The Meese Commission report unveiled a tremendous amount of interesting information about pornography. Unfortunately, none of it was what the commission was looking for. The commission's conclusions, circulated in the media, tried to put forth the case that pornography was dangerous and caused sex crimes and increased aggression, inspired sexism against women, encouraged pedophilia, and at the very least, was detrimental to "family values."

These conclusions were not supported by the top sexologists and psychologists in the country, many of whom testified. Two women on the commission, Ellen Levine, editor of such mainstream magazines as *Women's Day, Cosmopolitan,* and *Redbook,* and Dr. Judith Becker, the director of the Sexual Behavior Clinic at the New York State Psychiatric Institute, were so upset at the Meese Commission's recommendations to suppress explicit films that they published their own dissenting report. John Money, Ph.D., and Drs. Edward Donnerstein and Daniel Linz, testified and published conclusions from their own research that addressed the commission's conclusions, contradicting a causal relationship between pornography and sex crimes or increased aggression.

Veronica Vera was a member of a support group for women in the porn industry called Club 90. She testified for the Meese Commission about her experience in the production of sexually explicit materials. Veronica gave me a transcript and a videotape of her appearance before the hearings.

The first time I'd seen Veronica Vera was in 1992. She was standing on a stage in a Williamsburg Brooklyn art theater, dressed in the crown and gown of the Statue of Liberty. Veronica Vera's rendition of Liberty was personalized by draping the upper part of the gown around her belt to present the statue as topless, a state she maintained throughout the entire performance. I've always been impressed by one-person shows, having seen them about people like Emily Dickenson, Harry Truman, Roy Cohn/Jack Smith, and Truman Capote. This was the first one I'd ever seen where the person's breasts established their own stage presence, not an unfitting creative decision for a program entitled, "Bright Lights, Big Titties."

That evening she presented an oral autobiography with slides and music. It was alternatively thoughtful and ill-tempered, suggesting that the audience could go along with her or not, she didn't seem to care. Many of her anecdotes were given in a darkly sexual, edgy fashion as if the last way she would ever present herself would be as the sweet, accommodating, asexual, nonthreatening woman. She could be off-putting, blasting forth a heat too hot to touch. Still, in the end, speaking of her friendships and what she'd learned through her work, it was loving and involving. When we spoke backstage afterward she snapped that she was writing her own book and didn't want to be interviewed.

Two years later, after I'd run into her at film screenings and anti-censorship affairs and a number of her peers reported that I was okay, she spoke with me and passed on her personal Meese Commission archives. When I saw the videotape, I knew I was seeing something that hadn't been presented in the mainstream media, a woman who had acted in porn films who was willing to stand in front of the United States Senate and declare that she was perfectly comfortable with that. I'd never heard a woman say what she said, that she *didn't* feel degraded by her experience, that this was a subjective evaluation, influenced by the eye of the beholder. In fact, as the senator who questioned her concluded, what she had to say was really different.

"I certainly didn't want to appear as a pornography advocate," Veronica Vera declares during the start of her film, *Portrait of a Sexual Evolutionary.* It's quite an imperfect and very guilt-ridden medium, though I've grown in it. But I didn't think it would help women to beg the government to play Daddy and protect us from ourselves, and then at the same time, expect equality. It wouldn't help our own eroticism."

Veronica Vera appeared before the Meese Commission in a conservative blue silk dress. This image of a woman I was accustomed to seeing in her sexy, theatrical wardrobe of fishnet stockings, leopard-print clothes, and stiletto-heeled shoes was striking. The videocamera panned down the formal courtroom to where she smoothed her skirt and took her place at the table, facing a row of senators. This was Washington, D.C., October 30, 1984, Meese Commission meets porn star. She looked lovely and nervous, saying her remarks were based on her experience: "I consider myself very fortunate to be able to share them with this committee." She started by listing mythologies and misconceptions.

"MYTH," she read. "Women in pornography have unhappy childhoods." A still photographer crouched a foot in front of her and started snapping away. She missed a beat and continued speaking.

"REALITY: I come from a very loving family. That core of love has always been my strength." Here her voice quavered. She added that she was raised Catholic, and while she did not practice that religion . . . At this moment emotion choked the words off. "I mean what I say. Excuse me," she added, reaching for a glass of water to compose herself.

"I still feel that spiritual base. My family is aware of the nature of my work, and while they do not always understand what I do, we have always treated one another with love and respect."

Veronica Vera continued. She next listed the myth that women in erotic films were all bodies and no brains, responding that she had always been in the upper percentile of her classes, edited her high school and college newspapers and yearbook, and graduated with a BA in English.

"MYTH: Women in porn do not know how to do anything else to make a living." Before making sexually explicit movies, Veronica said, she'd traded stocks on Wall Street and worked in the oil business. She started by writing stories based on her sexual experiences for men's magazines, eventually deciding to act in an X-rated film.

This lead to her next myth, that making an X-rated movie was a sleazy experience.

"I was petrified when I made my first X-rated film," Veronica admitted. "I too, had been brought up with all the myths about what a terrible experience the whole business would be. But now I was meeting people in the business. Actors and actresses, magazine editors, and publishers, photographers, film directors and producers. They are mostly all dedicated hard-working people, people who take pride in their work, and are committed to making the product."

Veronica Vera went on to relate that she'd decided to perform in one of the films and discovered that it was real movie-making, through which she'd discovered a sense of camaraderie and pride. She said she'd never met anyone who was not participating out of his or her own free will. She declared that pornography did not degrade women.

"That is purely a subjective evaluation. Pornography concerns itself with the explicit depiction of sex. There are some people who are offended by what they consider a breach of intimacy. That does not make any of these aspects evil in themselves," she said.

Veronica Vera and an actress with the professional name Seka, who'd also appeared in erotic films, sat side by side at the lectern. Vera said that certain images, such as a woman with her legs spread wide, was "overused, unimaginative," and that she preferred to create her own images. It was a point she elaborated on, saying that now women in the industry were writing, producing, and directing films, as well as publishing magazines. "In short, we are expressing our views about erotica, and offering something different."

"MYTH: Women make very little money in comparison to all that is made from their bodies."

"REALITY: Wall Street has taught me that in any business this is

true. It is the people who risk time and money who make money. It is
the auto manufacturer and not the man on the assembly line who lives
in a bigger house."

"But the salaries paid adult film performers are certainly respectable,
and women are 'learning the ropes' of the sex industry. We are assuming positions of more financial control."

"I speak not only for myself but for every woman I know in the sex
industry," she finished. "We do not see ourselves as victims. We do not
need to hide in the shelter of being somebody's victim. We accept
responsibility for our own lives. We cherish that responsibility. Do not
make any laws to 'protect us.' We do not want them. Leave us our
precious right to choose."

There was a brief pause, in which she thanked the commission, and
Senator Arlen Specter thanked her. Then he began his questioning,
asking first whether Veronica Vera was familiar with the experiences of
Linda Lovelace-Marciano, whose published account of her experiences
while making the film *Deep Throat* had been referred to in numerous
testimonies and whose story of abuse while making porn films had
been highlighted in the hearings. Veronica replied that she had read the
book, to which Senator Specter asked if she believed that Lovelace's
experience was atypical for women who appeared in X-rated movies.

"They have not been my experiences, and in reading Ms. Lovelace's
book, I found that the villain in her book seemed to be the man she had
chosen to be her lover at the time, and not the sex industry," Vera said.

"Well, I think you accurately say the man was her lover," Specter
replied. "As she recounts the incident, she says that she did it under
coercion, she was not there voluntarily, and draws a broad generaliza-
tion, which you disagree with, as I understand it, women are not coerced when they are in X-rated movies, as a rule?"

"I have never met a woman who was coerced into participating," she
replied, adding, "I have met quite a few women who were curious to
know how they could go about being in an X-rated film."

"You say that the general characterization that women who are in X-
rated films come from unhappy childhoods is contrary to your experience, or are you saying that you did not have an unhappy childhood?"
asked Senator Specter.

"Well, I think there are certain stereotypes about women in this
business that have been allowed to continue, and about women who
will show off their bodies. There are quite a few people in the world
who think that is a degrading thing, and they must be forced into it,
and if they were forced into it, they must have been weak to start with,

and they were weak to start with because they had unhappy child-hoods."

The conversation next covered questions about underage participants in pornography, to which Vera stated that she only knew people who made adult erotic films, not child pornography.

"You say that in the business of X-rated movies the people are very concerned not to be involved in child pornography, and that there is a general feeling that child pornography is wrong?" Specter asked.

"I would say that, yes, sir."

The transcript goes on, like a vibration trace of two different wave-lengths. Hers, considerations of experience rather than stereotypes. His, a straight line: participation in porn, degradation, no separation between adult sexual choice and children. He seemed to think repre-sentations of sexual fantasy were dangerous.

"There is a depiction of you in what is called *Tight Bondage*. I am sure you are familiar with this publication," Specter opened the next topic.

Vera told him that the name of the publication was not *Tight Bond-age* it was *Adults Only*, and she'd done a photo layout depicting bondage fantasies, which she had always wanted to explore. She'd written about the experience, and now asked if she could read it.

"If you wish," replied Senator Specter.

"The photographs show me tied up in various ropes all over my body. Before we began the photo shoot I stood before the bathroom mirror and looked deep into my eyes," Vera related. She recalled that she thought of Betty Page, a famous bondage model from the 1950s, whose photographs continue to sell forty years later. Page had pos-sessed something timeless. Her body was both lush and athletic. Un-characteristic for women of that time, she lifted weights every day. Her skin was alabaster pale, her looks a mix of Cleopatra and a futuristic comic book star with her raven black bangs, chiseled cheekbones, and full crimson lips. Most unusual were the vividly sexual photos of her bound by ropes, intensely staring down the camera, radiating questions about the nature of power and exchange. Vera wondered what Betty Page had thought, doing this. As she watched herself in the mirror, a big tear rolled down her cheek, the release of which, she told the senators, made her come to an understanding. "Submission comes from within."

This may be the most interesting point Veronica Vera made in the Meese Commission hearings. The majority of the testimony presented was interpreted to say that women who participated in explicit films were forced to submit or were acting out of anything but their own volition (the discussion devoid of any context such as comparable pay offered by other jobs, or as Feminists for Free Expression leader Marcia Pally would later write, "They don't mind seeing women exploited with their clothes *on*"), the idea that someone could choose to submit, or choose, period, was a novel one.

Veronica Vera continued to explain the nature of fantasy to a committee with its own version of reality. "These photographs would not exist before you if I had not wanted to submit to this side of myself, and to reveal that image to you. Each day I tried to be in control of my life, because to reveal this side of myself would leave me vulnerable, but this is the stuff dreams are made of. My dreams, anyway." Great trust in her friends and the photographer made it possible for her to explore this fantasy, she added.

" 'I am the love toy, object of your desire, exposed and vulnerable,' " she read. " 'Picture yourself tying the ropes, keeping me as your prisoner, ready to be taken whenever you want me. Always open to your'— shall I go on?"

"You certainly may," responded Senator Specter.

"Always open to your cock and mouth," she resumed. "Enjoy me, take pleasure from me; as you do, you will understand through the purity of my surrender, you have become my captive, too.' Senator, I am very concerned that there is a whole layer of guilt laid on people because of their fantasies. Women, I believe, should take responsibility for themselves, and lift some of this guilt."

"I don't want to be a victim or considered a victim. I think it makes people unhappy. I do not think men should have this layer of guilt because they find pleasure looking at photographs, and I think we should be free to explore our fantasies."

Senator Specter stated that women who came before the committee feared that many women would be pressed into such positions against their will, and brutalized. "Do you think there is simply nothing to that kind of concern?" he asked.

"I think any woman who allows herself to be in such a vulnerable position, by someone she does not have extreme trust and knowledge of, is an idiot."

"She gets what she deserves?" Senator Specter asked.

"NO." replied Vera, to which he wondered if a law should intercede to protect her.

"Let us back up a second," she urged. "What sort of law?" The issue, Specter supplied, was to give a cause of action to women to sue the publisher. "Do you think that is wrong?" Vera replied yes, that she believed it was wrong to deny that fantasies exist.

"Well, if you talk about bondage fantasies, the level of damage is not nearly as extensive as rape fantasies," Senator Specter stated. Damage? From *fantasies*? Our next Senate Subcommittee will focus on testimony from the Food and Drug Administration, examining the issue of which is more fattening, dreaming about Haagan Das or cottage cheese. After that the Department of Motor Vehicles will look into the comparative dangers of fantasizing about drag racing or hang gliding.

"Would you think," Senator Specter asked, "that depiction of a rape fantasy which might lead women to be raped would be something that ought not to be in the protected ambit of the law?"

"I think rape fantasies are simply fantasies that people have," she replied. "I think they should be allowed to be explored . . . it is a very common fantasy, and I think that is part of what the whole field of eroticism is about, exploring our fantasies."

Senator Specter went on to speculate about the simulation of rape fantasies. "Are there movies that act out rape fantasies?" he asked.

"There are movies that act out just about everything."

"Are you personally familiar with one that has acted out a rape fantasy?" Specter asked.

Seka, the actress who was also testifying, suggested the scene where Rhett Butler carries a struggling Scarlet O'Hara up the stairs in *Gone With The Wind*.

"Is that the one where he leaves the next day, and the scene opens and she is smiling in bed?" Funny, the things that stick in Arlen Specter's mind.

"And he said, 'Frankly, Scarlet, I do not give a damn.' After he raped her," Ms. Seka offered.

"Those are two different scenes, I think," Specter interjected. "I think he leaves on that occasion—"

"I beg your pardon, Senator."

"He leaves on that occasion, after she wants to go to Ashley Wills." Senator Specter recalled.

Tara notwithstanding, Ms. Seka alternatively suggested the rape scene with Jack Nicholson and Jessica Lange in what she remembered as *The Mailman Rings Twice*. She mentioned genuine horror in Brian De Palma's film *Body Double*, where a woman has a power drill run through her abdomen.

Senator Specter endeavored to clarify. "Ms. Seka, a rape scene is different from a rape fantasy. And to the extent that there is a depiction of rape, that is something which happens in real life. It is something totally different to depict a rape fantasy, that someone wants to be raped, which is what is meant, as I understand it, by a rape fantasy."

"If you start talking about rape fantasies in the context that this is a common fantasy, as Ms. Vera testifies, then you raise an issue as to whether you are placing the idea in men across this country that it is a common fantasy in women, that they wish to be raped." This may or not be true, he concluded, but he personally tended to doubt it. "But I do not know all the answers and that is why the perspectives which you women are giving are really different."

The remarkable thing about Senator Specter's confusion is that it would appear he really didn't understand the difference between what a woman might fantasize about, and actually wish to do.

"Is it a common women's fantasy that she wishes to be raped?" he asked.

Veronica Vera tried to help him clarify. "Senator, what I am saying is that there is a fantasy of being taken, of having a strong man, or strong woman, take you as the love object. I don't mean actually without consent. That shouldn't be promoted. That's not what I am talking about."

"You are not talking about promoting a concept that there is the fantasy widespread by women that they want to be raped?"

"No, not that they want to be taken without consent," replied Vera "That is a horrible experience."

"How about women having a fantasy that they want to be in something like *Tight Bondage*?" he asked.

"Only consent bondage, knowing the person," she replied. "I do not think any woman really wants to meet someone who is going to actually rape and brutalize her."

"Ms. Vera, the problem arises, at least as testified by some women, that these pictures cause men to put them in these positions, contrary to their will, and Veronica Vera appearing in *Tight Bondage* is setting an example which could cause a lot of women a lot of pain, and you do not seem to think that is true?"

"No, sir, I do not."

"Okay," said Arlen Specter. "Well, that is a very substantial difference of view from people who have appeared before this subcommittee. I appreciate your candor, and we do agree with you that it is not easy to explore these issues, and there are some difficult questions." He thanked them and called the next witnesses.

WORKING SEXUAL REPRESENTATIONS

The trajectory of Candida Royalle's career has matched changes in the porn industry that developed over time, mirroring social changes. She acted in erotic films, becoming a porn star in the 1970s through the early 1980s. This woman was intelligent and political, and realized that the films she was in didn't represent sexuality in a way she and many of her contemporaries felt comfortable with. They formed a support group of women in the industry to talk about pornography and how they'd change it. At the same time, Candida entered therapy to examine her attitudes about her sexuality and her life.

She formed her own company, Femme Productions, which produced erotic films from a woman's point of view. Many of the women in her support group, also well-known porn personalities, would add their presence to the Femme films—acting in them, doing guest shots writing, producing, and directing—concrete steps forward for women in the industry. The process was different, and the product was different. Candida Royalle's work as an erotic revolutionary developed as a result of her own experience. The mainstream media began to cover what she was doing, and the work of this former-porn-star-who-makes-films-from-a-woman's-point-of-view received considerable attention.

Through the 1980s, more women and couples were viewing explicit films, due to the home video revolution. It was no longer necessary to go to a theater, which made many people uncomfortable and embarrassed. The privacy of their homes offered protection. Video sales and rentals suggested that half the porn audience was now women.

The time was right for the more egalitarian vision of sexuality that was being presented by Femme and other companies that followed. Ironically, just when this was happening, the antiporn contingent gained momentum. At this auspicious moment, it was a good time to meet the players involved.

I started to talk with Candida Royalle in 1991, and continued to the present. During this time there has been a sea change in the issue of whether or not government should restrict explicit films.

Beginning in the 1980s, a curious alliance formed between antipornography feminists and some politicians who spoke of getting government off the people's backs. Both endeavored to control decisions that should be made in the individual bedrooms of a free country. The antipornography feminists, especially activists Catharine MacKinnon and Andrea Dworkin, received a tremendous amount of press, which usually described their position on the issue as that of "the feminists," despite the fact that famous and influential women writers, actors, lawyers, social scientists, artists, filmmakers, political leaders, in short, "feminists" of all sorts, came out in support of eroticism in film and writing. These other "feminists" didn't want the government to protect them from sexual representations. I came to understand the importance of that position from the work of Candida Royalle. Instead of saying that pornography is terrible and we should get rid of it, she thought it would be a better idea to make her own.

It was all a mystery to me when I began to investigate what she was doing. I hadn't seen more than half a dozen porn films before the early 1990s. Five years later, I'd seen hundreds of them. Over the years I'd hear people pronouncing opinions on this issue. I'd ask how many films they'd seen, and they'd say, "None." or "A few." They'd talk about the degradation of women, and I'd ask how many women in porn they'd known. None.

The point was to take a closer look at the people and the films themselves, what they represented. The films were more than "dirty movies," they were a world of information about different people's concept of sex. Wouldn't it be a good idea to look first, then make up our minds?

WORKING PORN FILMS

"I think that I'm like any other woman except that I acted out more," says Candida Royalle, whose real name is Candice. "One of the worst things in our culture is the insidious messages that are sent to women. Our sexuality is the cause of danger to us. We tell girls, 'You have to be the keeper of the gate. Boys can go out and explore, but not you.' We're the provocateurs, the she-devils.' "

When she was thirteen she was attacked by a man who tried to rape her.

"I turned into a little animal. In the middle of it I had a vision of myself being found by my neighbors, face down and naked. I fought him off and he ran away from me."

"When I was brought home by the police, my mother, who was full of rage and fear, slapped me across the face and said, 'I told you not to go into the woods.' Of course she was remorseful afterwards, but the damage had been done. It's what we learn as young girls. Our sexuality is dangerous. It causes men to do bad things to us. The idea is it's our fault. It took me years to undo all these messages. I finally learned you cannot enjoy sex if you're always in control. Sex is about surrendering to the pleasure that's being given to you, and to the pleasure we give. I still have to coax myself into losing control. I think that's what submission fantasies are about for women. It's so unsafe for us to give up control. It's as if we have to pretend we're being forced to give it up. I think that comes from the very sort of things I went through."

In the 1980s, Candida started her own company, Femme, with the goal of making erotic films from a woman's point of view. A group of women from NOW, the National Organization of Women, came to see her work. "One of them was Florence Rush, who had been a member of Women Against Pornography," she recalls. "They watched it and said they really were pleasantly surprised, it was very egalitarian and so different."

"Then Florence said, 'But I wonder, at a time when women are still raped and abused, if it's safe for us to express our fantasies.' That was so depressing to me. I thought, 'My God, is that what it's about? We have to keep our sexuality under wraps? We have to continue to let men define it? To protect ourselves?' "

Candida went to San Francisco in the early 1970s, as she said, a very jubilant time. The influence of the 1960s was still apparent. "A lot of people who were in porn movies in those years came from that whole period of open sexuality," she points out. Ten years later, when she entered therapy, she found herself troubled. "I had so many gifts, so why did I go ahead and do this? Why did I do something that would prevent me from moving ahead with other things? I was trained in art schools from the age of fourteen. I was dancing from age ten. I was a performer, singing in jazz clubs. My father had been a jazz musician, and music was in my blood. Why? Why did I do something I was embarrassed to tell people I did?"

She was ambivalent about the films, although when she began she experienced what Veronica Vera tried to tell the Meese Commission. She was modeling nude when someone offered her work in a porn film. "I was horrified because I'd never even seen one!" But her friends encouraged her, so she visited a set. "It was very legitimate. The people were nice. There were scripts. There were auditions. The women were beautiful. It was not like I'd envisioned it at all. It was real movie-making. That's why I did it."

Candida Royalle became a star. In the mid 1970s through early '80s, she was a favorite of the pornography theatergoing audience, which in those days, was the only way to see pornography. The landmark obscenity battle was fought in 1970 and 1971 by Barney Rosset of Grove Press, who had imported the Swedish film, *I Am Curious Yellow*. The fight over that film went all the way to the Supreme Court. Rosset refused to accept banning of the film as obscene. "Norman Mailer was one of the most important witnesses in the trial," Rosset recalls, saying that Mailer testified that the film was "one of most important pictures I've ever seen in my life. I felt it was a profoundly moral movie." The Supreme Court decision on *I Am Curious Yellow* came in as a tie vote, but Rosset continued the battle over the country, with lawyer Ed De Grazia spearheading the hiring of top lawyers in various cities for preemptive strikes against the film being banned for obscenity. Grove Press went so far as to buy a theater in Minneapolis and show the film there. "When the run of the film was over we sold the theater," Rosset said.

"There's still confusion over *I Am Curious Yellow* as to what kind of film it is," Rosset supplied, describing its history. "It's a political film, not a sex film. It was serious. The sex is only one of the social issues of the story."

After my conversations with Barney Rosset, I watched *I Am Curious Yellow* twenty-six years after it was an international cause celeb. The much-celebrated scenes, including one in which the heroine and her beau (both are clothed) simulate sex outside the Royal Palace, would barely get an R rating now.

Barney Rosset added that the true irony of the battle over *I Am Curious Yellow* was that after Grove had fought to have the film shown, other companies released a flood of X-rated films. Grove was importing other quality foreign films by people like Jean-Luc Godard and found they'd created a monster. "Now the theaters we'd counted on showing our movies had no playing time for us!" Rosset said. "Suddenly it was all porno films. Everyone thought we'd won at the Supreme Court. We'd really lost on the tie vote, but we won in local jurisdictions. This in effect released the restriction, which in turn, engulfed us!"

Porn broke through to national distribution in 1971, with hits such as *Behind the Green Door* and *Deep Throat*. In 1988 the Freeman decision in the California State Supreme Court made it legal to shoot adult films because performers were considered actors rather than prostitutes. Prior to that, it was an underground community, with filmmakers frequently busted while filming.

Bill Margold is a California-based actor and filmmaker who, along with porn star Nina Hartley and political activist Bobby Lilly, heads up an industry-based organization called the Free Speech Coalition. Bobby Lilly also runs another organization called CALACT (Californians Against Censorship Together). Robert J. Stoller was professor of psychiatry at UCLA School of Medicine. He published numerous seminal books on sexuality. Before his death in 1991, Stoller spent months documenting Bill Margold's world for two books exploring the psychology of pornography. Stoller had come to the projects with an open mind, and did documentary interviews. Bill Margold is introduced with a cheerful self-description regarding his suitability for the business: possession of "a twelve-inch cock that is always, under any circumstances, ready. You can hang baby elephants from it, slash at it with razor blades, and the damned thing's ready to go. I can ejaculate three times in a row and be ready for the next scene in two minutes."

Margold, star of *Indiscretions, I through IV,* as well as many other films, spoke of leaving for work in the 1970s and telling his girlfriend he might be in jail by nightfall. "I'd liken it to *Les Miserables,*" he offered. "The vice cops were Javert and we were Jean Valjean running with our loaf of bread between our legs. They'd bust us with great glee."

He finds the laws they operate under now astonishingly hypocritical. "We can't use scenes in porn films that are common for sports and prime-time television. A film called *Henry, Portrait of a Serial Killer,* comes out and is hailed as art. A man in the movie sodomizes a woman and forces a child to watch. If I did that I would go to jail. In *Realm of the Senses,* a woman murders a man and castrates him. If I did *that* I'd go to jail." Again, it is an instance where local jurisdictions can decree what the community will accept. Decisions on pornography can be much harsher than the standards governing mainstream entertainment.

The meaning of their work? "Our primary purpose is to get people off. Once a man or woman has satisfied a sexual urge, they're relieved. They go to sleep. They don't run out and start raping people."

I ask about what it was like when Candida Royalle starred in porn films and Margold says some things haven't changed. "All the women in the business are perceived as whores. That's sad. Even if you hate me, at least you perceive me as being a man who makes X-rated movies, which makes me a kind of hero, because I get to have public sex with women. My worst enemies first ask me how I function under the pressure, and then how people get into the business."

Strangely, he found that it was his work in pornography that changed his attitudes about women. "I had notions that women were basically sex objects until I got into the X-rated industry and discovered what they really wanted to be were friends. When I speak at colleges I tell young people that if you're having relationships predicated on sex alone then you're not having a relationship. It's more important to sleep next to a person than to sleep with them."

Bill Margold had a great time for years in what he calls, "The Garden of Eden Above The Love Canal." To his surprise, he fell in love with a woman called Viper. "She was beautiful and the most incredible person I ever met. She had tattoos from tit to clit, had been a Marine, and a member of the American Ballet Theater. Producers would have heart attacks when Viper showed up on a set. They'd ask her to do one thing and she'd do nine. She could double fist fuck herself while being anally sodomized and invite another guy to have sex with her mouth. Most of her stuff would end up on the cutting room floor."

Offscreen, Viper taught Bill that love was more important than sex. "She much preferred to hug and kiss and roll around. When we had sex she'd say, 'Let's cuddly-mock.' She understood how little importance sex has to an overall relationship."

"I'd like to say that it's changed, the double standard of male porn stars being thought of as studs and women sluts," concluded Margold. "But it's like the rest of society. Not yet."

*   *   *

Candida Royalle acted in about thirty porn films. Dozens of titles listed under her name in industry directories such as *The X-Rated Video Guide* are repackaged films: compilations, edited versions, even scenes of hers added to other movies over the years, a frustrating and upsetting turn of events. "I went through these lists myself and couldn't believe the number of films I was in that I'd never heard of."

"In the five years I was in the business, I was in twenty-five to thirty films," she says. "It's very different now. Today they shoot what they call One- or Two-Day Wonders. The women that go into porn now do it as a career, a full-time thing. We had other things we were doing. This was just a great way to make extra money, so you had nurses and teachers and artists and performers who also did this. You'd shoot for an entire week on one film. I'd do a handful of films and then not work for six months. I never did it day in and day out, and I never got burned out. It was a different way of running your life."

So many aspects of her life contradicted my preconceived notions. Candida told me it was only in recent years that watching explicit films had become part of her life outside work. She and Per, her ex-husband, had worked together, initially for other people, then as a team when Femme started.

"On a sailing vacation in 1986 we put on some X-rated videos," she says. "I found other people making love was very arousing and permission giving, sort of like a rooting team, like, 'Hey! Yeah! Everyone's doing it!' I remember having a TV appearance right after that and feeling really comfortable saying, 'Hey, so what? It's good clean fun.'"

"Porn is masturbation material," Catharine MacKinnon wrote sternly in her book, *Only Words*, going on to describe the terrible things men who watch porn fantasize about doing to women (as if women don't fantasize, or watch porn). In MacKinnon's construction, sexual fantasy leads to oppression: "Sooner or later, in one way or another, the consumers want to live out the pornography further in three dimensions," she wrote. "Depending upon their chosen sphere of operation, they may use whatever power they have to keep the world a pornographic place so they can continue to get hard from everyday life."

MacKinnon has an eccentric and depressing view of men, not to mention porn and sexual fantasy (also not to mention the world, erections, and everyday life). She escalates her porn perspective to erotic reefer madness: "As pornography consumers . . . doctors may molest anesthetized women, enjoy watching and inflicting pain during childbirth, and use pornography to teach sex education in medical school. Some consumers write on bathroom walls. Some undoubtedly write judicial opinions." She goes on about the mayhem caused by porn consumers, sprinkling her thunderously accusing sentences with the lightly qualifying subject "some."

". . . Some gang rape women in fraternities and at rest stops on highways, holding the pornography aloud and mimicking it. Some become serial rapists and sex murderers . . . some make pornography for their own use . . . in order to make money to support the group's habit," MacKinnon goes on.

The antiporn activists exploited the cultural discomfort of admitting to sexual fantasy. The reoccurring phrase my working sex people used, "If I was feeling this, I realized that other people were probably experiencing this, too," was applicable here. "The first half of my adult life I was ashamed of my fantasies," Candida said. Later, she came to see the first films she made for Femme as a sublimation. "I was ashamed of my 'sick' politically incorrect fantasies. Being dominated? I was a feminist. So you close your eyes and fantasize, but you don't let anyone know." Fortunately, she decided to explore this dichotomy.

Before she was married and when she was making films, she enjoyed the wild life of a post-'6os, avant-garde, free-form community. When she entered relationships, though, she switched gears. "When I'm in love, I have no trouble being a one-man woman. I was married to Per for nine years, then I had a four-year relationship with another man."

Candida and one boyfriend did watch the early films she starred in, and she says she had a wonderful, delayed experience as a result.

"I was so far removed, and I'd come through my evolution. Watching them, I saw a sweet, troubled young woman who was very pretty, didn't know it, and was very insecure. I felt sad for her, because I had talents I didn't use. The real beauty was seeing how turned on my boyfriend got."

"What did he say?"

"It was what he did! He was my sex slave! He was in another realm. I experienced the power I had over him, on screen and sitting there. I realized that before, because of the guilt and shame, I never allowed myself to feel that power. It was after the fact that I experienced the upside of the whole thing. It was like a gift. I got to sit there and *feel* my power as a woman over a man. It completed that period of my life for me. I really got the goodies, at a time when I could appreciate it."

Late-breaking goddess. Insatiable whore. Frigid wife. The films Candida acted in were fantasy versions of sex. But whose fantasies? And how did they inspire this woman to switch the point of view and depict a woman's fantasies? To get there, we had to see where she started from.

We had a marathon Candida Royalle film festival, starting early in the morning and continuing until nightfall. Her four cats would take shifts, trooping over to observe, getting bored when they realized we weren't watching something interesting, like Femme's, *Nine Lives Hath My Love,* in which they'd had cameo roles. That film tells of a woman whose lover complains about all the attention she lavishes on her cats. In the end, he's magically transformed into a cat and so receives the same care. I had a laptop computer and tape recorder going all day as we watched the movies and she commented, "*This* is the kinkiest thing I've ever done."

WORKING IN FILMS

Candida Royalle acted in films from 1974 to 1980. "It was called the classic period of porn films because they shot on film rather than videotape. They'd shoot for a week, and there were scripts," she explains. "About the claims of us being forced into it . . . we had to go to script readings, tryouts. We did tons of auditions for this shit. I made between $1,000 and $1,500 for a week's work."

Responding to the victimization theory, she drily joked, "I tried to seduce the director, and he wouldn't have it. 'Nope! It's against my ethics!' he admonished."

The first film we watched, *Hard Soap, Hard Soap*, was a takeoff on soap operas. It starts in a kitchen where Candida and Leilani, who was one of her closest friends, discuss her husband, played by John Holmes, a famous porn star whose AIDS-related death was widely reported in the 1980s. Leilani also died at the age of twenty-nine, of alcoholism. Candida dedicated her film, *Three Daughters* to her friend.

"My marriage, I have to save it!" Leilani's character laments. The problem, Candida explains, is not enough sex. It's been "four whole days." Candida's character offers to spy on the husband, a psychiatrist.

In the next scene, Candida, wearing a ski mask, shows up in the psychiatrist's office. His diagnosis: "A girl who gives head, and she's ashamed of it, so she wears a mask! This will be a long difficult cure, but have faith in me." Instantly, with his piloting, she is on her knees performing oral sex on him.

"I liked dressing up in the clothes, but as far as the sex went, I could have been vacuuming the rug," Candida observes. We watch the scene, which is remarkably unerotic. Both are clothed, and nothing can be seen except when the man ejaculates. "Isn't it amazing? You don't even see his genitals, just the cum shot," she comments. "I once watched a trailer for a porn film, and the whole thing was a series of men ejaculating. I thought, 'This is what it's really about. It's their identity.'"

A couple of scenes later she's under the table, performing fellatio. "When I started Femme a distributer told me that I had to put more anal sex in my movies. The idea when we were making these older films was that wives wouldn't do oral sex, so you have all these blow job scenes. Ten years ago when I was starting my company the theory was that now the wives wouldn't do anal sex, so . . ." She ignored the advice.

On the screen the sex scenes contain dialogue like, "I'll be your first piece of ass," and "Who said you could come? Just keep humping." She shook her head, watching. "It's weirdly infantile, like bad high school daydreams."

"Now here's a porn political quandary," she said. The next scene involves Leilani's character getting into a charged sexual situation with a man who thinks she's insulted him. He grabs her by the shoulders and forces her to perform oral sex, then he turns her around and screws her from behind. It's tense and well shot, and both of us felt we should be ashamed to admit we find it hot. We're back to the question of fantasy.

And so is the current judicial/political climate, the result of which has been to relegate such scenes to the porn archives. "You can't do scenes like this anymore or you'll be prosecuted. The only way you can depict submission in porn films now is if there's no explicit sex. They've blurred the line between consensual role playing and actual rape and abuse," Candida said. Nancy Friday had written in her bestselling book that many women had rape fantasies. To hark back to the Meese Commission, this didn't mean they wanted to be raped in real life, just in their imagination, or fantasy depictions. We discuss being turned on by watching this scene, and how this illusion is separate from reality. Although the antiporn contingent argues that these scenes cause what they depict, the majority of studies don't support that contention.

"Well, you won't find scenes like this anymore," she declared, as the rape scene ended. "The line has been blurred between consensual role playing and actual rape and abuse. Europe, on the other hand, is into S&M fantasies, double penetration, the kinkier the better. American producers have to make an American and a European version, because they can't sell the American version in Europe. It's too soft."

Next is a nude scene with Candida in bed with a guy. "Of course it starts with a blow job," she muttered, watching. On screen, her character says, "Hey, I gave you head last night. Why don't you give me some head this time?"

"Very appropriate for the future founder of Femme Productions!" she laughed. The idea is introduced only to be rejected, because the very next scene has Candida going down on him, then there's a break while reels change, and . . . "Magic!" she declared as a new reel starts. "His penis is erect!"

She studied her body on screen. In her twenties, she weighed fifteen to twenty pounds more than she does now. "By today's standards, I wouldn't make it in the movies," she said. "I was too fleshy. My breasts hang like real breasts, not standing straight out. They would have told me to get implants."

Some of the shots are so unimaginatively graphic that they edge over the line into medical textbook realm. In one she's in bed with a man, and the camera zooms over to them. The next shot is a close-up from six inches away of what appears to be a brown furry creature under a blazing spotlight. It takes a moment to realize that it's her genitals filling the screen, with not so much as an inner thigh or bit of stomach to provide bearings.

A few scenes later she thoughtfully murmurs, "This is probably many men's idea of sex, isn't it? A little head, a few positions, and then come."

Watching John Holmes on the screen, she confirms his reputation. "He did have a twelve-inch cock, but more than anything he loved performing oral sex on women." She couldn't resist making love with him, and definitely enjoyed it. "I was in a very free community, and went through a period of almost compulsory experimentation. The irony is when I pulled back and was with one person, there was a lot more depth and pleasure to be had."

Onscreen, *Hard Soap* continues. Candida is in bed with a man when Leilani knocks on the door, saying the pressure of not having sex is killing her. The man Candida is with promptly has sex with Leilani, and again, withdraws for a giant close-up cum shot, immediately after which Leilani declares, "Boy, what a relief! Thanks a lot, you guys, I'll really sleep well now."

"Of course she's relieved after *his* orgasm," Candida sighs. "Okay, let's switch films. You get the idea here."

The next film is *Hot and Saucy Pizza Girls*, done in 1977. "We shot it in Berkeley. I remember being in the parking lot of the motel where they put us up, practicing our skateboarding." The movie opens with a cheery country soundtrack and a shot of Candida flying down the street on a skateboard, wearing red shorts and a black midriff top, her hair streaming behind her.

As people appeared on the screen, Candida recalled, "John Holmes was in this one, too, and Desiree Cousteau was the star. She was a very strange, very troubled girl. She was one of the first women to show up with fake boobs. They loved it that she was so Betty Boop cutsie pie, but as soon as the camera stopped rolling, don't touch her. She had no connection with the guys, it was all performance. I remember one saying he had trouble with her because she slapped him when the cameras weren't rolling."

The basic plot seems derived from an old sexist joke about the definition of the perfect woman being someone you could have sex with until when she turns into a pizza at midnight. The plot: The country girls deliver pizza and sex. "Let me get a piece of that!" the customers enthuse.

Onscreen, Candida delivers pizza, and within minutes is peeling off her little red shorts and having a man ejaculate on her face. "I'll tell you the truth," she said. "You had to do it, but it's awful. When I started directing I had to instruct the women *not* to immediately go for the guy's cock, because they were so used to scenes being paced that way."

"Look at this," she said, with a grin. She reached over and pulled open her clothing drawer. Sitting on top were the little red shorts with stripes and pearl buttons we were watching on screen. It was a funny moment, to whip out the same shorts, almost twenty years later. She'd kept them for nostalgia. Until she explained this, their presence in her bedside drawer was slightly startling.

Suddenly, she exclaimed, "That was my boyfriend Danny! I forgot he was in this! He's dead, too. The two guys in this scene are dead. He was very troubled, into drugs." On the screen, they are beautiful young people. Porn counterculture casualties from the time period are like '60s rock stars.

She shook her head, watching, saying it was a time when people pushed themselves too far and did too many drugs, and not everyone survived. "I look at the films, my photo albums, and it's as if while I'm watching they become little black holes. This girl Desiree, the star, ended up in a mental hospital. She shouldn't have been in films. She didn't have the balance." We talked about Candida's tough-girl screen persona. She thinks it was a role she acted for herself as much as an audience, underneath she was insecure and immature, but one thing that comes through is a hint of strength.

Onscreen, there is yet another cum shot on a woman's face, and she comments, "I guess what I hate is . . . when I watch a thing like that . . . is that they'd never think to say, gee females, what would you like? What would feel good to you? There were times when women were near orgasm and they shut off the cameras."

The Femme shoots have always worked differently, she said. "I take a scene from start to finish, but these old films staged and shot blow job to blow job, fuck to fuck." Even the finished product is edited like this.

"I loved the environment, I knew all the people. It was a small, tight knit community so it was like seeing your old friends. If directors and producers were nice that was a plus. This director, Damon Christian, was very funny and considerate, and so was the producer."

The next film was *Hot Rackets*, from the late '70s. It's a fairly elaborate production, starting with a split scene, with someone playing tennis nude, then a seaplane, aerial shots of San Francisco and a tudor mansion, where Candida is a bitchy, frigid wife "who wakes up with perfect lipstick on," she observed. Also a bad attitude. "Not now, hon," as she pushes aside her husband, who responds, "That seems to be the story of our marriage."

Fortunately, the French maid comes in when Candida leaves. "She's as frigid as can be!" he complains. "Aren't you supposed to be making the bed?" Instant oral sex from the maid.

Candida retires to a chaise longue to look attractive and unsatisfied. The butler comes in and stands helpfully by. "Where's my husband?" she asks.

"Being served by Sally," he answers, proceeding to ask, "Do you want it?"

"What do you mean?" she answers, startled.

"Would you like me to pull it out?" He has a husky voice.

"I beg your pardon?"

"The car . . . would you like me to pull it out?"

"The car! yes! Of course I want you to pull the car out! I'll be dressed shortly!"

The more we watch, the more the porn archives turn out to be a pathology printout, a valuable social document giving information about how differently men and women are socialized to see sex. The next sex scene is between her friend and a man, and watching, she commented on the style, which is photographed with close-ups only on breasts, genitals, and, she points out, no awareness of other parts of bodies being erogenous. "I hate the graphicness," she shook her head. "It's not pretty, not subtle. The people have wonderful bodies but you'd never know it. Their idea of showing sex is a bunch of close-ups of genitals."

Later, watching a scene where she is photographed masturbating with a dildo, she again observed, "It's shot from the foot of the bed at a bad angle. The point is to show it as explicitly as possible." The shot is clinical, harsh light, straight on, like an Army film. "If you had the camera running down my body, and you saw the dildo sliding in teasingly . . . This way it's nonerotic and foolish-looking. No wonder I had a complex. I'd see myself and think, 'God, I'm ugly!' But the way they filmed, everyone looks unsensuous." She shuddered and hit fast forward.

The camera presents the beautiful California neighborhood, suggesting sex is enhanced by a luxurious setting. The scenes of Candida driving a convertible through the palm-tree-lined streets and up the country club drive are elaborate.

"Check out my outfit," she laughs, as the screen Candida slinks out of the car in a low-cut sun dress with cross straps, wearing platform shoes and a floppy hat, while 1970s music wobbles on the soundtrack.

At the bar, the bearded, attractive bartender greets her. "This guy was very sweet. A lot of people doing porn were hippies and free spirits, and I remember he was very gentle." His character surmises her problem: "A lot of guy's chicks don't get much action at home so they join the tennis club and work off their frustration."

"Do you mean . . . tennis takes the place of . . . you know?"

"Do I ever. Do you want to know the truth? Tennis is a real sexual turn on. In fact, a lot of our players like to play completely in the nude! And others like to play scantily clothed and let their fantasies go crazy."

"I don't understand."

"Haven't you ever indulged in the fine art of fantasy?" he asks, pouring her a Grasshopper. "Sexual fantasy? I'll show you." He leads her to a mirror over the bar. Sound effects highlight his mirrored image— Poof! He's shirtless. "Keep watching," he offers helpfully. "If you let your fantasies get carried away, you might see something really far out!"

The magic mirror shows them taking their clothes off. The scene goes immediately to oral sex. A heartbeat sound overlays. He ejaculates and she pulls back. "Psychiatrist I'm not, Miss, but I do know what your problem is. You're a tennis widow. Get into the game." Watching the video, Candida drily observes, "Naturally it's presented that it's *my* fantasy to suck his cock. How did he know?!" Years later, when she started her company, the trailer to her films trumpeted, "Finally, there's Femme!"

A film called *Ball Games* had hints of sensibilities that were to come out in her own work.

"The director, Ann Perry, let me perform this scene the way I wanted to. It was unusual to have a woman director. The scene is better than most."

Although the setup was fairly typical (woman imprisoned for prostitution gets it on in jail), Candida, fast forwarding to a scene with a prison guard and the character she played having sex on a stairwell, points out how stylistically different this was.

The music is relaxing, and the scene has soft lighting. The cop puts a matt on the floor, and she puts her arms around him and they embrace. The pace is slow and sensual as she lifts her arms above her head to have him gently take off her dress. The camera is behind them, and while they can be seen just as clearly as in the other films, it looks flattering. He lowers her to the floor, and slowly kisses his way down her body.

The scene conveys a feeling of enjoyment, and watching it is sexy. The camera takes its time moving up and down bodies, stopping calmly to observe. There's a sense of pleasure rather than choppy, goal-oriented graphic couplings. Although this offers just as much detail, the sensibility and style is far different.

"It's like good sex, the way it's filmed," Candida remarked. "He goes down on me, it's downright revolutionary! See, there's whole body shots, kissing . . . licking . . . even the angle is lower, as if a woman lying down is looking up at the man." The sex acts depicted are the same, but the presentation is different. Explicit and erotic come together here. When she slides down to give him oral sex, he puts his hand in her long hair, and caresses her tenderly. The whole sequence is more tactile, confident, and mutual. "Almost shocking, isn't it?" Candida smiled, as the couple on screen finish with a slow, tender kiss.

The last two films she shows me are by Chuck Vincent, the New York director/producer that Per, the man she would marry, worked with. Chuck Vincent had a humorous take on porn films. He made comic explorations of male paranoia and sex role anxiety, while still managing to provide the X rating. If everyone in Woody Allen's films took their clothes off and had sex onscreen, it wouldn't be too dissimilar from the 1970s Chuck Vincent movies.

The Lucky Stiff is high camp, a man's view of men's weakness and vulnerability around sex. Candy Barber and Candida are in a New York apartment with so many hothouse plants it suggests a low-rent Garden of Eden. They're massaging a male client, and running up the tab. The women peel off their clothes, relieve the man of his, and proceed to fleece him via seduction, Candida making notes on a clipboard each time a new "service" is provided.

"Dual Breast massage? Let's *do* it. Rub a dub dub, Mr. Baker. Wooo," breathes Candy Barber, while Candida jots it down, announcing the price. "Perhaps we could interest you in a dual oral massage? That will be an additional twenty dollars. Love to work on you, Mr. Baker." They lead him through an "all the way massage," and then read him his bill, to his horror.

Fascination stars Chuck Vincent himself, as a young man struggling to be a successful bachelor. Candida plays his younger sister. His mother is so devoted she shows up unexpectedly to clean his apartment. "You'll probably catch a horrible disease! Who'll make your brownies! Or your bed! No one needs me! Sob!" His father tries to be a role model, "Yes, son, very few things ever got by your old man! You just call me if there's something you can't handle, if you know what I mean!"

Ernie, Chuck's character, sends for a copy of the book, *The Successful Seducer* so he can "learn the secrets of meeting girls and getting laid."

A sonorous Orson Welles-sounding voice-over periodically proclaims what Ernie's next move should be. "The first step in becoming successful with the ladies is to have a primary base of operation to execute your conquests. Every man must have a bachelor apartment, or *pad*."

"It's charming," says Ernie, touring his new apartment with his voyeuristic landlady-to-be. "Do the beer cans come with it?"

"I see you got a sense of humor. That makes it so much easier when the plumbing and heating break down," the landlady responds. Her parrot screams, "Breakdown! Breakdown!" and when Ernie says he'll take it, "Sucker! Sucker!"

Having "cut the umbilical cord," as the announcer recommends, Ernie is next seen dancing around in a huckapoo shirt, playing disco music while strings of lights flash on his ceiling. The voice-over instructs, "Now that you have your seduction pad in order, take the bull by the horns. We suggest for your first victim to call someone you know. Call, ask her for a drink. If she accepts, that can only mean one thing. Sex!"

It goes on with a series of disasters, all of which are observed by the landlady and parrot. Ernie's first date ends when her boyfriend comes crashing in, threatens to beat him up, and forces him to watch while he has sex with his wayward girlfriend. "Hey, would either of you like a drink?" A female obscene phone caller brings herself to orgasm describing her sexual fantasies about Ernie. "Hey, wait for me!" When he finally does have sex with a blond who doesn't like his apartment, shrimp cocktail, champagne, or the roast beef, but who, it turns out, *does* "like to suck cock," his mother shows up at the door, convinced by his heavy breathing that her son is having an asthma attack. "Softer but harder!" instructs another conquest. Eventually, after being tied up and relentlessly used by two demanding S&M-oriented biker-type women, Ernie just wants to be alone. The happy ending is provided when the obscene phone caller turns out to be his pretty neighbor down the hall.

It was evening when we quit. Candida said she didn't think it was being in porn films that was bad for people, but how it was viewed that was destructive.

"We live in a culture that tells us that sex is a dangerous force. And any woman who would allow herself to be seen actually performing sex is a very evil woman. *That's* what makes it a bad experience. It's not what we did, it's that we're told what we're doing is so bad. The way porn movies were made is a reflection of that."

Because we were looking at her past, she showed me the photo albums and scrapbooks of her life and marriage. So much for the evil scarlet woman. There were portraits of her, with her long brown hair, cuddled with her husband, a lithe young man with nearly white blond hair and Scandinavian features. Pictures of them together, with friends, at home, at meals, outside, all suggesting a warm, community life. Photos cut in heart shapes, surrounded by lace paper doilies.

"My marriage with Per came at a very important time in my life," she says. "I did these movies for five years, and four years into it I realized no matter how tough I wanted to be about it, I had feelings that conflicted."

"Six months into the marriage I made my last film, *Blue Magic* which Per produced. He was a very open-minded, liberated young man. The women on the set loved him because he was kind and respectful toward them. He never pressured me to quit, but I didn't want to make love to other men, or have men think I wanted them. It's work, but to make an effective scene the actors have to act as if they really desire one another."

The marriage lasted nearly ten years. She thinks it was "the place I grew up. Going into porn," she realized later, "had been a way for me to act out my sexuality without receiving any pleasure. That's really what porn was."

Candida packed away her videos of the films she acted in, the pornographic precursors to her own sexual expression. She'd certainly had the experience of acting out other people's fantasies. What she hadn't realized then was that she was moving closer to her own.

WORKING FOR FREE EXPRESSION

Shortly after my movie marathon with Candida in 1993, I attended a day-long workshop by Feminists For Free Expression. It was a radiantly beautiful May Saturday and some three dozen women had chosen to shut themselves inside, sitting crosslegged on the carpeted floor of Betty Dodson's apartment, passing around copies of Andrea Dworkin and Catharine MacKinnon's suggested porn laws, discussing the implications, and talking about why it was important to fight for women's erotic expression.

I was struck by the passion and dynamism of the group. FFE was a fairly new organization (est. Jan. 1992), a spiritual/political heir to groups like FACT, the Feminist Anti-Censorship Task Force. FACT was started to oppose the antiporn ordinance in Indiana. Feminist legal scholars Nan Hunter and Sylvia Law had written the opposing brief for FACT, and dozens of feminists signed it, including Betty Friedan, writers Rita Mae Brown and Kate Millet, and poet Adrienne Rich.

In response, Catharine MacKinnon had declared, "The Black movement has Uncle Toms and Oreo cookies. The labor movement has scabs. The women's movement has FACT." Every woman who signed that brief was a member of the women's movement, a feminist.

The court agreed with FACT's brief and the ordinance was defeated. Feminists like Ann Snitow and Ellen Willis and other FACT members met monthly until 1987, when the group disbanded and the women continued individual related work.

There was a need for new feminist organizations who were active in First Amendment issues, and FFE came together when the Pornography Victims Compensation Act, a bill that would enable a rape victim to sue the makers or distributers of porn films, was being heard by the Senate Judiciary Committee. It was a frightening idea—"The video made me do it." The rapist could go free, but a filmmaker could end up in jail. Teller, of the magic team Penn & Teller, wrote in *The New York Times* Op Ed Page, "When murderers claim the cereal box commanded them to kill, we lock them up. We don't accuse the corn-flake maker of murder."

Some FFE members had worked with FACT. Around the room this May day were people like FFE founder Marcia Pally, a former ballet dancer whose posture was like her prose—elegant, energetic. She would write a book on this issue, *Sex and Sensibility*, and speak of her beliefs of the fundamental misconceptions of the antiporn movement. "It's a movement that tells you that sexual fantasy causes violence. And it knows nothing about either violence or sexual fantasy."

Pally believes the antiporn people will always have an edge over free expression people, because the former movement preys into fear, desire . . . and fear of desire, surrendering to feelings. "We need fantasy arenas. They are a requirement of sanity," she says. "But at its core, sex is about abandon. Being out of control makes us vulnerable. So sex is something we all want and are all afraid of. It seems bigger than we are." One thing the antiporn movement offers is a soothing quick fix, she claims. "If you say, 'Sex is the problem,' it clicks," she declares. "Now if only we could get it under control . . . ."

Other FFE members that day included a young lawyer named Catherine Seiman, who gave a legal presentation, and Jennifer Maquire, who'd volunteered her public relations talents to write press releases on first amendment issues. There was Lavada Blanton, who was active in the Abyssinian Baptist Church of Harlem and employed at *Penthouse*. Lavada talked about her work around racial and sexual issues. Candida was there, along with porn star and performance artist Annie Sprinkle, and dominatrix Ava Taurel, who would periodically run cross town to where the National Coalition Against Censorship was having a weekend-long conference on women and pornography.

Perhaps the most impressive was our hostess, Betty Dodson. Betty was in her sixties now. In *Pleasure and Danger: Exploring Female Sexuality*, Carol Vance, writing a modern history of sex and the feminist movement, counted Betty Dodson's book, *Liberating Masturbation*, as a key text.

I couldn't imagine what it would be like for her, thirty years later, to still be opening her home for day-long meetings of women discussing sex and politics. She took her role model status seriously, but presented it humorously. She wore latex shorts and a T-shirt patterned with skeletons in different positions of sexual intercourse.

Dell Williams, a sixty-something, energetic friend of Betty's who ran the Manhattan women's sexual boutique Eve's Garden, said to me, "I'm glad to see you young ones will take over for us, to continue the work when we're gone." Watching Betty that day, I found myself thinking, "Don't ever go." I knew from reporting on her life that she'd worked for decades to educate women about their lives and sexuality, and still the same questions returned. I was starting to understand this could be a lifetime's work.

History tended to repeat itself. Carol Vance recounted the 1982 derailing of a Barnard sexuality conference, in which twenty-nine diverse feminist writers, activists, and academics would have met to discuss women's sexuality in our society, to see if there had to be an either/or choice of "Pleasure and Danger."

Reading Carol Vance's account of the Barnard conference fiasco is frightening. Antiporn feminists telephoned the college's trustees and officials, complaining that "antifeminist views" and "sexual perverts" had taken over. Within days, Vance reports, Barnard's president, Ellen V. Futter, interrogated the women's center staff and confiscated the conference booklets, *Diary of a Conference on Sexuality* to keep it from being distributed.

"Barnard's administration panicked," said FFE's Marcia Pally, who attended the conference. The Women Against Pornography used tactics she and others termed "unbelievable McCarthyism." If women had written about, for example, domination and submission fantasies, even in academic psychology papers, they were targets of WAP's attacks. One of Pally's friends who was to address the conference found her employers had been called and asked if they knew they had an avowed sexual pervert on their staff.

Arriving at the conference, Pally discovered the Women Against Pornography people had set up a table in the registration area. "On the table were fliers about speakers they didn't like, disclosing what WAP thought they did in bed that was impermissible, and for that reason they should not be allowed to speak." Her voice reflects shock. "I had never seen people's private sex lives printed on fliers and distributed at an academic conference! Barnard invites you to speak. You fly into New York for a conference, come trundling down with your attaché case to give your little talk, and you discover that your purported sex life is under assault! How would you feel? 'Who the hell is in charge here?!' "

Who, indeed. The conference booklets had been confiscated, but "that table remained up and functioning all day long," Pally recalls. Looking back, the one thing that upsets her the most is that she and the other conference attendees tolerated it.

But you can see how the tendency might be to freeze. It took me the first year of the four years I talked to people on the porn issue before I could clearly sort out how I felt about it. I'd had years of indoctrination that pornography was degrading to women and that there was something a little creepy or sad about people who watched it. Walking into a video store and asking for porn videos felt strange the first few times, as if some morals squad would descend.

The influential psychoanalyst Louise J. Kaplan had written in her book *Female Perversions* that what was really perverse are the crippling gender role stereotypes that we're all under social pressure to adopt: Men aren't allowed to cry or get emotional, women's ambition or desires are viewed as threatening or unwomanly. "Whenever a myth of primary femininity crops up—and it has appeared at least once in every century and two or three times in our own age—it is associated with reactionary social trends and with gender stereotypes of femininity," Kaplan wrote. Maternal sexlessness, intellectual vagueness, eternal caregiving, submission, are some of these characteristics.

If Kaplan wasn't right, books like Susan Faludi's *Backlash* wouldn't be *New York Times* bestsellers. The women in this room from FFE were there to work on these problems. They believed that porn was a potential messenger, a mode of communication rather than inevitable degradation.

They talked all day long, listened to presentations of legal, psychological, social readings related to the censorship issue. They discussed it, laughed, argued, questioned, there were even instances of tears. When they spoke of Catharine MacKinnon and Andrea Dworkin, whose positions on censorship they opposed, many still expressed respect for these women as active feminists. They just didn't agree with them on the censorship issue.

"If you don't like the porn you see, make your own," Annie Sprinkle had concluded. I was new to this group and their sensibility, and that unexpected sentence awakened me. I knew Candida Royalle's story, but on a deeper level, I was starting to realize what she had *done*. "Make your own porn." How . . . *active*. So much of the criticism, debate, Meese testimony, discussion, was about women as victims. What if we didn't like theirs, and made ours? It was like any shifting moment in history and politics. It didn't have to be one reality. People could make some new history.

WORKING IN A SUPPORTIVE ATMOSPHERE

"If, in fact, the bottom line of the feminist movement is for women to be able to do whatever they want to do, to achieve, to assert, to break with tradition, then, we've done that. If anything, you should be in our corner, cheering us on."
—Gloria Leanard, from "Deep Inside Porn Stars"
at performance space Franklin Furnace, 1985.

Ten years ago, these women in porn were starting to enunciate a message that would slowly make its way into the mainstream consciousness. First, they needed to reinforce it themselves. The time was the early 1980s. Candida Royalle was a porn star. Her business was sex, but she needed to get more deeply in touch with herself, and her own sexuality.

Candida needed to sort things out. Through friends, she found a therapist, someone she trusted. She continues to go back now and then when new issues trouble her. "This woman had been a prostitute at one time in her life, and I thought, 'She won't judge me.' I've sent a lot of women in the sex industry to her since then. The first thing I did was to march into her office and say, 'I have to understand why I did this. I need to come to terms with it. I want to be able to understand it so I can live with it and go on with my life.' "

Candida was willing to look down the barrel of society's prejudice. Self-acceptance was critical. All these years of work later, she says the old stuff can come back. "Let's face it, in society's view you're basically someone who broke the worst taboo. You are a ruined woman who is used and unworthy. I still have buttons that can be pushed to bring out the old shame. Like, a man must look at me and see damaged goods. I know that there's an ugly little worm in me that crawls around, and certain things can trigger that worm to be very big and take over my being for a day or so.

"People always ask me, would you allow your daughter to make these movies? How would you feel? I answer: I'd explain to her that I don't think it's such a horrible thing to do, but society does. And you are going to have to live with that the rest of your life. I understand the ramifications so much more now than I did then."

She pauses thoughtfully. "I never grew up wanting to make sex movies. I don't think there's anything wrong with that, I just didn't. My reasons for making sex movies were that it was I thought they served a need and it was a great way to make extra money. On the other hand, I know there were destructive reasons as well. Because of the society I live in, doing these movies can be an act of destruction."

In her heart of hearts, she didn't believe that consensual adults acting in erotic films to be viewed by other adults was wrong, and later, she spent a lot of time examining how she would feel about employing people to do the same.

The freedom of what she was contemplating, making porn films from *her* point of view, was an extraordinary idea. A lot of the old-style porn worked hard to make sex dirty, she thought. "Turn of the century depictions of 'bad' girls, as opposed to the wife at home." She believed it perpetuated shame-based views of eroticism, as well as stereotypes. "I longed to experience sex that is exciting because it feels good." Not to say that all sorts of fantasy couldn't be explored. But whore, bimbo, bad girl, stud, would have to go.

WORKING CLUB 90

I think the wisest thing that Candida Royalle and her friends did was to realize that if they were going to try something different in their industry, they would have to support each other. She and a number of women who had worked in porn formed a support group called Club 90. Many of her Club 90 compatriots also entered therapy and found that this supportive environment helped them with issues of sexuality.

The culmination of their work together was when they were approached by the alternative performance space, Franklin Furnace, and asked to do a show based on their support group meetings. They did, and got rave reviews. Audiences seemed to identify with what they were saying.

Gloria Leanard, one of the longest established stars of Club 90, came on first in a magenta evening gown with a lavender feather boa, to declare that she and these other women considered themselves feminists. She added that they and she hoped the performance might influence the viewer to consider things from a different point of view.

The women, Annie Sprinkle, Candida Royalle, Veronica Vera, Susy Nero, Veronica Hart, and Kelly Nichols, appeared, first in fabulous evening gowns. As the evening went on and they began to tell their stories, each stepping forward to the spotlight, they'd metamorphosize, slipping into casual clothes, jeans, nightgowns, comfortable dresses, to illustrate that they were just ordinary people, albeit with an exotic livelihood.

"I guess I'm not what you expected, a porn star with a baby" said Jane Quarterheart, whose screen name had been Veronica Hart. She told of enjoying the business "getting paid for two things I loved to do, act and have sex," and that "one thing about the X-rated business, I never had to sexually audition for anyone." She enjoyed her run in the business, then married and had a baby. "Now I'm a wife, and a mom, and an actress, and sometimes a director and producer."

But a question remained that she posed to the audience. "Why could I never work in mainstream projects? Can America accept a girl like me who is honest about what she's been through and where she's been?" She raised her eyebrows and challenged the audience. "What do *you* think?"

At different points, the women sat on a couch and swapped stories.

"I was on a set doing a girl-on-girl scene and the producer told me I wasn't going to get paid that day because sex with two girls is not sex!"

Another woman, Kelly Nichols, pulled off an elaborate curly wig and stepped into the spotlight to speak of the glamour the business had brought to her life. She told stories of being in films in Paris, the Everglades, San Francisco, appearing at the Jerry Lewis Telethon. "This is stuff that a little girl from West Virginia could never experience if she had stayed a waitress at Bob's Big Boy!"

Annie Sprinkle, having changed to a flannel nightgown from an electric green sheath, spoke of having been born Ellen Steinberg, and that Annie was the kind of person Ellen could never be. "Ellen was fat and ugly, but Annie was voluptuous and sexy!" She half-sang the words in her baby doll voice. "Ellen wore sensible orthopedic shoes, but Annie wore eight-inch spike heels." And so it went, a classic alter ego that reinforced what Candida had told me in the very beginning: "I'm like any other woman but I acted out more." How many people fantasize about their secret lives? For this woman, being in porn had given her access to hers.

Annie went on, talking about Ellen's flannel nightgowns and Annie's fetish lingerie, Ellen's sensible eating, Annie's penchant for Famous Amos chocolate chip cookies . . . and thank goodness for Annie, who paid for Ellen's art school. She spoke on conflicting desires, Ellen's wanting to be a wife and mother, Annie wanting fame . . .

"Some day I hope I get it all together!"

Veronica Vera spoke of traveling to countries like India where erotic images were "carved in stone and treated with reverence."

And Candida, when it was her turn, stood in her fishtailed evening gown before pulling a sweatshirt dress over her head and mused about what she had been through, that she was in a process of examining where porn had helped as well as hurt her, and that "I see myself as a revolutionary of sorts, maybe one day making women's films to replace the tired old men's films that exploit women and promote archaic sexuality. After all," she said, "I'm still young and I have a lot of dreams."

I watched this taped performance near the end of my research. Ten years later she's realized her dream, and employed many of these same women to codirect and write her Femme films. Making these statements on a stage and saying no, being in porn hadn't destroyed them, that it had worked for them, was way ahead of it's time, and took courage. The reviews provided encouragement that gave them hope.

FANTASIES

The experience with the Franklin Furnace project strengthened Candida's direction. "With home video being more established, all my movies were re-released. Candida Royalle was not going to go away."

"That was when I started to put together my own company, Femme, wanting to prove to the old boys' club that I could do something better. It was 1983."

Candida teamed up with a close woman friend, Lauren Niemi. Per's father was involved with Scandinavia's largest video production and distribution company. He agreed to finance her first film.

In February of 1984 Femme officially started. The first film was *Femme*, in April of 1984. *Urban Heat* and *Christine's Secret* were made that summer.

They were different. People noticed and started writing reviews and doing interviews. There was a lot of interest in a former porn actress who made films from a woman's point of view.

The films were celebrated as being for women, although it was a man who first told me about them, and said they were wonderful. They are a lovely, sexy pleasure to watch. She gave time to establish mood, as in *Christine's Secret*, where a woman arrives at a friend's country place for the weekend and looks up to see a shirtless man standing in a window, watching her. Or in one of the segments in *Femme*, in a Soho art gallery where three people circle each other like a dance, looking at the art, looking at each other, taking *time* to develop both tension and expectation before moving to a dream sequence where they all make love. Ten years before the celebrated eroticism of *The Piano* her film *Three Daughters* had a scene where a woman and man play the piano together, gradually moving closer and touching fingers, hands, before moving to bodies.

And there are cautionary tales about being sensitive as a lover. In *The Photographer*, starring Rhonda Jo Petty and Jerry Butler, a male photographer has whipped a woman into a near orgiastic frenzy, seducing her with his camera, then abruptly announcing, "okay, that's it." She challenges him to a strip poker game and then proceeds to turn the tables by arousing him, then abruptly announcing, okay, that's it! He protests. She can't leave him like this, then apologizes for his thoughtlessness and asks if she'll give him another chance. The next scene is perfect.

The male and female figures are both standing. Before a sequence of lovemaking that is explicit and erotic, this scene of two bodies equal, facing each other makes a striking visual point, and is in stark contrast to the typical fetishized, disembodied parts that are central to previous porn movies.

Candida claims that her second film, *Three Daughters,* may be the film that comes most "from the heart." It portrays the sexuality of three young women in a family, especially the coming of age of a teenage girl.

"When I was thirteen, I started this thing with my twelve-year-old neighbor. We would practice dance together, and it turned into a game where we took turns being the boy. Whoever was the boy would undress the other. We'd touch and caress each other's bodies for hours. It never got genital, but it was a sensual awakening. There's a scene like that in the movie."

Three Daughters was about rediscovering a time when every feeling was new, and the slightest touch or kiss was exciting. "I realized how we forget about that as adults. You forget about nuances and buildup."

Praise for *Three Daughters* came from the commercial movie review community and the psychological/sexological community. The American Association of Sex Educators, Counselors, and Therapists featured it at their annual invitational film festival, which made her the first erotic filmmaker to be accepted into the organization. Jami Bernard, reviewing for the *New York Post*, described it as "taking the thorn out of porn." Bruce Williamson at *Playboy* said it made the competition look like "greasy kid stuff."

"I wanted to show a young girl coming of age without the guilt and shame," Candida says. 'That's why you see she's gone from being a kind of tomboyish kid in shorts and at the end she's driving off, a young woman who's come of age. There's no talk of happy ever after. It's about, 'She's become a woman, and this is hers now, this is hers to keep.' "

Recognition increased. In 1985, *Glamour* magazine published an article that started with the words, "Finally, there's Femme . . ."

"It was my first mainstream article, talking about the issue and featuring me as the first woman doing this. From that the Phil Donahue show called. I was on with Catharine MacKinnon and sexologist Lonnie Barbach. Right before I went on my former partner, Lauren, gave me the loveliest piece of advice. 'You have nothing to defend,' she said, 'You are the lily that rises to the top of the muck.' " That piece of advice helped calm her, and she was able to talk about what she was trying to do. Later, Catharine MacKinnon would refuse to appear on programs or panels with women who represented a healthy view of explicit films.

After the *Glamour* piece, *The New York Times* wrote about Candida, followed by United Press International. Femme was launched in a major way.

"That it's a woman, Candida Royalle et al, behind the camera, doesn't matter to us," Norma Ramos, from Women Against Pornography was quoted as saying. "Her films do exactly what other pornographers do, which is reduce women to body parts."

But they don't, I thought. I would soon begin to interview members of the sexological and psychological community who disagreed with Ramos.

FEMME

"Most of what I did as an actress, I wouldn't ask women to do in my films," Candida said, sitting in her light-filled Soho office. She uses married couples and lovers most of the time, and shoots in a cinema verite, continuous way. "It's not stop and go, stop and go," she described. "I think this realistic method of filming what's really happening instead of staging it is more human and sensuous."

Much of her technique derived from what she didn't enjoy doing herself. "The women were all made to look like total little bimbettes. In most porn, they still are. The way you're kind of splayed out, and the camera is shoved up your legs. I mean, it's embarrassing. 'Get into this position, and when we turn the lights on, we want you to go from this position to this position, and then we'll film that for a while. Then we'll move the lights and cameras and you move to this position, and we'll do that for a while . . .' There was no sensuality, no natural approach to it."

The films she acted in were made in what she describes as formulaic and mechanical ways, almost assembly line fashion. If the lead actor loses his erection, they'd have a "stunt cock," she said. "That's happened to me and it's terrible. You're having sex with one person, and then they switch and you have another man's penis in you."

Or, the man could take advantage of the situation in between takes. "He'll ask the actress to suck him to keep him hard. Some women would, some wouldn't. That's why fluffers came about, girls who were brought in just to keep the guys hard. I would get really angry about it, and say, 'Hey, this is *his* job!'"

"How common was it that the actress would comply?"

"It was only expected if you let it be!" she declared with humorous grimness. "There were women who were much more accommodating than others. I wavered somewhere in the middle. I didn't like being taken advantage of. If they couldn't get it up again when it was time, that's their problem! I shouldn't have to keep them hard for the fifteen minutes they were setting up a new scene."

"The first guy I worked for was gross. He took advantage of the girls. He'd shoot girls giving him head and sell it on the underground market. He'd take up a girl's day doing eight- or sixteen-millimeter shots of them, saying 'You have to prove you can really do it for you to get this work,' not pay them, and then sell the film."

At media appearances and lectures, Candida Royalle often spoke about how something that is a part of society, but disavowed, keeps sex workers underpaid, unprotected, and exploited. Seeing sex workers as victims rather than people who made a work choice, people who provide a valuable service that is popular in our society, does the same.

IN A NEW DIRECTION

Back in the 1970s, when Candida was starring in her films, Dr. Robert Stoller, who would later study Bill Margold and his coworkers, wrote in one of his books that the differences in men and women's response to pornography might be due to childhood experiences and socialization of the sexes. "Men, judging the pornography of women, make the same mistake as when judging the pornography of anyone dynamically different; not stirred themselves, they cannot see that the material might arouse others." As society changes, he allowed, more women would discover a taste for such products.

Before he got to the part about society changing, Stoller wrote, "A few words may be in order regarding the puzzling fact that attempting to sell pornography to women would lead one to starvation."

Candida Royalle, the former porn actress in films whose audience was primarily men, now a decade later was making her own films, the audience for which was primarily women and couples.

She didn't starve.

* * *

Sandra Cole is a former president of the American Association of Sex Educators, Counselors, and Therapists (AASECT), as well as an internationally recognized expert on sexuality and disability. Talking to Cole was fascinating. She was able to point out that yes, these films were important and good for people and they did a lot more that just "reduce women to body parts." Henceforth, I thought I might print snippets of her comments on cards and bring Femme films as hostess gifts.

Sandra Cole found out early about Candida's films and was very impressed with them, calling them "a great departure." Sandra and Ted Cole were founders of the Human Sexuality program at the University of Minnesota Medical School. In the late '60s and early '70s, they were using explicit films with patients who were sexually dysfunctional. The films demonstrate techniques, how to take time, how to demythologize the belief that both have to come simultaneously, the stuff which makes people dysfunctional in the first place.

Cole drew a distinction in erotica, between eros (love), and thanotica (violence and death). Snuff films and violent pornography she saw as the latter category, but allowing for complexity, she stated that "the whole spectrum of human behavior is extremely important to document, and that includes S&M, bondage, or anything that's compliant sexually and emotionally or fantastically arousing to people." Thanotica she believed was more about violence than sex, and she didn't value it.

Upon discovering Candida's Femme films, Sandra Cole called and said she was very interested in them. "They're valuable because they're made for independent use, away from the therapeutic model. There's a need for people to have films for enrichment without the stigma there's something 'wrong' with them. There's a whole population of people who wouldn't be caught dead going to a counselor."

Candida and Sandra Cole talked about how her films could subtly educate men to please a female. "We discussed guys who never talk about what they're doing with their partners, don't even know their partners aren't satisfied. Men who have learned that if it's good enough for their buddies and it's good enough for them it ought to be good enough for a female."

"Will they change lovemaking for men?" I asked.

"For a woman to risk trying to train her partner, to put it crassly, she has to have a vehicle if she doesn't have the words. These films are helpful because if he participates he will be influenced. With exposure comes change."

Most men believe the point of sex is ejaculation, Cole pointed out.

The movie equivalent is the ubiquitous cum shot, money shot, the four-star focusing in on the penis ejaculating over the woman's body or in her face, which is to the majority of porn films what the *1812 Overture* is to the finale of a Boston Pops concert.

Much of the antiporn critique of the cum shot labels it the final insult. Candida, who has had a number of them in her face, allows they aren't among her favorite memories of her acting days. I've read social scientists who actually analyze what they define as the sexism ratio in each porn film according to how many cum shots it has.

Why is *that* the definition? I thought. Couldn't they be interpreted in a lot of ways, such as evidence of male anxiety, a sort of "Look, Mom, I did it!"

"Men are socialized that ejaculation is the focal point," Sandra Cole told me. "So they don't know what they don't know. They insist on completing their own erotic arousal. There's the whole myth of 'Blue Balls. Once we start we shouldn't stop or I'll die, I'm going to explode.' Well, it's not true. His penis will become partially flaccid. He will wish he could get off. She may buy his myth and never talk about it, or she's a 'nice' girl, don't make waves or ask questions. Who knows where it goes? Ignorance about sexuality has a life of its own. We're trying to grab the tail that wags the dog and put sexual enrichment, health, and intimacy back into a society that's become very sex negative." The Femme films, Sandra Cole declared, were a major contribution. "Candida's a visionary, and she has the ability to translate her vision into products that are helpful to people."

In the 1970s, Robert Stoller wrote that a person making erotic films must "develop a daydream that is not idiosyncratic. He must extract out of what he knows about his audience those features all share in common. If he does not, he runs the risk of selling only one copy. He therefore has to create a work precise enough to excite himself and general enough to excite many. Thus, pornography for the researcher is a sort of statistical study of psychodynamics—a more colorful and more powerful method than the opinion poll that is sometimes foisted on us as rigorous research."

He . . . or **she** could create the work. Candida Royalle's career was gaining ground, mirroring a change in society. As Stoller had said, if she wasn't producing work that the audience identified with, it wouldn't sell. Femme was turning out to be a reflection as well as a product. The evidence she produced could be documented in dollars and cents. It was a powerful method by which to study the culture.

WORKING ON

Femme grew, and Candida continued to make films. She and Per broke up after ten years of marriage, and her original partner Lauren Niemey left. She found herself writing, directing, raising money, producing, and doing her own distribution. It was too much, and she didn't know how long she could keep it going.

In 1993 Candida had a screening party for *Revelations*, an ambitious project she'd written, produced, and directed. It was set in an Orwellian, repressive future, when the state controlled sex and decreed where and when it would be experienced. She'd been inspired by political events of the past few years. The lead character, a beautiful young woman who is frustrated by her militant husband, becomes curious when she sees police take a neighbor to jail, and that night, finds her way into a secret room where the neighbor hid sexual images and films. She risks exploring, despite the danger. . . .

The screening was at Manhattan's Club USA. The audience was a large circle of writers, journalists, friends, FFE members, political and legal activists, other film people, musicians. Candida looked lovely and very nervous. Later her accountant told me she rolled double or nothing getting this one produced. The film was enthusiastically received. As I was leaving, a couple of prototypical New York club kids, boys about fifteen years old, squeezed their way in to check out what was going on. One asked me and I told him it was the premiere of Candida Royalle's newest film. He craned his neck and nudged his friend.

"That's her. Yeah, I've seen her and that other one, the older lady who teaches masturbation, on cable."

"Betty Dodson?"

"Yeah. That's wild. Was her film good?"

"Yes, it was very good."

"Cool," he said, punching his friend on the arm. "Women do all this stuff now."

The film has an effective ending. Those who have explored outside the sexual parameters set by a totalitarian government are punished, taken away by gun-toting soldiers to a world of barbed wire and prison. But the woman knows her hidden room remains.

"In certain ways," Candida says thoughtfully, "It's about women in general, people opening up. We're all shut down, some more so than others."

THE PSYCHOLOGICAL COMMUNITY

The time was 1993, at the American Psychological Association meeting in San Francisco. The topic was "Creating Adult Erotica That Presents Positive Sexual Role Modeling." Candida Royalle and Helen Singer Kaplan, Ph.D. the founder of the Human Sexuality Program at the Payne Whitney clinic, were presenting.

Two years later, in the summer of 1995, Helen Singer Kaplan died of cancer. She was a major contributor to the treatment of marital therapy and sexual disorders, writing dozens of papers and many books on the subject. It was like her to open up such an interesting and complex topic. Many of the back and forth comments, between Kaplan, Candida Royalle, and the psychiatrists, showed the intricacies of working with sexuality, fantasies, and patients.

In recent years, an increasing number of people who work in the sex industry have presented at such conferences, I attended ones with Candida Royalle and Ava Taurel, a dominatrix who later entered New York University's Human Sexuality graduate program.

Ron Moglia, the head of New York University's graduate program in Human Sexuality, one of the largest programs in the country, discussed the complexity of this with me. Just getting his field considered legitimate had been a long road.

Because it was sex, it was suspect. He would always run into people, unfortunately often in funding positions, who couldn't wrap their minds around the idea that sex could be legitimate academic work.

I could sympathize. I remember once having lunch with a male journalist I considered very intelligent. When I mentioned interviewing the head of NYU's graduate sexuality program, he thought it was hysterical. "Oh, come on! A graduate degree in sex! What next?"

So I was interested to consider the APA doctors meeting an actual erotic filmmaker.

In 1993 at the San Francisoco meeting, Helen Singer Kaplan's opening remarks contrasted sharply with the writings of antipornography writer Catharine MacKinnon, who had declared that showing pornography to a man was like saying, "Kill!" to an attack dog. Kaplan spoke of the formulation of sexual fantasies. She said that children learned from early sexual stimulation, and that this was usually a healthy progression.

The process went awry, she claimed, when events interrupted what should be a normal developmental process. "There is a mechanism by which people form these fantasies, and that is children trying to cope with emotional trauma by libidinizing or sexualizing them. It is similar to the mechanism described by Ana Freud on identification with the aggressor," she added. "The child attempts to deal with conflict, turmoil, and pain that disrupts families by sexualizing these events. A striking example of this is concentration camp survivors. Many of these women had fantasies of having sex with Nazi guards. This is anathema on an intellectual level to these women, but it's their erotic fantasy. It was programmed very early in life."

In *The New York Times* in 1994, Catharine MacKinnon stated there was "overwhelming documentation" of the fact that pornography resulted in antisocial, abusive activity in its consumers. In interesting contrast to this claim, Helen Singer Kaplan said that you couldn't make a man sadistic by showing him S&M erotica. "Men, as well as women, become sadistic or masochistic or a pedophile as a result of certain childhood experiences."

The continuum of sexuality is often addressed in different contexts. The human psyche is an amazing and complex thing, and there is no pat ABC formula of how individual sexuality develops. Regarding Kaplan's point about S&M, professional dominatrix Ava Taurel suggested that among her clients, the fantasy-experience tradeoff may not be a completely literal progression from what happened to them in childhood. She'd seen adults become interested in being spanked during S&M sessions who claimed they'd never been spanked as children.

"Maybe," Ava suggested, "they have encountered a woman who has enjoyed a few friendly slaps and they like to go in this direction." She also suggested maybe they got the idea from films and wanted to know what the sensation was like. (Consensual experimentation is a different construction from the antiporn contingent's monkey-see, monkey-do construction, in which the claim was that merely seeing something on film would induce someone to go out and do what they saw.)

"There is a big distinction between people who add S&M as an element, and those who have it as a major component from childhood." Ava said she supposed that Dr. Kaplan, as a therapist, had seen more of the latter.

Kaplan was sticking to the theory about sexual fantasy being rooted in childhood. "Not only that," Kaplan countered. "If it doesn't happen psychodynamically, why should the person find being spanked erotic? Why not find asphyxiation erotic?"

"Yes," sighed Ava enthusiastically. "That is a wonderful fantasy."

"It *has* to be something in the personality otherwise it wouldn't be an addiction as an adult. But this is a philosophical argument," said Kaplan. "If a patient has it as a component I try to work it into their sex life, and I'm sure you do the same thing. You don't have to eradicate these things." Later I would come to appreciate the sophistication of this psychiatrist making this link between her work with patients and the sessions of dominatrix Taurel. More therapists seemed afraid to make that kind of acknowledgment.

Taurel and Kaplan's ruminations on where fantasy comes from are interesting questions that people in the field of sexuality and psychology ponder. Dr. Charles Moser, M.D., Ph.D., is a professor of sexuality in California. He wrote, "How humans develop specific sexual interests, or aversions, is a basic and essentially unanswered question in sexuality. One should not presume that there is only one process that determines these sexual interests."

Ava said she thought many people had common fantasies and would like to find therapists who understood, who could help them.

Kaplan finished the thought for her. "Help them integrate it. With cross-dressers our approach is to help them integrate the fantasy into the relationship rather than eradicate it. To go back to the last point, if someone has an antisocial fantasy, rape or pedophilic, we really try to teach them to stay in the fantasy rather than acting it out. I don't think we have the techniques to eradicate a fantasy without doing violence to the personality, cutting off a piece of them and causing depression."

Sound idea. Instead of considering porn as a depiction of fantasy, *creating* behavior, it could be used as a therapeutic adjunct. In other words, watching it could take *off* the heat, or give it an outlet.

Helen Singer Kaplan later gave another telling example from her cases, of a husband and wife with a major sexual impass. He loved anal sex. She thought it was disgusting. The differences in what they desired had resulted in a standoff. In treating them, she suggested the occasional use of a porn video depicting anal sex that he could watch when they had vaginal sex, so in effect, both got what they wanted.

It's a fascinating discussion, and the opposite of the conclusions drawn by the Meese Commission, as well as the antipornography stance of Dworkin and MacKinnon. Later in the presentation, Kaplan would point out that years ago rigid ideas of "normalcy" had lead to experiments with behavioral deconditioning that tried to rid patients of unwelcome fantasies.

"They used to take homosexuals and give them electric shocks when they saw a beautiful male figure, and play sweet music when they saw a nude woman," she recalled. She used this as an extreme and prejudiced example, to point out the danger of labeling individual, subjective fantasy. "I make no distinction between healthy sexuality and fantasy driven sexuality," she added. "It's one and the same for me." She thought a bit and further clarified. "In the case of antisocial fantasy, such as pedophilia, a more workable approach would be the use of anti-androgen medication combined with psychotherapy."

"It is clear," Kaplan continued, "adult experiences of watching erotica can't influence behavior in either direction. If they could we could take a pedophile, show him a nice porno picture of adults having sex, and he'd be cured. That doesn't happen and vice versa. You can't take someone with normal sexuality and show him S&M footage and make him violent."

The presentation segued into desire disorders. Kaplan pointed out that patients with inhibited desire often turn themselves off, entering the bedroom with anxieties about the partner and sex. She said one of the exercises they used was to assign the patient to take responsibility for their own thoughts and feelings, and be active in getting into the mood. To do this, she asked them to watch erotica ahead of time, "to come into the bedroom with an erotic feeling already there, instead of sitting there like a lump waiting for your partner, saying, 'Okay, turn me on.'" Here explicit films are helpful, rather than harmful.

The program, which included segments of Candida's films, followed with a question and answer period. I thought the questions proved that when it comes to sex, psychiatrists have just as much to learn as the rest of us.

The first question was from a psychiatrist from the Harvard Medical School, who had just written a book. One of his case studies was a man who "had an addiction to purchasing pornography, a furtive, secretive procurement ritual, really an ego dystonic behavior that he did not want to be doing. He had found pornography as a young boy among the possessions of his father and this really turned out to be a form of grief involving the lack of a good relationship with his father. I, too, am completely supportive of the kind of films we saw today but I have some concerns about the issue of sexual addiction and pornographic addiction."

Kaplan responded, "I have never in my practice seen a negative effect from introducing people to erotica. It gives people permission and releases guilt about sexual fantasy. I think if the person is going to be compulsive or addictive they're going to find something to do it with. I see no apparent danger. I don't think it's an addictive substance."

Another psychiatrist expressed surprise that in the film they'd seen, the man didn't have a constant erection, which to him was "a total turn-off. I'd also be intrigued to hear the experience of the female actresses. Are they simulating? How often when they pretend or seem to have an orgasm are they actually having one?"

Candida answered this one, saying while sometimes you try to enjoy it, that acting in porn films was the hardest work she'd ever done. "There's an image of people going to the set and having a grand old time, orgies and all." But it was exhausting, she added, with long hours in front of hot lights, physically depleting work.

"As for your comments about the male erection, well, unfortunately, that's the result of the fact it's long hours in front of crews and camera. Even in the most intimate setting men don't have a nonstop erection. You stop, you go down on the woman, you do things and your erection might go down but it certainly doesn't mean you're not excited." The people in the film, she added, were married, and her assumption was that the man was turned on to his wife. "I hear a lot of complaints from men saying men in porn films always look like studs. Constant huge hard-ons and I can't measure up. It's good for them to see the guy isn't a nonstop piston, that he's human, like anyone else." The audience laughed.

"What do you think of that question?" I asked weeks later, as we reread the transcript.

"I think he ought to reexamine some of his attitudes about male sexual performance," she answered.

The next man asked about the effect of "liberalization of pornography in our society and the effect it would have on children."

"We're not going back to Prohibition because we don't want babies to drink liquor," Kaplan answered. "It's always been an excuse for government intervention to say 'yes, but the children will be harmed.' I don't think children should see this, but I think there's a greater hazard to society if we start censoring people's sexuality."

The discussion went on to everything from the Meese Commission to individual variations on common fantasy. In concluding, Helen Singer Kaplan said that if the sex therapy assignments given to a patient were boring, there was something wrong with the assignment. "One of the principles of sex therapy is that you never do anything without desire. If you don't feel desire, then it becomes counterproductive and creates a link between boredom, mechanics, and the sexual act.

Same with erotica", she added. "If you find it boring and mechanical, you should rent a different film."

THE FEMINIST SPECTRUM ON PORN

In 1993 the Maidenform bra company ran an ad they hoped would appeal to their customers via identification with their political beliefs, a visual statement suggesting the linkage of their lingerie and solidarity with the following causes.

It pictured a big white bra surrounded by international NO signs, the circle with a slash through it.

International NO sign: NO RACISM.

International NO sign: NO POLLUTION.

International NO sign: NO PORN.

"So, we write a letter about the bra ad, agreed?" asked Marcia Pally, as members of Feminists For Free Expression passed the ad, a large bowl of popcorn, and bottles of wine, soda, and juice, around the Chelsea apartment living room. This day's FFE representatives, an eclectic sampling of lawyers, writers, academics, and magazine staffers, looked it over and nodded. They did not want the Maidenform company equating porn with pollution and racism. "Okay, next item is about the next Feminism and Free Speech series . . ."

In *The New York Times* Sunday magazine of March 13, 1995, Catharine MacKinnon, whose book *Only Words* advocated laws to outlaw pornography, debated First Amendment lawyer Floyd Abrams, with Anthony Lewis moderating.

MacKinnon complained that a "form of trouble for the First Amendment" was "a lack of access to speech by those with dissident views not allowed to be expressed in the media, by a publishing world that excludes these . . ." This from the woman *The New York Times Magazine* had now, for a second time, featured as a "feminist legal scholar on pornography." The first time was a cover story in October, 1991.

"The literature and media is flooded with feminist antiporn points of view, and there's very little of the opposing viewpoints being represented," Leanne Katz, director of the National Coalition Against Censorship, told me in 1993. "Women came to us at NCAC and said we need to form a specifically feminist response."

At numerous visits to NCAC over this several year period, Leanne

Katz would express their frustration with media coverage of the censorship issue, especially the difficulty in getting the mainstream media to stop referring to the antiporn movement as "the feminists."

Leanne Katz is a true believer, "a First Amendment junkie" who talked her way into a temporary secretarial job at the ACLU in the 1970s. She's been executive director of the NCAC since its formation in 1974.

Katz told of hours of interviews with reporters about NCAC members who didn't believe censorship was good for women, and then the article would feature the antiporn contingent's views, quoted as "feminists say."

"The news isn't when women say they don't like censorship! The news is when women say they want censorship!"

From her years of experience, Leanne Katz feels manipulation of this issue has "been going on sub-rosa for a very long time. It's an intensely divisive issue among academic feminists, so much so that the mainstream feminist organizations are afraid to talk about it. The reason they're afraid to is because the antiporn women do not want open discussion of these issues. Instead, they've created an atmosphere of intimidation."

A lot of women feel that supporting the suppression of pornography is wrong, she adds, but they're afraid to say "Wait a minute." "The censors have learned to play on the fears and anxieties that so many people have about sex."

NCAC would host a conference on feminist women who took a pro-expression position on pornography, including people like journalist Molly Ivans, and writer Judy Blume, award-winning author of young adult fiction. Judy Blume read hilarious and heartbreaking letters she got from kids begging for the facts of life "in order of importance" and asking questions about menstruation and masturbation, afraid something was wrong with them. Blume talked about the danger and cruelty of censorship, and recounted a story about being on *Crossfire* with Pat Buchanan, who'd highlighted passages of her books dealing with these topics. "Finally, I just turned to him and said, Mr. Buchanan, are you hung up on masturbation or what?"

NCAC Working Group member Betty Friedan declared, "My own book, *The Feminine Mystique*, which helped start the modern women's movement, was suppressed as pornographic."

Leonore Tiefer, psychotherapist at Montefiore Medical Center added, "Female sexuality is a joke without freely available information and ideas."

Other NCAC Working Group members included Wendy Kaminer, Erica Jong, Nadine Strossen, former NOW head Marilyn Fitterman, Nancy Friday, Fay Wattleton of Planned Parenthood, and Nora Ephron. Many of the FACT, NCAC, and FFE members intertwined.

All discussed their passionate conviction that censorship had never been good for women. These were famous, influential women, women at the top of their fields who'd been active for years. It was moving and inspiring to hear their words. Why did it take so long to make known the fact that a spectrum of feminist opinion existed on pornography, not just that the antiporn contingent did not speak for all feminists?

Chris Finan is director of the Media Coalition, an organization set up by the trade groups governing the publishing, video, software, and recording industries.

The Media Coalition's mandate is to protect the First Amendment rights of their members, not, he drily pointed out, as Catharine Mac-Kinnon stated in an address to the National Press Club, "to protect sexually explicit materials." The day after MacKinnon was in *The New York Times Magazine* again, we spoke.

"We don't agree with her," Chris Finan said. "It doesn't mean we're trying to silence her because we disagree with her. Much of her moral power comes from this pose as a leader of an oppressed segment of the population."

One of his projects had involved preparing a synopsis of MacKinnon's writing for distribution to their members. "We felt that the media didn't know enough about her agenda, that in effect she is a censor. They'd picked someone who wasn't representative of feminists as a whole."

Finan found the MacKinnon synopsis tough slogging. "It's difficult to read because it's so unremittingly hostile to men. It's hate speech. I read it for several months and I began to think every time I saw a woman, 'She must loathe me!'"

* * *

"I've hardly watched any porn films," my editor from *New York* magazine mused over lunch. She was the editor I'd worked with on all of my stories for *New York* magazine Her youthful good looks—blond, blue-eyed, slender—belied the fact she'd been there since the inception of the magazine, the Gloria Steinem, Jimmy Breslin, Tom Wolfe days. I'd always liked her tremendously. She was a superb editor. She was naturally the person I would call to talk to about a story I wanted to do for the magazine.

"How many porn films have you watched?" she asked.

"A few hundred now. But my point is, there are all different kinds. Hardcore. Softcore. Films for couples, some from a woman's point of view, like Candida's Femme films. Gay porn. Lesbian porn. Bisexual porn. Transsexual porn. What you read all the time, what MacKinnon talks about is too narrow and limiting a description for what erotic films represent, and what they can do."

I told her that there was a spectrum of people who watched porn. A spectrum of people who made it. That as many women as men watched it. I talked about the women involved with FACT, NCAC, and FFE, and what they believed. That even some of the feminists who had originally been against porn had reversed their opinions.

She got it. She asked questions, and said she hadn't thought of it this way before, and that yes, this sounds like something that should be covered in *New York* magazine. She asked if I would write a proposal that she could submit. I did that night, and called the next day. Overnight, she'd developed a very adverse reaction to the idea. I was bewildered at the change.

"If you write a query, I'll pass it on to someone else here. But I'm afraid you'll have to find someone besides myself to work with you on a story about. . . ." her voice shook as she said the dreadful word, "pornography!"

"Don't feel bad," Leanne Katz consoled when I stopped in the National Coalition Against Censorship to thank her for the material and tell her what had happened, how I'd met with another editor at the magazine, written a six-page proposal, and *then* had them say no.

"It was as if I was talking to two different people," I said. I knew that my editor had been concerned with feminist issues for many years. She'd told me about related work she'd done for *New York* in the 1970s. The indoctrination that porn was poison had been established back then. Still, it had seemed during our conversation that she'd understood what I was saying.

"I've had things like this happen many times," Leanne said. "Sex is a very complex and loaded topic for most people. It's why there should be more discussion and information. It's why we do what we do, to try to break through that barrier. It's important," she sighed.

I didn't talk to my editor from *New York* for some time. When we did speak again, she was starting a new job at a woman's magazine which had just hired a new editor-in-chief, Ellen Levine.

"Do you know that Ellen Levine was one of the two women who

publicly dissented from the Meese Commission's conclusions about pornography?" I demanded.

Her voice sounded bright and innocent. "Why, yes, a friend of mine mentioned that!"

I wished her luck before we said goodbye.

WORKING FAMILY VALUES

"Our average customer has a family, two or three years of college, washing machine, car in the garage," says Phil Harvey in his Washington, D.C. office. Harvey is the owner of Adam & Eve, the largest provider of mail-order erotic products in the country.

Between 1984 and 1994 Adam & Eve went from a twenty-million dollar business to an eighty-million dollar business. "It's a white collar, upscale middle class, suburban profile, one and a half children as it breaks down statistically."

What the success of Adam & Eve finally illustrated to me was that the production and distribution of explicit films was a profitable, completely mainstream business. It had a lot to do with family values, because family people were buying it. And that could be a good thing.

How did he get into the sex business? Condoms. From 1964 to 1969, after graduating from Harvard, Harvey had worked for CARE in India. During those years the Indian population grew by 18 million a year. He became convinced that providing food to countries with hungry people wasn't the only answer. Affordable contraception and education was. He went to graduate school on a Ford Foundation scholarship and studied family-planning administration, at that time a primitive science. "No one knew much about it. They could teach demography and reproductive physiology, but when it came to planning itself it was the blind leading the blind. It's still relatively primitive as a discipline."

Phil Harvey and another Ford fellow, Timothy Black, started the condom business, in 1970, originally as a graduate school project. It was illegal to sell condoms through the mail. An Anthony Comstock law dating from 1872 still categorized condoms as obscene, therefore unmailable. "No one was doing it, and it was a very substantial market. While we and our attorneys waited with some nervousness, the orders poured in." He and Black didn't know much about business, but they could see that more money was coming in than going out. They decided to proceed. The initial idea was to experiment, see if they could promote contraception through non-clinical means, but instead the business grew more quickly than either had anticipated.

Twenty-five years later Adam & Eve sells four million condoms a year. One of their advantages has always been the embarrassment factor, which has diminished in the past few years because condoms are out from behind the counter. Now, Harvey points out, you can take them off the rack so there need not even be an exchange of words. Adam & Eve, selling at lower than drugstore prices, offers sample packages, where you can try multiple types.

The catalogue is an A to Z guide to accessorizing one's sex life. Besides the X-rated videos, there are pages of such toys as glow-in-the-dark dildos, vibrators, massage oil, the Holiday Babydoll Lingerie Set (Santa Hat included), thongs for men, nostalgia erotica collections featuring stripper Candy Barr, Marilyn Monroe, and Betty Page, poker cards faced with nude men or women, flavored lubricants, and Delay Spray which promised to help a man "be an all night lover!"

In addition to having fun, Americans also apparently want to learn as much as possible about sex. Some of the most successful products have been instructional videos, which Harvey's team selected through consultation with sexologists from AASECT, the American Association of Sex Education, Counselors, and Therapists, who screen everything in the Adam & Eve catalogue to be sure the material does not depict violence or anything they consider damaging. The Femme line sells well.

"It's nice for our employees to feel good about what we sell, like when Lloyd Sinclair, from the Midwest Center for Psychotherapy in Madison, Wisconsin, comes around and says, 'You people are important sex educators. Most Americans are not going to have the time or inclination to come to people like me for clinical sessions for sexual problems, but the material you sell teaches people good things about sex.'"

There are videos that show how a man can maintain ejaculatory control. There is the popular *Becoming Orgasmic* based on a program for improving women's response rate. There are instructional videos so people can learn different sexual positions.

Harvey speaks of the factors contributing to the products' popularity. "What they do is combine the permission giving of a nonthreatening but professional authority who says sex is good for you and you should learn to have a more intimate and exciting sex life. They also have explicit sexual depictions, which are inherently interesting, but also teach how other people have sex. In order to do it, you *have* to be explicit, you can't do cable version videos if you're going to teach people how their parts work together."

These tapes have been very successful. They're advertised in major national publications, because of the quality and the educational value. The list ranges from *Ladies Home Journal* to *Good Housekeeping*, *The New York Times*, *Omni*, *U.S. News and World Report* to *Soap Opera Digest*.

Why are these instructional sex videos so popular with Americans, as well as viewed so approvingly by the psychological and sexological communities?

Watching the tapes with a computer booted up and rewinding to check quotes I could see why these tapes are such a success.

Sexologists use the term "permission giving," a lot. Watch these tapes, and you understand that term, as ordinary people get to explore something that they've previously felt awkward or shy about. The act of watching passes that permission on.

Instructional sex videos, such as *The Better Sex Video Series* by the Townsend Institute, and the Sinclair Video Library's *Ordinary Couples, Extraordinary Sex*, use couples who first discuss, then enact how they worked through sexual situations that were new to them, that improved their sex lives. They use all kinds of people, some of whom are gorgeous and sexy, some who could be the folks next door. The message is that no matter what you look like or how old you are, you're a sexual person and it's okay and right for you to open up and enjoy sex more.

Most people can relate to these stories. I found that they encouraged reassessing and resensitizing. You watch these people having all this Better Sex, slowing down and communicating and having fun and being sensuous and playing, and it can't help but make you think . . . hhmmm, like to do that. Looks good. Can identify with her. Really? A man thinks *that*? It's enlightenment as humanistic exhibition and voyeurism. Talk about safe sex.

In the *Better Sex Video Series* by the Townsend Institute, Dr. Judith Seifer and Dr. Michael Kollar, two highly qualified sex educators and counselors (they go through the list of their affiliations and achievements in the beginning) are introduced.

Dr. Judith Seifer, a likeable and warm figure, sits on a chair, and faces the camera. She starts by saying that most people don't know how to talk about sex. Dr. Michael Kollar continues by saying that we don't have a process for learning about sex. As adults we're just supposed to know.

Both doctors explain that people need information, and the permission to ask what they want from each other. Seifer says it's important to discover what people like, and what they don't like.

What I especially appreciated about the *Better Sex* videos is that the couples dramatize the bad sex they used to have. I thought that was very generous of them.

You start off with them sitting in chairs, wearing nice clothes and introducing themselves, like the good-looking Mary and Robert. A high-school health teacher, she's got a lovely refined Dutch accent and blond ringlets. Robert, a musician, is a strikingly handsome man. "Robert learned to change positions, delay ejaculation, and loving play helped Mary and Robert have a more intimate sexual relationship," voice-overs Dr. Koller.

We cut to the back seat of a car, which represents them dating in high school. "I had an awful time, really," Mary's lightly accented voice describes the sight of them making out while he adds, "I was cocky, thought I knew it all."

While crickets chirp, high schoolers Mary and Robert go from petting to Robert pulling off her underpants and maneuvering her around to have perfunctory sex. Dr. Judith Seifer narrates, "Men have been taught by our society that intercourse is what sex is about. Kissing and foreplay is what you do to get to the real thing." High schooler Mary looks hesitant, then uncomfortable as Robert proceeds.

"Women grow up taught that sex is for the man, and we are less than respectable if you desire sex. Oh, we've all been taught the wrong things," sighs Dr. Seifer. Robert and Mary finish, and Robert says, "What do you want to do now?" "Go home," Mary responds stiffly.

We next see our friends dressed and sitting in their chairs. "Sex after marriage was pretty much the same as sex in high school, except we had a bed," Robert tells us.

Now the scene goes to their bedroom, all dark, lights out, under the covers. "I'd get on top of her and ejaculate, it was like releasing a load," Robert recalls, as the screen figures accomplish this at just that pace. Doctor Koller, speaking fast, adds that "It's normal for most men to ejaculate rapidly through intercourse."

"After we did it, the lights are off, it's dark, and he rolls off and turns his back to me. I would think, what is this? There isn't anything there. Not anything." Onscreen, poor Mary crosses her arms over her chest and shrugs.

Fortunately, they explain, Mary brought home the coursework she used for her class, Masters and Johnson's *Human Sexuality*. "Through that we learned to start experimenting," Mary offers.

Mary and Robert demonstrate how they brought communicativeness and playfulness to their sex life. Now we've got these two attractive people in their bedroom, daytime. Mary is in her pretty lace blue underwear, Robert in shorts. No longer appearing to have been offered a $100,000 prize if they can wrap it up in under five minutes, they look at each other, kiss, embrace. They're rolling on the bed, caressing. They back off and touch each other.

"It's just so romantic. Before it was so cold. Now it's . . . nice. I like it," Mary says as you see them playing, his palms softly flickering across her thighs, up her breasts and neck, on her hair. "When sex includes a whole spectrum of sexual play, both partners are more likely to enjoy their sexual experiences. Intercourse is only one part, and it doesn't have to be the focus of every single sexual experience," Kollar interjects.

The tape cuts back to them in bed, nude, him running his hands over her face, down her body and legs, sucking on her toes. She sounds wonderstruck. "I always thought sex meant you just lay there. I never thought you could enjoy it. I'd never seen my parents show feelings to each other. I didn't know what I do now."

"Going down on her used to be like diving into salt water. I'd close my eyes and think, 'I'm not supposed to be here,' so I'd do it for a few minutes, and then climb aboard and finish," he says, while onscreen, they perform oral sex that manages to be what Phil Harvey had described, both educational in detail and pleasurable to watch.

The delight they take in each other continues. Mary explains, "The first time I went down on Robert I didn't like it. But now I do. He plays games, and it's more fun." They show her licking and sucking and stroking, explicit and very instructive, with her mouth on his penis, illustrating tongue and lip stimulations. "The best way to extend sex is to not do one thing for too long," Dr. Kollar adds over the action, "Repeatedly build up and cool down. Often by delay, you can achieve a more intense orgasm."

After they embrace in bed, they return to their chairs, with Robert earnestly saying, "It's a great thing to please somebody else, and they return the favor." Mary says it's like being kids and doing what you want, pure pleasure, rather than goal-oriented adults. "I enjoy it more and I think he does too."

That's the general format. You first meet each couple sitting in their chairs, then you voyeuristically get into bed with them and have bad sex, then you all go back and talk, then to bed and have better sex while the counselors come up with the wise, instructive commentary.

The case histories and situations are all slightly different. Dr. Seifer next introduces Laura, who "like many women, grew up inhibited and sexually nonexpressive. Her husband David wasn't a mind reader. They decided to work on it together . . ."

This time we meet a nice, blond-haired woman with a sweet face, and her moustached husband who looks, as he says, like a partner in a health club. Laura, a social worker, tells how her friend fixed them up, saying she knew this guy who was a "hunk," but she didn't believe it until the door opened and there he was. Now, married six years with two kids, they want to have better sex.

Another subtle permission-giving benefit of such programs is that the people are familiar, with average bodies, which frees the viewer of feelings of inadequacy. The husband here is in good shape, but he's big, almost heavy and she has a womanly body, with a belly, not the shape of a fashion model. Also, "married six years, they want to have better sex," is a brief phrase, but a big concept that could inspire a lot of video viewers.

Their situation is that lack of communication held them back. This is demonstrated with a bedroom flashback. He's licking and kissing, going down her body while the camera cuts up to her face, quiet and immobile with her lips pressed together, serene and silent. Sort of, you alive up there or what, Laura?

"I was discouraged," confesses David. "She gave me no response to tell if she enjoyed what I was doing. It was tough."

First they work through how Laura's religious upbringing (sex was never discussed) affected her, and they agree that she will try to talk, show him, vocalize, make noises, and otherwise stand up and be counted in the bedroom. While this process is enacted, the counselors discuss how people are aroused by combinations of things, one of which is seeing the response of the partner. "It's important to show your arousal and that you're having fun. Making sex fun can make it possible to laugh at what doesn't work and try new things."

By the end of the video, formerly repressed Laura is in the kitchen, taking David's cup of coffee out of his hand and undoing his bathrobe. They wind up screwing on the counter.

I recently told a magazine editor about these videos, and he asked for an example of the sexual problems. I related the David and Laura story. There was a silence at the end of the phone, and then he said, "My first marriage broke up. I was convinced my wife didn't think I was a good lover. She certainly never told me I was. Years after the divorce, I asked her. She said, 'Oh, God, I've never had a better lover than you. I loved sex with you so much I used to have to clamp my lips shut to hold back because I thought you'd consider me disgusting, like some slutty wild woman.' Our marriage ended and we never knew how the other felt. Maybe if we had something like those tapes," he actually sighed. "They sound like a great thing."

The videos include the multiple-orgasmic wife who must learn that it's not her husband's sole responsibility to provide all the fun (their bad sex scene has the poor exhausted man pretending to be asleep), G-spot stimulation, both taking turns with initiation, and again, communication. A formerly promiscuous pilot and his publishing exec wife decide they want to practice hot monogamy, and so act out their fantasies. In all the stories, certain explicit situations are dealt with, ranging from how to accommodate an extra large penis to such personal admonishments as "we all like to feel that our partner is making love to *us*, not our erogenous zones."

Pretty eye-opening stuff. In a similar mode, a scene with two mature, divorced and remarried people adapt the skills she learned through therapy to "practice the idea of touching and loving, not so much doing as being." This may *sound* esoteric, but they manage to show you what they mean. I was surprised to encounter one of the most intimate sex scenes I've ever seen.

Becoming Orgasmic by the Sinclair Institute, employs the "play within a play" device, in this case, an instructional sex video within an instructional sex video. A pretty young wife reads about the *Becoming Orgasmic* video-book program in a magazine and sends away for it. The video follows her while she reads the book, reevaluating her attitudes toward sexuality, and does progressive, day by day sensitizing exercises in which her stream of consciousness is heard. "Go to a mirror and think about what I like about my body? Ugh, my enormous butt. Touch myself? It still feels wrong to me somehow."

Her young loving husband is supportive, listening when she tells him about what she's learning. His assignment is to understand she can't have intercourse for some weeks while she's going through this. He is amazingly open-minded, at one point watching a video with her that goes through the physiology of a woman's orgasmic response, discussing why she has so much to overcome, and cheering her on. "Honey, that's wonderful, you had an orgasm. Maybe it'll be more intense if you keep going!" It's very clever, and again, a good example of "permission giving."

And so it goes, through the things she and her husband tentatively try in bed, starting with small touching exercises and moving to mutual masturbation. The theme of the process is not so subtly underlined, with him in bed saying things like, "I really love you. I didn't realize how much you had to overcome. You're doing a terrific job."

It progresses all the way to them experimenting, in the shower, or with vibrators. The use of good explicit imagery opens up possibilities for everyday eroticism. The sex scenes are sensual, and very clearly detailed.

The last scene has him dressed for work, saying "I'm really glad you got that book and video, although I admit I had doubts." She says his support meant a lot to her, and it ends with her thinking they've become closer. Simplistic perhaps, but undoubtedly popular and helpful.

The New York Times reported five years ago that home video viewers rent and buy more adult tapes than exercise, music, sport, how-to, or classic films. Only children's videos and new movie releases are more popular. The *Adult Video News* reported that women and couples make up forty-eight percent of the people who rent erotic films.

An interesting thing about Adam & Eve sales is that they're not split between, say, recreation and education. The same consumers who buy *Becoming Orgasmic* or the instructive Sinclair tape may also send for the Red Hot Cotton Chemise along with a couple of Pleasure Rings and some Whipped Delight Edible Gel. "After two or three purchases, everyone has bought from two or three categories," Harvey states. "We give the customers what they want, and it's been consistently clear that they were interested in things with explicitly erotic content."

The company also publishes the informational newsletter, *Sex Over 40* which addresses the questions and concerns of a mature population. Recent articles have included, "How Talking About Sex Can Improve Your Pleasure," "Arthritis and Sex," "All About Orgasm," "Erectile Dysfunction," "Exploring Ways to Get More Sex in Your Relationship."

Phil Harvey became a millionaire through Adam & Eve. Most people would have stopped there. Harvey runs a nonprofit campany, DKT, a charity involved in family planning and AIDS prevention in the Third World. DKT and other organizations have used what Harvey calls social marketing, selling contraceptives in neighborhood kiosks and stores rather than clinics that were only opened in limited locations, enabling them to reach more people. People are reluctant to go to clinics and hospitals if they are not sick.

"If people pay only a few cents for something, they're more likely to use it than if it's a giveaway," Harvey explains. "It also gives us a way of measuring our reach." DKT and PSI, an older organization also founded by Harvey, are the largest distributors of contraceptives and health aids in the Third World, with programs in thirty-two countries providing contraceptive services to six million people.

In 1994, the *Washington Post* reported that during President Jean-Bertrand Aristide's three-year exile, Phil Harvey had provided millions of condoms to the people in Haiti most at risk for contracting AIDS. "The last national survey in 1989," the *Post* reported, "had shown that seven to ten percent of the population was likely to test positive for the HIV virus, twenty times the rate in the United States."

So what did the Justice Department do in the late 1980s to this extraordinarily effective guy who was working with the U.S. Agency for International Development? Bust him.

In the late 1980s, Phil Harvey's company was sued for obscenity by Project Post Porn, created by former attorney general Edwin Meese, a sort of Sons of the Meese Commission. They went after companies who sold erotic material, prosecuting for obscenity under community standard statutes.

It's strange to watch something that's as beneficial as, say, the *Better Sex* videos and to think that the federal government actually came to the offices of Adam & Eve and treated them like criminals. But they did. Your tax dollars supported this action.

"Obscenity laws are based on Federal rulings. The laws in Alabama are the same as Alaska," Harvey states. The Supreme Court in 1973 *Miller v. California,* defined as "obscene" works that "have no scientific, educational, artistic, or political value, appeal to the prurient interest and are patently offensive to community standards."

Harvey runs his company within those guidelines, and it isn't easy. "Same laws but each community may impose its own standards," he says, "and some areas are pretty conservative. There are people in Alabama and Mississippi who are furious we won't sell to them, and I don't blame them because they are deprived of their rights."

Project Post Porn took advantage of that geographic schizophrenia. Harvey filed a motion citing harassment after federal agents conducted a day-long raid of the premises, photographing and interrogating employees, photocopying subpoenas and handing them to people as they left.

The jury took only five minutes to find Phil Harvey and PHE not guilty of obscenity charges in nearby Alamane County, North Carolina, and spent fifty-five minutes debating if they should try to get an apology from the prosecution for bringing the case to trial. When

Adam & Eve was acquitted, the editorial page of the Raleigh, North Carolina *News & Observer* called it the "end of a foolish crusade" and suggested "the taxpayers had a right to know why public officials carried on with this crusade of harassment."

This wasn't Harvey's first legal battle of this sort, and it probably won't be his last. Candida Royalle had known him for years, as Adam & Eve carried her videos. But around this same time, the porn squad bought them closer . . .

Adam & Eve had filled an order that included *Urban Heat,* one of Femme's films, to an APO, a military address on a ship, and for some reason, the shipment was returned through New York customs.

"They grabbed *Urban Heat,*" Candida relates. "They confiscated it and declared it obscene, and said they'd destroy it unless Adam & Eve wanted to fight. They messed with the wrong guy."

Harvey knew his AASECT panel had recommended this material, and decided to fight the case to establish a precedent.

"The attorney for the government, who got wind of it, decided they should look at the movie they busted. When they realized what a mistake they'd made, they came back with their tail between their legs and said they wanted to pull the case," Candida said. "I demanded it in writing, for the record that this never should have happened, which they did. It was victory. The last thing the government wants are pornographers who are proud of their work and willing to go to court over it."

It was a good collaborative effort between principled, talented, and strong people. What Candida Royalle and Phil Harvey didn't know then was that later they'd form an even stronger allegiance.

WORKING REWARDS

By the time 1995 was halfway over, Candida told me she was in a "holding pattern." Femme was stronger than ever. Her film sales were up thirty percent that year.

"I'm forty-four," she said. "At this age you realize you're at the midpoint of your vital years, and it's frightening." She was wondering if she wanted to have a baby or accept that she never would. She loved writing, directing, and making films and wanted to do more of those things, but the distribution/business end was keeping her from the creative part. She was exhausted. Finally, she was trying to fight buying into a fear of aging. "I look at pictures of women in magazines and most of them could be my kid!"

Candida, Betty Dodson, and others I met were women who changed my view of my own life. I had been raised in a culture that glorified youth and disparaged age, especially in women. These women, whom I met when I was thirty-one and had watched for five years, gave me a different set of expectations. Candida and her friends were in their forties and demonstrated that a woman could be beautiful, dynamic, and sexual at that age. Betty was in her sixties and radiated a sexuality some women never have. It came from how they lived, and who they were. Attitudes are honest self expression. They liked themselves and so others liked them.

"What direction do you want your life to go in?" I asked. "What are you thinking of doing?"

She responded that she was exploring selling the distribution part of her business, leaving her free to make films and write a proposal for a book helping women to learn to get what they want sexually.

"Any prospects for a sale?" I asked.

"Well," she said, leading me to the history of her work with Adam & Eve, "There's this person called Phil Harvey. Have you ever heard of him?"

A few weeks later, I was in Washington interviewing him. When I heard his story about starting Adam & Eve, of helping to distribute condoms in Third World countries, I believed he would be the right person to support the next stage of Femme and Candida Royalle. He was like her, someone whose life illustrated that promoting good sex could be healthy and significant work.

By the start of 1996, Phil Harvey's company took over Femme's distribution and set up financing for her next films, leaving Candida Royalle free to continue and expand her work.

4

Sex and Strippers

Maureen Dowd of *The New York Times* is one of my favorite Op-Ed writers, a position that nearly swandived on September 21, 1995, when she wrote about strippers.

I admire the fact that commentators from *The New York Times* are troubled by issues of sexism. Sometimes I think they stretch points a bit far, such as when Dowd's fellow *Times* writer Frank Rich tried to protest what he considered unrealistic, sexist standards of beauty by lodging a one-man protest against the *Sports Illustrated Bathing Suit Issue*, which sold five million issues in 1996. He was trying to be a sensitive modern guy but his piece still ended with one of those moments "What were you *thinking?*" when he declared earnestly, "These women aren't even attractive!"

Maureen Dowd discussed sex in the movies, noting that sex had become "an instrument of upward mobility. There are more fallen women rising," Dowd declared. "Demi Moore plays a table dancer—a step up from lap dancing—in *Striptease*. She got $12.5 million—the largest paycheck ever given to an actress—for undressing (again.)"

Dowd makes undressing sound like dipsomania. "Keep an eye on that women or she'll start tearing her pants off. . . ." I think Demi Moore's undressing provides us with a valuable mirror.

In 1990, *Vanity Fair* magazine put a pregnant, nude Demi Moore on the cover and the issue became their number-one newsstand seller, moving 547,248 copies. A national debate ensued in the form of 95 separate television pieces, reaching an estimated audience of 110 million people. There were 64 radio programs on 31 stations, and 1,500 newspaper articles. The idea of a woman's pregnancy as lovely, glamorous, and powerful was an unfamiliar concept.

Maureen Dowd posed for *Vanity Fair* with every last stitch of her clothing on. And so did Frank Rich, along with several of *The New York Times* stable of hot writers, Alessandra Stanley, and Alex Witchell. They looked fabulous. Not only were they good writers, the layout suggested, they were good-looking.

Many were struck by this, particularly the sight of pretty, redheaded Dowd, the Washington reporter, who for sexist, ageist reasons, people had expected to be . . . well, dowdy! "Misogynists have often reproached intellectual women for 'neglecting themselves,'" wrote Simone De Beauvoir, "but they have also preached this doctrine to them: if you wish to be our equals, stop using make up and nail polish. This piece of advice is nonsense. Precisely because the concept of femininity is artificially shaped by custom and fashion, it is imposed upon each woman from without."

Is attractiveness different if one is clothed, wearing a bikini, or nude? As long as you don't undress, attractiveness is okay?

Dowd wrote the critical *Times* review of Michael Crichton's goofy what-if-a-woman-sexually-harassed-a-man book. But there was a moment in the movie version that impressed me, when the villain Demi Moore, busted for her sex crime against innocent Michael Douglas, made an unapologetic, defiant speech about women being sexually assertive. It was a different film representation of women's sexuality. Dowd started her column by pointing out how in the cinema past, female sexuality called for atonement: Vivien Leigh in *Waterloo Bridge* had to jump off the bridge as self-punishment for being a prostitute.

But Dowd was also displeased with a woman making a living through her sexuality. "You might say that Hollywood is doing what it has always done: making glossy movies with nubile, semi-clothed women jiggling. Sex not only costs; it also pays. And the women like Demi Moore who are cashing in are not pandering any less than the men who are paying them. What really arouses all these people is money," Dowd concluded.

Where do I start? I'll go for the sentence about nubile women.

This is a fine line. Because Maureen Dowd is honorably trying to change the world, to free us of sexism, she seems not to see this is oversimplifying and judging in a way that doesn't help. Then again, I wince when Dowd quotes Camille Paglia calling a prostitute "the ultimate liberated woman." On this topic, somewhere between Maureen Dowd and Camille Paglia lies truth. Not to mention context.

"Money's money and how you make it is your own business," said Dianah, the stripper who ended up educating me. In the past year, every time I wanted to stop writing this book the thought of Dianah spurred me on. I called Dianah recently to see what had happened to her, a year after I last wrote about her life. She was in Kentucky, where she'd started out, dancing and supporting her mother, a forty-two-year-old woman with no medical insurance who'd had two heart bypass operations.

Between stripping and writing about stripping lies a big gap. "Women like Demi Moore." What *about* women like that? They "choose to," or even "have to." Women like Maureen Dowd and I don't have to strip. We're educated and we know how to write. I don't know about Maureen Dowd's life but when mine goes off track I have family and friends I borrow money from. There's always someone I can turn to for help. For women who don't have these supports, stripping beats a lot of other jobs. I followed Dianah and other strippers around for their twelve-hour shifts. Between the physical demands, and the fact that society doesn't give them much of what Aretha Franklin called R-E-S-P-E-C-T, it's some job. Writing's easier.

But what about women who choose to even if they don't have to? What if they decide it's their best option? "She got $12.5 million—the largest paycheck ever given to an actress—for undressing (again)" is what Maureen Dowd writes of Demi Moore.

We're talking about $12.5 million. Moore is the first woman in Hollywood to make that kind of money. Do we expect Demi Moore to say, "I'm sorry, I can't accept your filthy money for this degrading act. Take it back." Maureen Dowd, I don't know what they're paying you at the *Times*, but for *half* that, I'd have my shirt off so fast. . . .

The Dowd-on-stripping conundrum mentally kept after me in the fashion of my cat Joe, when he walks up and down my body to persuade me to make his breakfast. I shoo him away, fall asleep, and he hops back until I wake up. I couldn't stop thinking about Dowd's mental processes. Something odd happens with writers whose work you like. When they do something disappointing it almost feels as if one of your friends let you down.

I went back and read the column half a dozen times. It was cranky, judgmental, even prissy, none of which characterized her work. The subject had to have something to do with her tone. Sex. Commercial sex. Women being paid for being sexy. Why did that topic hit the "Override" button of a brainy woman writer whose hallmarks were context and compassion?

I recalled a table full of writers, a grouping with the loving, supportive atmosphere of the Romans at the Coliseum the moment the Emperor decides if the lions should be released. At one point something Maureen Dowd had written came up.

I know writers who are inspired by other good writers. I call them "secure." I know more writers who are raging neurotics. What was scary about watching each of these guys set upon her was to think what the others would say should someone be fool enough to go to the bathroom. None were.

I did pick up that all of the critics would have given their pointy little wolves' teeth for Maureen Dowd's job. What I didn't realize at the time was I let them intimidate me. I was with older, more accomplished writers (translation: pages published) and the only woman present. "I think she's awfully good," I responded. They informed otherwise, for reasons I later realized were matched to each critic. If the person had a Ph.D. in political science, Dowd didn't. If the person was supported by major foundations, she was commercial.

If this was what colleagues say about a woman with one of the top jobs, where was I? I had a glimpse of what was in store for a woman who competed on what had been exclusively male territory.

An article about strip clubs in *The New York Times* quoted an executive woman as complaining about the amount of business entertaining that takes place at strip clubs. "How can you be taken seriously when there is some woman on stage taking her clothes off?"

I think I know why Dowd jumped on Demi Moore. She's under tremendous pressure, not just to do her job, but in combatting how people react to the fact she has her job. Sexuality is a card that's played heavily against women in professional competition. It's often hidden, but it's there in a major and terrible way.

I wish Demi Moore and Maureen Dowd could compare notes. They'd probably find a lot of common ground. As for the executive and the stripper, both of these women are trying to make a living the best way they know how. The day our sexuality isn't used as a threat against us, maybe we'll realize we should be supporting each other in our right to do our work. It's hard and complex enough without adding judgment to the equation.

DIANAH AND KIRK, AFTER THE STORY ENDS

Recently, I talked to Dianah King and Kirk Hill, two professional strippers who were in love with each other. I got to know them both and followed them around for a year. This chapter is their story. What happened with their love affair illustrates how being an exotic dancer differs for a man and a woman. The resultant pressures destroyed their relationship. This was the first time I'd talked to them in six months. They broke up a year ago.

"Going to Maine to get rid of her stuff kind of finalized things, even though hope and dreams are there," Kirk said, sounding wry, affectionate, and bitter all at once. "She sent me a letter saying if she didn't have a friend like me, she wouldn't have friends at all. She keeps asking me to take care of myself for her, because she says she knows I won't do it for myself."

Kirk didn't quite know in what direction he should focus his energy. He was in Florida, where he'd originally planned to have Dianah come live with him. For most of the year business had pursued him. He'd toured, dancing when the gigs were good. Jesse Tyler, his gay porn persona, had been in demand. A gay male friend who'd introduced me to Kirk thoughtfully sent me *The Zeus Shopper*, a mail-order catalogue of hard-core VCR features. Jesse was on the cover, his nude bodybuilder frame reaching in a V to the sky, enlivened by a raging hard-on. He looked very healthy.

I'd never seen men as such blatant sex symbols before I'd known male strippers, but sex symbol work fits certain constructs of society. The Kirk-Dianah story was that she could make money dancing for men, but he couldn't make much dancing for women. For male dancers, the big money was on the gay dance circuit, hustling on the side, or doing porn films.

How stripping worked for men and women could illustrate something of sex roles. How the law regulated stripping could, too. Deconstructing stripping analysis in Supreme Court decisions such as *Barnes v. Indiana*, the 1991 decision that upheld an Indiana club's enforcement of the wearing of pasties and G-strings, providing some of the choicest tidbits of the gender-role buffet I'd ever seen. "Degradation of women," was one of the reasons cited by Supreme Court justice Souter for supporting the application of uncomfortable shiny pieces of material.

If wearing pasties prevented degradation of women, what prevented degradation of men? Or did Souter believe only women to be degraded by nudity? And what was it about a pastie, the cover-up value of which could be accomplished by slathering your nipples with glue and dipping them in glitter, that would prevent "prostitution, sexual assault, criminal activity, degradation of women and other activities which break down the family structure" as Souter wrote?

While concerned citizens on the Supreme Court and Op-Ed page of the *Times* tried to save women from what they, not the dancers, considered degrading, Kirk dancing as Kirk couldn't get enough work dancing for women, so Jesse dominated.

It was interesting to hear what Kirk told me now, a year after breaking up with his girlfriend. When he moved to Florida nobody knew Kirk so his more famous persona had taken over.

"I felt people would like Jesse more, because Jesse was wilder and more outgoing. I just lost myself and my direction, being Jesse. My best friends were asking, 'Where's Kirk?' " Currently trying to normalize his life with a regular job running a carpet cleaning business, Kirk says that he liked dancing but was tired of hustling. "How I make the most money will determine what I do," he sighed.

He'd had a tough time finding a direction that would make him happy. Building his body had provided him with both a living and an identity. If society was different would Jesse and Kirk peacefully coexist instead of being dueling parts of the same man? Masters and Johnson had written that everyone fit somewhere on a sexual preference continuum and during the course of a lifetime that position could shift. Kirk and Dianah's experience illustrated this.

I called Dianah in Kentucky, and when we settled down to talk she told me the day before had been her twenty-fourth birthday. I asked about the club and she said it was not very big, maybe five girls per shift. She could make $100 to $300 a night, but had to work hard to make the money. "It's blue collar, everyday Joes come in. Lots of drinking. This is the South, everybody drinks. The club requires you to sell five or six drinks a night. We're drink hustlers, basically." She was talking to another owner about managing a club, but for now, this job paid the rent. She wore pasties in accordance with Kentucky law.

She was as upbeat and strong as ever, but I knew she'd been through a difficult year. She'd fallen in love with a club owner in Puerto Rico after she and Kirk had separated. The affair was a disaster. We figured out that when she'd been in New York last, we'd missed each other by a few days. I was traveling.

"I tried to call you but you were gone. I ended up settin' around," she said lightly, but my heart sank for her, knowing what New York could be like if you didn't know anyone. Memories of covering Dianah's life flooded my mind while she talked. She was gorgeous enough to cause a firetruck to smack into a Park Avenue meridian when she leaned out of a cab once and yelled, "Hey! Come light my fire!" She loved sitting in front of the television and watching Bette Davis movies on Sunday afternoons. And there was nothing like seeing a nervous stripper clasp her hands in prayer five minutes before her appearance on cable TV's *The Robin Byrd Show*.

She said she was thinking of doing photo layouts to restart her career. "My mom is doing better, but she still can't walk really well. She had a slight stroke. I'll go back to photos and featuring as a dancer, but until I know she's okay, I'm staying put."

When she'd first gone home to Kentucky, she'd wanted to quit stripping, she told me. "I tried painting for three weeks. I made $250 a week. I could live on that, but not with my mom's bills."

"Of course not," I said, thinking, degradation? Next person I hear use that term might just be pounded into the floor. She invited me to visit her in Kentucky, and I invited her to visit me in New York. "I miss you," she said.

WHO'S DANCING FOR WHOM?

Kirk and Dianah fell in love one year before I met them. They were living together in Maine, enthusiastically planning their careers. What they couldn't anticipate was how the work would affect their relationship. The business of exotic dancing in the United States is defined by societal gender roles.

There's a big gap between the sexes in strip club patronage. *The New York Times*, on the subject of "gentlemen's clubs" (upscale establishments where women strip for men), reported that "some 10 million customers spent $3 billion last year at such clubs."

How many exotic dance clubs of different sorts are there in the United States? The best place to go for statistics turned out to be guide books for erotic entertainment, sort of the Zagats' of stripping.

Don Waitt publishes *The Exotic Dancers Directory*, a national guide to topless or nude clubs where women dance for men. He realized there was a need for such a book because the Yellow Page listings of strip clubs varied widely from state to state. Some list clubs under "Exotic Dancers," some under "Entertainment," which can be confusing. "You had to guess by the name of the club. Names you'd think would have exotic dancers didn't, and vice versa," Waitt explained.

How many strip clubs feature women dancing for men? Don Waitt said that his directory listed over 2,000 clubs. "My guess is that there might be another 500 smaller ones," he adds. "I'd put the total at 2,500 in the United States and Canada."

Bill Brent is the editor and publisher of *The Black Book*, an alternative sexuality resource guide that lists gay dance clubs, among other resources. He estimated that there are probably 200 to 300 places in the United States where men dance for men.

Gina Gatta is the editor and publisher of *The Woman's Traveler*. She and Bill Brent explained that many gay clubs rotate their entertainment, but estimated that there are 200 lesbian clubs throughout the country where women dance for and with women. "In the late 1980s there was more of a trend of women stripping for women, but the emphasis has changed. Now the predominant thing is go-go and box dancing. Women in the clubs want to join in and participate rather than be spectators. So the dancers who are working for the club are more party enhancers than entertainers." She adds that in her opinion, women don't hire women for private parties, meaning stripping and/or sex, the way men hire women and men.

As for the total number of clubs where men strip for women . . . Don Waitt says that it's a fraction of the business. "We've only come across about a half dozen clubs that have a steady diet of men dancing for women. The LeBears, Chippendales . . . I'd say less than ten nationally. You have male reviews that dance at your traditional single's bars on a specific night, Ladies Night from eight to ten . . . but it's pretty limited."

"I'd like to interview you for a novel I'm writing," one of my old boyfriends called to ask. He was a prolific and successful writer, alternating between nonfiction and novels. One had been made into a major movie. He told me the book he was thinking about writing involved stripping. I asked when he would interview some actual strippers. "Just go to a club and tip well. They'll talk to you on their breaks," I urged.

"Oh, I wouldn't do that. I don't like those clubs. It's a degrading atmosphere for women," he said.

I'd been working with Kirk and Dianah for a year at this point. "Let me get this straight," I asked. "You're writing a book about a stripper. But you won't go into a strip club because you think it's degrading? That's great, to have your mind made up about their world *before* you write a word. Don't let that reporting thing trip you up." He told me when he wrote a book about the Chernoble nuclear accident he hadn't considered it necessary to go there, either. Nice analogy.

Not everyone thinks of strip clubs as degrading. Some people consider them home away from home. Dianah and many strippers have "regulars," clients who come in specifically to see them, who tip lavishly and bring gifts. A lot of them are lonely and it provides a form of company that means something to them. One young man gave Dianah a poem that likened the strippers to stars coming out at night, "and just like those heavenly bodies, our world they beautify."

I liked his perspective:

"We each see something different
as we look into each face
yet to me the most important thing
is the beauty and gentle grace
that shines from deep within the soul
yet is all too plain to see
for all you have to do is look
to see what they mean to me."

"To see what they mean to me." What they mean to this guy and someone who considers it degrading is obviously very different.

And what does it mean to look? The numbers of clubs and who goes to them marks a big difference between men and women. I think it's a socialized difference. When the VCR came into people's homes, soon half the porn rentals were by women. It's men who visit nude dance clubs, but does that mean women are less visually stimulated?

I spoke with Donald Moser, Ph.D., a Lifetime Achievement Award Winner of the American Association of Sex Educators, Counselors, and Therapists, an honor held only by a handful of doctors and psychologists. He does not believe there is any biological or genetic difference between the sexes that is responsible for how men or women respond to visual stimulation. He does, however, believe that there is a difference in the way men and women are socialized, affecting what they find exciting visually. His studies have concentrated on sex differences in response to pornography, but when asked to speculate about the differences, he says that if men and women were socialized in similar ways, we wouldn't see the gap in strip clubs for men and women.

"When you look at the literature of attraction," Dr. Moser said, "You see that physical attractiveness rates a bit higher for men. In our society we learn the importance of physically attractive women. Take a male film star like Dustin Hoffman. He's not a physically attractive man. It's difficult to find a parallel woman film star."

Moser continues, "Women aren't usually placed in a context in which they view men. It's not a social norm. Socialized emphasis traditionally has had women place more value on relationships, and men on excitement and novelty."

He thinks that things have changed a great deal and will change more. He speculated that women who attend exotic dancing or enjoy explicit films were more assertive and achievement oriented than the traditional stereotype of a passive and receptive woman.

Personally, I found the more I researched, the more I loved going to the Gaiety, a theater in New York where men stripped for audiences that consisted of gay men and me. I liked it much more than the showy, giggly, all-male reviews offered for audiences of bridal shower parties. America's gender role assignments are clearly reflected in the mores of strip clubs. How would it play out for a man and woman who set out to have careers as strippers?

INTRODUCING DIANAH AND KIRK,
NEW YEAR'S 1994

I met Dianah King and Kirk Hill a few days after Christmas, when they came to New York to do *The Robin Byrd Show*. They didn't do the show under their own names. Dianah used the name she always uses, Crystal. Kirk was Jesse, the name he uses for dancing in the gay clubs. Dancing for women in all-male reviews and bachelorette parties, he's Bo. Jesse was not just another dancer on the rotation. He was a feature performer, having made a name for himself in porn films and magazine layouts. He danced at venues all over the country. Although there are strippers in every state, good strippers who have what Jesse, Bo, and Crystal have, are hard to find. Good strippers have the body (genes, gym, and/or surgical augmentation). Good strippers not only have the face, charisma, and talent, but are professional and reliable. Bo got a fraction of the work Jesse did. Crystal made more money than Jesse and Bo put together.

"The myth is that strippers make a thousand dollars a night," Dianah said during our first interview. They make good money, but not *that* good. "Typically my goal is $200 a night." In clubs in big cities she can make $500 or $600 nightly.

After chasing around the country trying to find steady work at the few clubs where men dance for women, Kirk finally realized that his real money-making opportunities as a dancer wouldn't be there.

"Women aren't as sexually explicit and aggressive as men," he says. "But it's slowly changing."

Having a tan is a requirement at a majority of clubs. The tan was the first thing that stood out about blond, square-jawed Kirk, the tan and the body. He stayed on the diet, put in hours in the gym training with professional body builders, and it showed. When introduced, he takes a half step back, to permit a better view.

Meeting Dianah was different. She came in quietly, distrustfully, for a long time she wouldn't look up. The first impression was of a slender figure huddled in a leather jacket, a lock of very light blond hair shielding her eyes, which turned out to be the stunning combination of very pale blue, with intense dark brows. Dianah wasn't sure about sharing her story. For female strippers, having it known you have a boyfriend is not good for the fantasy, and that fantasy is business.

Before we went out to dinner, our mutual friend remembered that he taped their appearance on *The Robin Byrd Show*. Kirk was a veteran, having appeared on the show numerous times, but this was Dianah's first time, not just on Robin Byrd, but on television, period. "I've never seen myself dance," she murmured as they found the tape for the VCR.

In New York City, Robin Byrd is a stripper's best friend. *The Robin Byrd Show* is a cable television program that has been on the air since the late 1970s. The show is a cosy showcase for men and women erotic dancers and performers, who are introduced, perform, and at the end of the program sit around after putting some of their clothes back on. Robin conducts interviews with her guests and takes phone calls from the viewers. The inimitable Robin sports the same outfit every night, a crocheted black bikini top with lavender ribbons ("I'll wear them until they find a cure,") over the nipples, and a tiny black string bikini bottom. She has tousled shoulder-length blond hair and straight bangs, the hair a shade of blond best accomplished by the application of multiple cans of Sun-In. Robin Byrd has reached such a state of institutionhood that her program now begins with spliced clips of her mainstream television appearances, from Howard Stern to Joan Rivers.

The Robin Byrd Show kicks off to the strains of an electric guitar, while onscreen a neon heart encircles the title, and shapely women's legs straddle the heart. After ads for Robin's porn pal phone lines, domination and submission fantasy phone lines, talk-to-body-builder lines, hot horny women just waiting to take your call phone lines, hot horny men just waiting to take your call phone lines, Robin comes in. "Hello, we are live! I'm Robin Byrd, and this is *The Robin Byrd Show*! I'm here, you're there! Lie back and get comfortable, but first, go run and get your rubbers and your dental dams! Not the ones for your feet, the ones for your dicks! Last week I showed you a dental dam and how if you use a petroleum base, it eats through! Look! It makes it weak, so don't use a petroleum base for lubricant!" She snapped the little piece of plastic to illustrate, then advocated the scrubbing of teeth, a particular sticking point with Robin. Often the first five minutes of her show will consist of Robin rubbing her teeth, putting on makeup and lipgloss while chatting about the lineup. This time, her lineup included Crystal and Jesse.

Tonight Robin was in an especially festive mood, offering additional cheer after exhorting her audience to lie back and get comfortable with loved ones: "And if you don't have a loved one, you always, always, have me, Robin Byrd!"

After the first dancer, first commercial bank, Robin announced, "For the first time on *The Robin Byrd Show* and hopefully not the last, all the way from Kentucky! My goodness, all the way from *Kentucky!* Here is Crystal!"

We were all sitting on the bed of my friend's apartment in New York City. Dianah and Kirk smiled at each other, excited. They looked like any two good-looking young people in blue jeans and leather jackets. But this young girl was on the television, making her debut.

White satin lapels over tanned flesh. Silver studs on the white satin. When the camera pulled back and up past her heavy silvery necklaces it was right into Crystal's face. She smiled so radiantly you'd never know she was nervous. She was all gold skin, gold hair in a shag cut, and the kind of white teeth Robin nagged her audience to work towards.

She rocked her hips and arms with the heavy drumbeat and electronic waves of music, turned and bent, lifting her skirt to exhibit the tiny white satin thong she wore "I have a nice butt so I'm comfortable showing it," she explained. With the artfulness Philip Roth once wrote illustrates "the difference between a flasher and a stripper," she undulated her hips to show off her firm rear end, then whirled and faced front again, dropping the long skirt back into place and smiling, holding her arms out to model her showgirl finery.

Quickly her hands dropped to the skirt and unfasten the buckle. Three white satin studded strips holding a tiny white bikini triangle in place remained.

"You know a stripper is nervous when the clothes go off that fast," Kirk instructed, watching the video. Dianah half laughed and nodded. "You can't see but my hands were shakin' so bad I could hardly work the catch!"

We could see the a brief frown of concentration on her face as she worked at getting the skirt off, but when it was tossed to the side her smile returned. Her hands tousled her hair and ran slowly up her torso, then unfastened the breast plates, cupped her breasts, and slid the satin top off.

Dianah and Kirk eyed each other and laughed. "Don't worry, it always happens when you're nervous," he consoled. What always happens when you're nervous? "My hands went right to the scars from my boob job, and then to a scar on my stomach," she said, frowning critically. "It's what you have to tell yourself not to do when you're nervous, don't lose the clothes too soon and keep your hands away from your faults," Kirk said.

On the screen the beautiful blond woman with her tiny waist and full white breasts threw her arms out, then turned, bent, rolled her hips, straightened and smiled at the camera. She looked gorgeous, singing to her music, lowering her spangled thong teasingly over her hips and putting it back in place. ("I was too scared to take it off.") Crystal blew a kiss and finished her dance projecting pure joy.

Her face flushed as the freeze-frames of her performance ran up the screen right before the commercial break. She could see how good she looked and how well she did. When she sat back to watch the next dancer, her boyfriend, Dianah seemed quietly and deeply happy.

Her song had been undulating, slow, and sensuous. Kirk, now Jesse, came ripping out of the starting gate. "Oh, yeah!" sang a voice as a guitar riff wailed. The screen filled with a man's navy blue trunks with white stars, topped by a white jacket with the American flag. He rocked and rolled all over the screen to a superfast song, ". . . if you got something for me, I got something for you!" The jacket was off, and Jesse ran a commanding hand along his weight-lifter body, turned and flexed his v-shaped back over an unbelievably tiny waist. "Baby, it's a party! Party! Party!" shouted the music. He lowered the blue star-studded field as far down below his abdomen muscles as he could without giving away the whole show, then offered his backside to unveil his muscular buttocks. Whipping around, he skillfully tugged his briefs down, each lowered notch perfectly syncopated with the guitar cords. "Party! Party! Party!" A white crocheted G-string popped up in a surprise appearance and Kirk danced it up and down and around the screen. "Baby! It's a party as long as you're there!"

Unexpectedly, he started to laugh and say something to someone off camera. He teased with his crocheted cover, lowered it below his buttocks, spanked himself, then flung it at the camera.

Off camera, Robin was mad. "Now you're not going to take your bottom off just because your girlfriend didn't?" she had demanded, prompting his final move. On *The Robin Byrd Show*, there are things you just don't not do.

* * *

When either Kirk or Dianah was in New York, I'd go to the clubs they danced at, watch them work, and meet them for a meal so we could talk. Sometimes they'd come to town together. I'd known them for months before I heard their life stories. But when I knew their backgrounds, I understood a lot about their choices: what it meant to have your work involve sex.

Sex therapist Helen Singer Kaplan said that only a small percentage of people end up being with a partner who is their sexual fantasy. Kirk, Dianah, and most of the people I interviewed were so charismatic, sexy, and attractive, that they *were* sexual fantasies. They could make a living doing it because they matched so many people's fantasies.

I think our sex industry is a mirror of dreams and fantasies and projections. A sex industry would never survive if it didn't serve the society it reflects. As for why we disavow it . . . I think it's a mirror we're reluctant to look into. Even if it's just a mirror of our own fantasies, that can be frightening for us.

Both Kirk and Dianah, prior to dancing, had considered themselves strictly heterosexual. Because of the realities of the business for men, if he was going to make a living, he'd have to expand his sexual range into bisexuality. He did, then found it enjoyable. Dianah said, "You find yourself getting this new perspective, and wondering, 'What about me? Do I have this tendency?'" Both found themselves exploring sexual activities they'd never before thought possible.

HOW'D YOU GET THIS JOB? / KIRK

Speeding along the ramp to get to the turnpike in Grey, Maine, in 1990, Kirk felt the motorcycle go into a wobble and tried desperately to stop it. Before he could steady the bike the front wheel hit the guard rail. The last sight before hitting the ground was the beautiful blue sky of the spring day.

"Don't move! Don't move! You might have hurt your back!" people were saying. He couldn't turn his head, but out of the corner of his eyes he could see them waving the traffic on. He sensed his leg bent at a crazy angle. This accident would leave him in worse shape than the first one. His back was broken. His leg was broken. He had broken fingers, a fractured right scapula, a destroyed right kidney. At this point, though, all he knew was that he was in tremendous pain.

They started the series of operations, three in all, cut him open to rearrange his back, fixed the leg, cut him open again and took some hip bone to fuse the lower back disc.

The doctors cautioned that he might not be as strong as he was before. Actually, at first they weren't sure if he'd ever walk again. But Kirk was sure. He was accustomed to training, and went after his physical therapy with the same drive that had built the body that saved his life.

While recovering, Kirk had time to think about his life. He believed God was trying to tell him something. Confronted with dying for a second time, he realized how depressed he'd been since he got out of the military. Now at age twenty-seven, and smashed up to this extent, Kirk felt good, as if there was a purpose for him.

*   *   *

The *first* motorcycle accident had left Kirk for dead. They were about to use the electric paddles in the emergency room of the hospital in Orange County, California, when his heart restarted. They'd had him pegged as dead. Not unusual when a tractor trailer collides with your motorcycle.

The police were looking for identification when they cut the jacket off him. That was when they found the coke.

A few months before this, Kirk had left the military. A native of Maine, he'd always wanted to travel, be independent. His father was an instructor at the Maine Correctional Center. Kirk came from a close-knit family, and had three sisters, which he claims always made him especially conscious of being male. Being a man, he thought, made it unsuitable to live at home as long as his sisters had. Kirk was always the funny one. He used humour to overcome shyness and get attention from women. Years later, becoming a body builder boosted his self-confidence in the same way.

Much later, after dancing in gay clubs, Kirk realized that he'd been confused between ways he felt and ways he was supposed to act. "I grew up a sensual person but with men always having to act masculine, I didn't feel right being fully sexual with a woman. I didn't feel I could let myself go and be romantic. There are certain ways a man is expected to be."

Interviewing him, I realized his sexuality had been formed by this conditioning in such a way that to actually reach cut-off parts of it, he'd have to enact them in another sexual context. There were ways of being that he'd been raised to think weren't "manly." The only access he had to those ways of being was when he started stripping in gay clubs.

This is the same concept that sex therapists talk about when working with sexually dysfunctional couples, getting them past rigid ideas of performance, the belief that the man is solely responsible for erection, intercourse, and orgasm. There was a refrain I heard from heterosexual guys who'd started hustling: "We would think of ways to touch each other I never would with a woman." Sure, sheer construction is responsible for some of that. But conditioned ideas of performance are also part of it. When I went to gay clubs and contrasted that presentation with men dancing for women, it was a world apart. The sex performances were sex *roles*.

Kirk thought something was wrong with him for enjoying things that weren't how "a man is expected to be." He also enjoyed being passive, having the woman take over. He liked having his body grabbed by his girlfriends, to be taken, even having his nipples played with. Later, he felt that dancing changed this for him. "It exposed my sexuality to the fullest extent."

Kirk attributes his discipline, the extreme sort required to build a Superman physique, to his father. "I'm like him in that I'm a perfectionist," he claimed. Work hard at everything you do, and don't complain. That soft stuff, emotions and empathy, he identified with his mother, with females. "When I was growing up I never got his praise. He was distant." It wasn't that he was a bad guy, Kirk pointed out. It was just the way he thought men should teach their boys to be men.

The military was good for Kirk. He liked the challenge of the Marine Corps, and acquired self-respect when he found the natural satisfaction of hard work and discipline. "They yell and scream and burn and torture you but it's all part of making you a man," he says. In boot camp, Kirk was known as "The Smiler."

This nickname came when the drill instructor had him do push-ups at the rifle range for some infraction. "I was sweating so bad I had a puddle underneath me but I kept smiling. The drill instructor could never understand why I smiled so much. So finally one day he took me aside and asked, 'Why the hell are you always smiling?' I told him, 'No matter how much you yell at me, I am only going to be able to do what I can do!' "

Kirk started body building at this time. He'd fallen into one of the service's occupational hazards, a serious drinking problem. "Basically, you drink whenever you have time off." His drinking had started in high school and intensified over the years. "I was painfully shy around women. Drinking and partying were ways to get over my shyness." Sent to rehab, he got into weight lifting as a means to quit drinking. He sculpted the body he'd always wanted.

In April 1988, Kirk left the service. He worked temp jobs, but to make ends meet, some guys he met at one of the jobs convinced him it was a good short-term idea to deal cocaine. The motorcycle accident occurred a few months later. "I read the whole thing as a sign that God didn't want me involved with drugs." He transferred his probation home to Maine, got back on his feet financially, and seemed to be leveling out, although he didn't feel happy. Then he crashed his motorcycle again. Now in the hospital, he thought he'd try a different direction.

HOW'D YOU GET THIS JOB? / DIANAH

"When I'm working, every man I look at I think, my life is dependant upon this person. *I need his money.* That's sad but that's the way it is," Dianah said over dinner in New York. She nodded at Kirk. "When I walked up to him that first time, I wasn't concerned about him being good-looking or a nice guy. I wasn't concerned about having a relationship with him. I wanted his money."

In the Marines, Kirk had seen strippers all over the world. He was very particular. Since he'd become a stripper himself he was hard to impress. At Pure Gold in Lexington, Kentucky, this young blond woman impressed him. "She approached me, asked if I wanted a table dance, and she had that pretty little smile," he remembered.

With Crystal, he found himself getting aroused. He didn't like buying drinks in strip clubs because he knew what a rip-off it was, but he asked if he could buy her a drink. He was impressed by her honesty when she confessed that a gentleman nearby had bought her a drink and she should go talk to him, but she'd return.

"A little bitty cup of coffee not even this big costs you seven bucks,"

Dianah indicated. "She didn't say sure, take a sip of the drink and then leave, which she could have," Kirk added.

Dianah returned shortly and sat with him. They talked, and he found himself more and more attracted to her. Then she asked what he did. "I blushed and smiled and said, 'I do the same damned thing as you.'"

Kirk told her the story of how he'd started, at a successful club in Portland, Maine called Mark's Showplace. Kirk had run into guys he used to ride motorcycles with and they told him about the Amateur Night competitions at Mark's. The prize was $300 and with Kirk's build, he'd win, they said. So in December 1990, Kirk decided to compete, knowing strippers made good money. He'd thought about exotic dancing since he was in California, but then wasn't confident enough about his body. Now he was. His family supported the idea. His sister Noli sewed sequined G-strings for him.

Kirk learned some valuable lessons on that night. "I thought that every girl wants to marry a doctor, so that would be my costume. Well, if you come out wearing a surgical mask, even if you have a buff body, it scares people. I came out to "Doctor Feelgood," a Motley Crew song. When I saw they were negative to the doctor thing I knew I'd better take some clothes off fast."

He made forty dollars for two songs. He thought it was a great start, especially when Mark's invited him back, but Mark's only had men dance for women on "Girls' Night Out" evenings, which only happened every month or two. Dancing at Mark's, Kirk met Dale, a young man who looked so much like him people thought they were brothers. The two became fast friends and decided to form a dance team. They traveled around New England, finding spots to dance for women. Trouble was, there weren't that many gigs. Men dancing for women was a small part of the business. And it wasn't the part that paid well.

"When women come to see men dance, it's usually a special occasion, someone getting married or a party," Kirk said. "They take a bunch of friends and cut loose. The pay can be good if you're dancing, where you'll get paid for group work plus tips. The bad thing is that when I do private parties for women, they don't think to tip."

He believes this is socialized behavior. It's incredibly frustrating for Kirk trying to make money dancing for women. "Everyone wants to see the stripper at the party, but when you go up to women they run into the kitchen going, 'Eeeeeeeee!' It's not that they're scared, it's how they think they should act." In contrast, it's hardly standard behavior for a man to run away from a naked women in front of his friends. "A man will try to impress a woman by giving her more money. Women don't do that. They do tip, but not much or for the same reasons."

In the clubs, with a group, women will spend more, he added. "A woman will hold money over her friend's head to embarrass her. They're more interested in teasing the friend than seeing naked men. I can tell I've done a good job if they're laughing. Sometimes the quietest ones can go wild. You'll hear, 'I can't believe she's doing that, she's never like that!'"

He wondered if the group doesn't give women license to act out. "I think women are really just as horny as men, fantasize as much as they do," he suggested. "The older lady next door is very nice and caring and everyone calls her Granny. She somehow always ends up in the yard when Dale and I are laying out getting tanned in G-strings. When we put the tanning bed downstairs and tanned nude there was a doorway we shared with Granny. I'd hear, 'How you doing!' and I'd wonder if she'd been watching the whole time. I used to think the older you got the more you lost your sexual drive, but now I find that's not so, it's just society sees older women as not being sexual and that's how they're supposed to act."

Kirk claimed that another difference in dancing for women is that they want the dancer to have more identification than just being a naked man. "Women want the fantasy of believing what they see up there. They want to know it's that hot construction worker on the corner, or the cute mailman, or Superman on TV. They know he's gorgeous and has a great body, so if someone comes out as Superman, the fantasy is created. It's story oriented." Dianah added that she uses costumes and personas too, but it works more to enhance rather than facilitate the performance.

A couple of months after they started, Kirk and Dale reevaluated their dance team, Fantasies Unlimited. A female stripper in Portland told Kirk that most male dancers she knew made a living in gay bars. "But we're heterosexual," Kirk told her. "There are more heterosexual guys dancing in gay bars than gay or bisexual," she told him.

Dale was not up for this idea. Kirk needed the money. The plan was to make enough to finance their own troop to compete with the big ones, like Chippendales or some of the traveling male revue shows that toured the country dancing for bachelorette parties and performing at special functions like Girl's Night Out.

"A couple of months later we met someone who told us to send photos to the owner of a gay bar in Rhode Island," Kirk related. "We had no fucking idea what they'd want, so we got on the floor and started dancing together. I took his shirt off, pulled it down and rubbed his body. The customers standing around took an interest, so we thought, all right, and we asked the manager if we could take our pants off because we were wearing G-strings." When the manager said yes, they did a bumping and grinding simulated sex act, half expecting at any moment to get laughed off the floor.

"After we were done they came over and said, 'Oh, my God! We've never seen anything like that in our lives! It's so sexy!' The owner said, 'If you cut your hair I can book you in San Francisco for two weeks, $1,200 each.'"

Kirk told Dianah the story sitting there in Pure Gold in Lexington, Kentucky. How they played a circuit of clubs but the goal was to have their own troop. How most of his work came from dancing in gay clubs. How he'd created the character "Jesse," who'd done magazines and porn films, finding out quickly that he got paid $200 for a scene in a heterosexual porn film, but $400 to $2,000 for a gay porn scene. How once you had those credits you were a name and you were paid more as a feature dancer.

She was open-minded. "Money's money and how you make it is your own business." She was intrigued, having never seen *men* dance. Kirk told Dianah about the club in Maine, a much bigger and better club than this one in Kentucky. He knew that with her looks and her accent, she'd make a killing. He asked if she'd go to breakfast with him when she got off work. "I usually go to breakfast at a place nearby," she agreed.

*   *   *

In two days, Kirk and Dianah had fallen in love, and Kirk made her a business proposition. "She said she wanted a boob job, and I said, 'If you want that, I'll help you save the money. You won't have to pay rent, no expenses.' I made everything strictly a business deal because I wanted to get to know her better. She could sleep on my bed and I'd sleep on the couch if she didn't feel comfortable. I said, 'Sex is entirely up to you, whenever you say no or yes. And if you come to Maine and don't like it you'll have a plane ticket back home.'"

Dianah cautiously started to like him. "He was the first nice guy I'd met in months. I'd been married before my eighteenth birthday, and was married three years. But Kirk was the first person I thought I could talk *to*. It was a good feeling."

Kirk and Dianah agreed to try. First he had to finish two weeks of a tour that would take him all the way to Texas. On the way back, he'd swing by Kentucky and they'd go on to Maine together.

"The next day we said good-bye and I thought, 'My God, this girl, I can't believe I'm leaving her behind.'"

"He was supposed to be gone two weeks," she remembered. "Two days later, he was back."

And so they found themselves trying to explain things to Dianah's devastated mother, who'd returned from her factory shift to discover her daughter about to leave home with a stranger. "Mom," said Dianah, "I know you're afraid but I'm going to take this chance. He seems nice, and this is an opportunity. I've never been anywhere. I stayed at the same job at the factory. I just haven't seen anything my whole life."

That day in June 1993, Darlene King watched her daughter drive away with the stranger to a new life in Maine. It wasn't the first time she'd lost Dianah.

* * *

Photographs of the first summer Dianah and Kirk spent in Maine speak eloquently: they were in love and it was a happy time. The photographs are in the woods, on top of mountains, with trees sharply green, the sky intensely blue or colored by vivid sunsets. There are pictures of her in bathing suits or nude, lying on a rock overlooking a valley, smiling a sweet smile with her knees and arms tucked, hiding. There's one of her wearing hiking boots. She fluctuates from sensuous and sexy to looking like a jock. There are shots of him flexing his v-shaped torso in the kitchen, a towel around his waist. In the first photographs after the boob job, she posed like a 1940s sex siren, head tilted back over her shoulder, bending backward to thrust out her new silhouette, more what she thought she should look like than was used to.

Dale, Kirk, and Dianah would practice dancing in the apartment they all shared, part of a small red house up a quiet road with tall pine trees. "I learned so much watching those two men," Dianah recalled. "Dale does physical moves, floor kicks and spins. Kirk is more sensual. He'll do the tight, slow hand rub your muscles, show everything you got poses. I learned how to incorporate it all."

A few weeks after arriving in Maine and working out in the gym, Dianah entered the Mark's Amateur Night Contest. Mark's Showplace was the biggest and best club in Maine, maybe in New England. Kirk and Dale came to support her, and the hundred-dollar tips made it seem she wasn't an amateur. She didn't win, but Mark's offered her a job. She started dancing nightly, and soon became one of the most popular attractions.

Fantasies, Unlimited, meanwhile, wasn't getting much work on the straight side. Dale and Kirk were fighting. Dale urged Kirk to get serious and move somewhere where they would have more luck setting up their own dance troop, somewhere with more clubs, like Las Vegas, Atlanta, or Florida. Dale went to Florida. And for the next ten months, Dianah continued at Mark's while Kirk took the occasional out-of-town booking.

ON THE ROAD

The following winter in New York, Kirk was tired from traveling. He's been on the road for weeks booked through agents. He'd flown to four clubs in the past four days in Texas, from Dallas, to Houston to San Antonio. He says this trip worked out well. There is a tight network between the club owners, so it was worth it to them to import a feature stripper like Kirk. The clubs were packed. It was all good business for everyone.

This trip was well-planned, which is unusual, Kirk added. He was even picked up on time. Unless you are a very big name, going through agents can be ghastly. "Agents in this business get twenty percent and most screw up arrangements. You find yourself flying under other people's name, so the club owner gets the frequent flier mileage. If we crash they'll be looking for Harold Butthead, not Kirk Hill."

Dianah's first feature experience, six months later, was unhappier. She was booked on a week-long trip to Ohio through an agent. The agent told her the club would pay for her airfare and hotel. The night she was to leave the agent said, oh, yeah, they decided they're just paying for the hotel. Dianah, who knew that booking a flight under such short notice would be costly, protested. She'd lose money, or just break even. What was the point of going?

You have to go, argued the agent. You're booked. You let these people down and you'll get a bad name in the business. Dianah felt she had no choice. Waiting for the limo she'd been told to expect, she became even less happy when the club owner showed up instead. They weren't a mile out of the airport when his hand was on her thigh and he was telling her how pretty she was.

"The tips were terrible. I made $52 a night. I try to average $200.

The club closed at 1:00 A.M., but they'd make me wait until 3:00 A.M. to get paid. It was awful."

"When I arrived, I opened the door to my room. The club was paying for it—all of $113 for the week. There was a bucket of piss standing next to the toilet, which didn't work, and the rug was covered with mildew." Dianah canceled the next week's trip. The hell with the agent.

"I'm fed up with the whole ordeal," Kirk sighed. "All hassles. It's not as easy as everyone who's not in the business thinks it is. I did movies and magazines and that gets me better jobs in gay clubs. In straight clubs I have no credits. Maybe if I did a calendar. But women don't come out to see certain men the way men go to see feature centerfolds or female porn stars. Women go out to see groups of men dancers." He says that he and Dale have talked to individual investors about helping finance their group, but trying to make a living has made this hard to concentrate on.

He and Dianah had been in separate places for weeks at a time, and this took its toll on the relationship. Dale was in Florida, impatiently calling Kirk to come down so they could get their act together. Until Kirk made the mistake of telling Dianah to move with him rather than asking her, she'd considered joining them, but that approach got her back up. Things were going well in Maine. She'd had a husband order her around and no man was ever going to do that again. If Kirk wanted her there, *ask* and she'd think about it.

WORKING THE GAIETY

While trying to work out life with Dianah and Dale, Kirk was also preparing to dance at the Gaiety in New York. The Gaiety Theater is located above the Times Square Howard Johnson's, on Broadway. One flight above street level, it's got a stage with a runway where men with the bodies of professional body builders, dancers, and models dance for men. The rules are strict, no touching on the ass, cock, or balls. Other clubs have different rules. A more conservative area like Maine has a no-touch policy for the dancers, and bouncers strictly enforce it.

Dancers work weekly shifts at the Gaiety. Many of the dancers supplement with hustling on the side. They're paid hourly, but unlike women strippers, the male dancers aren't tipped as they dance. It makes a serious financial difference.

"I don't like hustling for a living, but I'm safe about it," Kirk said. "I wear condoms, they wear condoms. They know I'm straight. Most of them even know I have a girlfriend."

For Kirk, the experience raised questions about his sexuality, about sexuality in general. "I'd rather be with Dianah. It's a job and I treat it like a job, but it got weird for me in the beginning when I found I could enjoy what was going on. I think everyone has bisexual tendencies, but not everyone acts on them."

And then Kirk went on to describe a phenomenon that seemed so telling about male sexual conditioning and performance that it amazed me:

"Many of the guys who work at the Gaiety are straight. When a woman comes in they'll bust their balls trying to impress her. And because they're trying so hard to impress her, when they're backstage all they can think about is, 'There are girls in the audience!' and then they can't get hard. Nerves. I had the same problem, it's psychological, performance anxiety."

People seem afraid of their sexuality, Kirk says. "I think people know how much they are capable of, and that scares them, as if they think they won't be able to control it if they ever let go. People hide from themselves, not just society."

Dianah tried to keep an open mind about Kirk's work. Her attitude had changed since she started dancing, in a way that had affected her understanding of life and sex. "If I'd so much as walked around the house nude when I was married, my husband thought that was improper," she remembered. Now she walked around the dance club half nude, and felt fine about it. She was sure she'd married for life, that she would never love anyone but her husband. Well, that belief had been revised, too. Kirk's work involved things she'd never encountered before. Yet she knew he loved her. Maybe love was more complex.

Before she'd left Kentucky, she and her mother had run into her best friend from high school. "My Mom said, 'Guess what Sissy does now?' She said, 'What?' 'Sissy's a dancer at Pure Gold.' She said, 'You mean, you show your titties?!' That's the reaction I got from my best friend. She said her husband goes there. 'You don't show your titties to him, do you?' And I said, 'If he gives me ten dollars, I do.'"

* * *

At Chippendales in New York, men dance for women. It's an extravagant show, with choreographed routines, music, loudspeakers, costumes. And as Kirk said, they are built around fantasy themes, male prototypes like military uniforms or marshal arts. The audiences consist mostly of bachelorette parties, girls getting married next week with their friends, or divorcees getting remarried next week with their friends.

A handsome young man in a tuxedo selects a young woman from the audience—how she and her friends SCREAM!—and he takes her by the hand to a central table set up for dinner, where he lip-syncs a romantic song to her, peeling his clothes off—Eeeeeee! and finishes by rubbing his hand up and down the shaft of the candle. The audience sighs. Then they scream as guys in neon G-strings work the floor for money.

At The Gaiety Theater, men dance for men. At the top of the stairs is a glass-enclosed ticket booth. Inside, Denise, the red-haired proprietress, sells tickets. There's a small theater with a stage that extends out to the audience on a short runway platform. The audience is all men, ranging in age from young boys to seniors. As quietly as I tried to enter, I was always stared at.

The curtain over the stage was silver lamé. It's dark except for small aisle lights and a spotlight. Over the loudspeaker, the DJ announced each performer. "Please welcome . . . Devon!"

The music started, unbearably plaintive. A woman sings in a low voice, "Are you happy now? I could never make you so. You are a hard man, no harder in this world. . . ."

Erections get a big hand at the Gaiety. The audience clapped when Devon, a big blond, walked out with his. The man's beauty and sexuality is rated by applause. Unlike the frenetic theatrics of Chippendales, this was more like a horse show where the whole idea is to study the specimen in the spotlight.

He was nude except for white socks, which accentuated the nudity. He had a perfect long body, slightly tanned, his ass the color of pale cream. He posed, knees bent and arm muscles flexed. He knelt down within touching distance of two men next to the stage.

The music had a primitive drumbeat over electronic scales. A woman's voice rose over it in a wailing cry.

Devon lifted his arm up to the sky, stretched his torso and took a deep breath, rippling from his chest up the line of his throat. He had an ethereal, angelic expression. The music throbbed, rushing like blood.

He stopped in the middle of the stage under the light and pretended to pull a rope down from the sky. Muscles rippled his arms, shoulders, and chest. He sank to the floor in a hamstring stretch that left his cock pointing at the audience. He sat up, closed his hand between his legs, and ran it down the shaft. His hand traveled up his abdomen and chest with slow twisting, moves. He looked down and his hair, the color of wheat, fell over his eyes. He turned his back and offered his rear to view, spreading his legs and sliding back and forth on his white socks. He stood straight, pirouetted, lifted his arms up and rotated his hips in an undulating series of thrusts. The audience clapped as he exited.

The pace of this was so different than Chippendales. This was for slow, luxurious looking. Donald Moser had said that women aren't usually placed in a context in which they view men. It was true. I'd never seen anything like this. I found myself settling in like a cat in front of a warm fire.

The next dancer, a big, solid, Italian-looking guy, came out wearing a black sweatshirt and loose drawstring pants. His music was cheerily philosophical: "Some people can hold it together. . . ." He caressed the front of his shirt, his hand moving up and down his chest. He had a classic Roman head, thick short dark hair. He looked like someone you'd see behind the wheel of a large truck, but his movements were languid and flowing as he removed his clothing, particularly sexy because his rhythms belied his appearance. His body language was receptive, tentative even. He put his hands on his stomach, slid his pants up and down, and rolled his buttocks.

His next song was a soft, guitar solo ballad. "The night . . . the night is yours alone . . ." The guitar strummed slowly. "Are you sure . . . you've had enough of desire?"

He was totally nude except for black sneakers. He was large, very toned. He brought his hand slowly down his body to the shaft of his penis, and held himself as if for a moment's study. He lowered himself on the stage as if joining another body. He traced his fingertips as if touching a face.

When he regained his feet, this big lovely man exhibited his body, showing himself off the way we expect of a woman.

Looking at these men, I realized why men love looking at strippers. The pleasure of looking over nude bodies is to enter a state of altered consciousness, a sort of erotic visual drunkenness in which you can take your time. I felt as if I'd had sex with all of them. My painter friend Elliot and I once talked about why when we came back from art museums we were completely exhausted, and he said, "Because it's active to really look at art." So was this. Looking at every part of them was as active as touching every part of them.

The body language was different from the presentation at Chippendales, which was so assertive. In their relation to the viewer, the

Chippendale's dancers never seemed to lose the dominant position even when they had their clothes off. Chippendales was in your face, not in your eyes. This was more about being seen, which was calmer, more open. What Kirk said about being surprised by how many different sexual things men could do is true. But you don't get to see them all in society's limited presentations of men, which focus on images of hardness and masculinity rather than vulnerable sensuality. I found this incredibly sexy and intimate.

When Kirk came out, his body was so perfect it was hard to accept, as if one of the statues from the museum had hopped off a stand and strode over. He stood in the lights and turned, slowly offering every muscle, every part, as if the beauty of a man was something to be celebrated, too.

WORKING CRYSTAL

From the parking lot, Mark's Showplace in Portland, Maine, could be a bank. In a quiet shopping mall, the building is a large understated red brick structure. Driving in, Dianah remarked that the parking lot was nearly filled.

The deliberately discreet design of Mark's Showplace is characteristic of how club owners work to avoid community conflict. Maine, like much of New England, is conservative. Owner Mark Deane, who came from nearby Bangor, knew that to run a club successfully he would have to work with the local community. "It helps the local economy," he said. "We have 125 employees, and contribute $30,000 a year in taxes."

Peter Sandor Gardos is a sexologist and editor for the Society For the Scientific Study of Sex, one of the nation's oldest research organizations concentrating in human sexuality. He is an expert witness, often testifying in cases where local authorities try to ban or restrict nude dancing.

Gardos says that as he worked on cases, he became aware of the paucity of research in this area. He was disturbed by movements made by politicians and legislature. "I didn't see that it had any empirical validation."

Gardos concentrated on the question of harmful secondary effects: i.e., if this club comes in, there goes the neighborhood.

In the cases in which Gardos testified, he found that conclusions were often drawn on limited or skewed evidence. "They'll bring in a case that cites the 1970 Indianapolis study. The defense always concedes it. In one Atlanta case, the data was fudged. They did comparisons, basically took three areas with nude clubs and one area without. They tried to compare crime rates. Not a bad idea," he says, "but for the areas with the nude club they used three years' worth of crime and the area without the nude club they used one year."

The question of whether nude clubs lead to increased crime is one Gardos continues to study. "Is it true only for them, or is it true of any location with several hundred people drinking alcohol? The reality is often that the nude club has less violence." He claims that one of the primary causes of disturbances in a nightclub is fighting, based on "were you looking at my girl?" or "I saw her first." Those pressures don't exist in a strip club. "The mores and norms are well established, and anyone who violates them, they're out of there."

Finally, just as club owner Mark Deane found in Maine, a club's acceptance can depend on presentation. Most people will express reservations if you ask them about a strip club coming to their town, Gardos finishes. "But if you say, there will be no windows, no loitering, it'll be clean, well run, not within a thousand feet of any of the following types of things, and it will bring in revenue and not increase crime, you'll find the majority of people do not object to it."

In June 1991 the Supreme Court upheld *Barnes* v. *Indiana*, the ruling that states may ban nude dancing. Professor Stephen Gillers, a Constitutional law expert at New York University Law School, discussed it in an interview, saying that Rehnquist created a gradation of First Amendment protection by this ruling, claiming that some speech is more valuable than others and will get more protection. Rehnquist wrote, "Nude dancing of the kind sought to be performed here is expressive conduct on the outer perimeters of the First Amendment."

"What does he mean, 'of the kind sought to be performed here?' " queried Professor Gillers. Was Rehnquist saying the Supreme Court would now distinguish between what goes on in a strip club or an avant garde ballet? "Up until now, you were protected or you weren't, and the Court didn't distinguish between artworks or modes of expressions. Rehnquist then goes on to say, 'We can balance the First Amendment interest of this sort of nude dancing performed here, the kind that gets less protection in our view, against the state interest.' "

That interest, Gillers points out, is public morality. "People get upset if they see naked bodies. We therefore find the interest in public morality is stronger than the marginal First Amendment interest in this performance. What does that do? It makes the Supreme Court into a censor."

Prior to this, obscenity was not protected. "This dancing was not obscene, everyone agreed to that," Stephen Gillers noted. "What Rehnquist had done is to say, no, even if it's not obscene it can be prohibited, even without a compelling state interest, just a generalized interest in morality."

Justice White dissented, saying that anyone who was in a strip club went because they wanted to, so who was hurt by strip clubs? "What Rehnquist said was that the state has an interest in morality abstractly," adds Professor Gillers. "It's really astonishing. He is saying that people who may never go into the bar are affronted that it's there and they can translate their repulsion."

Gillers points out that Rehnquist's decision cited *Bowers* v. *Hardwick*, a case upheld by the Supreme Court holding that Georgia could forbid consensual sodomy.

If Americans get teary-eyed over our free country every Fourth of July, they should think about this Supreme Court fiasco. The most frightening part of George Orwell's *1984* was the couple in bed with Big Brother watching behind the picture on the wall. The Bowers case began when a policeman walked into a man's bedroom to serve a warrant for a minor offense (the fine of which had already been paid), discovered him in an act of mutual oral sex with another man, and arrested him. Harvard Law's Lawrence Tribe, in the petition he wrote requesting Supreme Court reconsideration of Bowers, suggested that the question that Court should be considering "is not what Respondent Michael Hardwick was doing in the privacy of his own bedroom, but what the State of Georgia was doing there."

"In drawing the line between Bowers and Barnes, Rehnquist is saying the state has an interest in suppressing what they consider immoral conduct even if those who would suppress it are not in any way exposed to it personally." The issue, Gillers adds, is whether or not morality can be used for laws infringing on First Amendment rights or a claim of privacy.

Justice Souter's opinion was the most interesting, Gillers added, because at the time, he was the most unknown. "He says, 'I want it clear I'm not equating the nude dancing that went on in this bar with nudity that may occur in other settings like sunbathing or a dance concert. I want to make it clear that for me public morality is not a legitimate state value that can justify the infringement here.' What is? Souter credited a secondary effect of nudity in these establishments: Violence,

prostitution, criminal activity. Because of the correlation of such dancing with these evils the state can forbid it. In his footnote he says those
secondary effects would be more questionable if the state were to seek
to enforce laws against, say, *Equuis* or *Hair*."

Great. We're back to "the negative secondary effects caused by strip
clubs." What is this based on? What research did Indiana and Justice
Souter use? How does he make the leap that exotic dancing causes
crime?

Speaking of insufficiently substantiated conclusions, according to
Souter, the unhappy secondary effects of nude dancing include "prostitution, sexual assault, criminal activity, degradation of women, and
other activities which break down the family structure."

Nude dancing causes prostitution and degrades women? That's interesting, especially since we've seen that it's much easier for a woman
to make a living just dancing. More men supplement their dancing
incomes with prostitution because unlike women dancers, that's the
way to make good money.

DIANAH'S WORK NIGHT IN MAINE

"A lot of clubs prefer that you have your makeup on, hair fixed, and
wear something decent when you arrive. At Pure Gold in Kentucky the
front door is the only way in." So saying, Dianah stepped out of her
truck wearing loose drawstring pants, a sweatshirt, and a baseball cap.
Inside, the sound system pumped music that reverberated in the soles
of your feet.

The interior lobby of Mark's Showplace opened up to the huge space
of the two-story club. The main floor had three different stage areas.
Dianah pointed out the table dance area by the far wall. In Maine,
which Dianah complained was a national low for table dance rates,
dancers got five dollars "for a whole song!" In Kentucky, it was twenty
dollars. Nonetheless, her attitude helped her. "Hell, I'll go out and ask
everyone in the crowd. 'Somebody get a table dance off me, I'm a dyin!'
I'll find somebody if I have to ask everyone."

It was early evening, and already there was a decent crowd around
the two main stages, where pairs of women danced topless. Lights
flashed, pulsating with the music. Dianah stuck her head into the enormous control room where DJs played the music. She said hello to the
two working this night.

"It's going to be a good night," one declared. On the way upstairs to show me the VIP stage, she explained that there's a feature dancer tonight, Amber Lynne, who will draw a large crowd.

Dianah pointed out that bouncers are right next to the dancers. "Guys can get close but not that close." Other things about the VIP stage bothered her more. "If a girl has cellulite on her ass you can see it a mile away. If you have any marks on your body or if your belly sticks out, you can see it all the way downstairs. That's why I hate going up there. It's the worst stage, the lighting's harsh." But it was still the best place to make money. "Most girls make six bucks, but I'll make fifteen or twenty, because I'll play each guy until he gives me his last buck. I'll reach out, grab hold of him, and shake him. A lot of girls won't do that."

Did the men have the nerve to stand two feet away from her, look at her, and *not* tip? "Some do, you'd be surprised. I feel like knockin' em over the rail, which would be easy to do. If I'm working and a guy is standing in front of my stage mmhhh hmmmm hummmmmm, turning their back to me and looking downstairs. Whewww!" She feigned walking around to the guy. " 'I'll tell you flat out, if you don't want to look at me, that's fine, but please don't take up space at my stage!' I'll say it nicely at first but if I come back and the guy is still turned around I'll tell him, 'Get off my stage!' "

Nine women shared the locker room. Bright, well lit, and clean, it features huge mirrors ringed by lights. She introduced me to some of her friends, her dancing partner, Joy, and a woman with alabaster white skin and punky short black hair and dark eyes named Xavier. She paused significantly after saying "And this is Rakelle. . . ."

Dianah and Rakelle were rivals from Dianah's first day. Kirk attributed it to a difference in their approach. Dianah's energy and personality resulted in her making good money. She was competition. So now it's a psych game, Kirk related. "She'll say something like, 'Aren't you gaining weight?' or 'That outfit looks stupid.' If someone puts doubt in your mind, it affects how you do." Rakelle and Dianah dress in different areas.

"They furnish us with locks for the lockers," she murmured, and opened hers to show what could be a mini-costume room for a Broadway show. She had racks and pockets of G-string and bra combinations hanging in rainbow hues on the door and inside her locker. Hangers displayed one elaborate spangled outfit after another. Nine months ago she had nothing, she added. Now she could go anywhere and feature.

To be a feature dancer is the goal good strippers aspire to. Feature dancers get their names on special billing and draw a crowd. They're paid much better. The handful of top ones make phenomenal money. A feature is a headliner who can pack a club by virtue of her name. That name recognition comes from either porn films or erotic magazine layouts. The very top features are as well known as strippers throughout the country as Cindy Crawford, Claudia Schiffer, and Linda Evangelista are known as models.

Dianah pulled out her elaborate costumes to provide a better look. "This is my pink tux, which I paid $300 for." It was satin, with spangles and studs, piped with black. The next was a jeweled red, white, and blue bustier and a denim jacket, matched with tiny denim shorts cut down to string bikini size. A 1950s outfit included a poodle pink satin miniskirt complete with an aqua halter top that stripped off to reveal a tiny white bra.

She lead the way upstairs to the office lounge of Mark Deane, the club owner. He mentioned that Amber Lynne, a well-known porn star who is tonight's feature dancer, will be paid $15,000 a week, plus expenses. On the way back downstairs, Dianah paused to watch Amber Lynne on the Main Stage.

Amber Lynne wore a white flounced petticoat, a camisole with roses covering her bodice, garters, high-heeled white shoes, elbow-length white gloves and a hat with trailing streamers. She was a gorgeous woman, with long blond hair and a fantastic body. Her persona was an X-rated Victorian May Day fantasy. When Amber Lynne kissed a photograph she was about to give away, and lifted herself on her high heels, the crowd roared. Dianah turned to go downstairs to get ready for her own show.

*   *   *

I watched while Dianah changed into Crystal. She wore leather high-heeled boots over a thonged outfit, making up in front of the lighted mirror.

Joy, her dancing partner for the evening, entered. She was Crystal's age and height, petite, slender, with long legs and a beautiful face. She had pretty brown eyes, a straight nose, and long shiny walnut-colored brown hair. She showed me her five-inch steel heels, which screwed in to her shoes like spikes.

A tall, blond woman arrived. She was fuller figured, with large pink-tipped breasts. She greeted Crystal and Joy, and said she liked the feature dancer. "She's so much prettier than her pictures! Her outfits are great."

"Trixie Tyler and Natalie Smith wear great outfits too," offered Joy, speaking of other headliners.

"She came over to my house to take dance lessons," Crystal said.

"Can someone be a feature and not be a proficient dancer?" I asked. A chorus of "Oh, yeah!" from the women. "A lot of them can't dance," Joy said.

The schedule was posted. In the course of the evening, Crystal and Joy would dance for alternating half-hour and fifteen-minute shifts at 6:45, 7:15, 7:45, 8:45, 9:45, 10:45, and 12:15, rotating to every stage at the club. It was a physical challenge. By the end of the night, just following them from stage to stage and interviewing people, I was exhausted. Pamela, the voluptuous woman, joked about getting too old. She was thirty-eight, a Physical Education major in college who started dancing at age thirty. "It's great money and hours. I can take off a couple of weeks, a month." She worked as a house mom, then went back to dancing. "Being a house mom is demanding. You have to be there, you can't take off whenever you want. There were forty girls, and to take care of that many girls, all menstruating at the same time, give me this, give me that, Mom Mom Mom. You do everything a mom would do, get costumes ready, help them get ready, be a psychologist about boyfriend trouble, working at the club . . . after three years, I was ready to go back to dancing!"

Pamela said she enjoyed the job, money, and the flexibility it offered. "The majority of the men are nice. They can't touch you, which is good. It's exciting to feel a sense of power when you're out there. But it's not a sexual thing, in fact sometimes you get grossed out by things they do and say. It's not like, oh, this is such a turn-on doing this. But you try to look like it is."

She was in between jobs when she waitressed at a topless club, saw how much money the women were making, and thought, "I could do that!" It was only supposed to be for six months, but, she said, "Eight years later, here I am!"

Crystal went out to dance, greeting two of the bouncers. Bouncers provide protection. The main rules are, You Touch, You Go. As far as fights, the bouncers don't touch the customer unless he touches a dancer or the bouncer first. Most of the time the crowd is fine, Crystal claimed, except for Friday and Saturday nights, which are "asshole nights." "Figure it, it's the guys who don't have dates." This night the house was full, and on the whole customers seemed mannerly and friendly, and happy to answer questions. A lot of them asked me questions about reporting on dancers. Dianah's "regulars" came over to introduce themselves.

Every dancer has "regulars," men who come to the club to see a favorite. Crystal greeted four rather shy, sweet guys who hovered in the hallway wearing matching caps that read, "Perverts R Us." The Perverts were regulars. One nice thing about regulars was that they could be quite protective if anyone acted badly. All evening they helped me keep track of Crystal. "She went to the VIP stage. Now she's over there. . . ."

On the Main Stage, Crystal strutted to a high stepping show tune. She bent over and flashed her butt playfully to the guys lining the stage, tossing her hair. She and Joy met in the middle of the stage and exchanged dance moves. Crystal kicked her legs up and Joy kissed her on her G-string. They hugged to end the set and walked around, collecting tips.

The music switched to heavy metal, "I Love Rock and Roll." Crystal took off her top, shrugging her full breasts out and tying it behind her neck to frame her chest. She acted out a wild and sexy persona, doing splits, touching her breasts to the floor, going down slowly sinuously humping. She rolled over and crawled, showing off her lovely nude buttocks and uncovered breasts framed by the glittering tong. The guys next to the stage were enthusiatic. One reached over to tip her. Her hair down over her eye, she gave a sweet smile to him, managing to look pretty and hot at the same time. She shimmied her shoulders.

On the same stage lithesome Joy danced, spreading her legs out on high heels. She was graceful, willowy, now practically upside down in the yoga bridge position, nearly nude, swinging back and forth on her spiked boots and hands. The song ended. They picked up their money, and a bouncer helped them off. Both headed bare breasted back to the dressing room.

WORKING SMART

Amber Lynne has danced for ten years. She started out as an adult film star and graduated to dancing when she was engaged to a club owner. She spends thirty-five to thirty-eight weeks a year on the road. "I'm the highest paid act in North America," she said, which is probably true. She makes $200,000 a year.

Amber Lynne sat in a chair next to a lighted mirror. She wore a filmy white robe and looked quite the glamorous sex star with her shapely tanned legs crossed, cornsilky blond hair cascading down her back and curling at the ends, makeup highlighting pretty features. She had a great, husky, sort of whisky voice, and was plain spoken.

A decade ago, she was tired of doing porn films when someone asked her about dancing in a topless club. "I was the girl in high school you couldn't get on the dance floor. They said, 'We'll pay you $10,000.' I said, 'I'll learn. I'll learn!' My girlfriend helped me, we practiced in my living room and I was sooooooo bad, I couldn't even walk in high-heeled shoes. The first time on stage I froze. Thank God I was booked with one of my friends, Tracy Adams. My legs started shaking, and she literally had to grab my arm and hiss, 'Come on! There are 500 people here! Let's go!' "

Now she did her shows with elaborate costumes, acting out different parts. She traveled with a dresser, a quiet woman who sits in a chair nearby minding the rack of wild and beautiful outfits Amber uses. She learned to trust her instincts. "I was an adult film star when I was eighteen years old. I learned things about sex I never knew. There was a camera and crew and a whole staff of people. Once someone stands and watches you have sex with someone else, what is there? First it was scary, then I grew from it. When you strip yourself naked and stand up with no prop to work with except your body and who you are, that's when your personality really takes charge, when you have to draw from the loving and humorous part of you."

What I realized speaking to her was that Amber Lynne was a smart business woman. She said she didn't feel exploited because she wouldn't let herself be, and I believed her. She had thought out her career, planned and acted wisely. There were many writers, journalists, and psychological experts whose work I admired, but I disagreed when they insisted that what someone like this did was degrading, exploit-ative, or self-destructive. Or unconscious, for that matter. This woman knew what she was doing.

Amber Lynne said she was twenty-nine years old and was consider-ing what she'd do next. Her idea was to start a full-service agency for female strippers that would help dancers avoid the pitfalls of the busi-ness. "It won't just be an agent calling up and saying, 'I have a booking for you' but an adult entertainment clearing house for clubs and ser-vices where they can also find anything they need to about the industry, whether it be who does the best costumes or who rips people off." She believed that the more educated a woman was about the business, the more she could work it to her advantage.

When she started in the industry, things were different. "Girls were afraid of speaking out and saying, 'I want this much because I'm worth this much.' I went into clubs and asked, 'How much more money did you make at the door and the bar the week I was there compared to a normal week?' Well, if they were making $60,000 or $80,000 more, then I'm worth $20,000!"

When club owners reacted as if she were insane, Amber Lynne merely said, "Okay, then, I won't work, how's that?" She got the money.

Amber Lynne believes that it is important for women in the sex industry to see themselves as powerful and conduct themselves accordingly. She pointed out that without women acting in erotic films and dancing, a multimillion-dollar business wouldn't exist. Her agent's mother, who is seventy-five, was Rita Atlanta, one of the most famous burlesque strippers. "This industry has been around for seventy-five years," she stated. She was infuriated by the double standard that makes money from women but tries to represent them as crazy or defective, powerless. She thought mainstream media didn't shed light on the business because it provided no context to the decision-making process or options that make women choose sex work. I agree.

She spoke of a friend of hers, a *New Yorker* reporter who said that until knowing Amber Lynne, she hadn't envisioned women in the sex industry as being go-getters like her. "This is a business," Lynne stated flatly. "We make our money, we go home. For the most part, this is just a job." At home, she lives a conservative and domestic life. "I'm an entertainer. That's what it's about, a show. Nudity just happens to be part of the show. As any actor will tell you, even in love scenes in a movie, you act."

She ticked off stereotypes on her fingers. "They say exotic dancers are drug addicts or alcoholics. Right off the top, you'd have no longevity in the business if you are, period. Just to handle being on the road you have to be healthy; that's why rock stars burn out after three or four years, or O.D. and die."

When she began dancing she realized she could make a lot of money over a long period of time. "How many people do you know who make over $200,000 a year? How many people at age thirty can pick and choose what they do next?"

You do give up a lot to be in the industry, she added. Her biggest problem was relationships. "It's not just because a guy can't handle having the woman he loves get up and take her clothes off in front of 200 or 300 screaming men waving bills at her. It's because of the long road trips. But I figure anyone who is really worth it will put up with it."

Weighing her options, Amber Lynne considered how far she's come and where she's going. What she wanted was to continue seeing herself as powerful and imparting that sense to other women who work in her field. The extent of her power was evident after she was approached to do a benefit for the Youth AIDS Foundation in Los Angeles. "We raised $70,000 in one night."

Being in the sex industry, she was advised not to do it because of the association of sex and AIDS, but that appalled her. "How can you say no to a thirteen-year-old kid on the street who's going to die?" She helped approach rock and roll people, and the combination of their audience and her fans made it work. Maury Povich asked her to do his show afterward, and she realized he never had a porn star on his program until then. She *was* the mainstream. The false separation was over.

SHOWTIME

Back in the nonfeature dressing room, Pamela pulled up white fishnet stockings and freshened her makeup. Joy and Crystal changed into their next outfits. Joy wore a grass green spangled bathing suit that plunged to a tiny bottom, Crystal, a sea green bra with the pink satin tuxedo jacket belted over it.

"In a club like this you make most of your money on stage," Pamela explained saying that in a club she worked in Dallas, table dancing was the big financial return. "There we were on stage once and the rest of the night you'd sit with customers and make twenty bucks per table dance. Here it's five dollars, so it's good to have all the stage time."

Crystal and Joy were due on stage. They placed top hats on their heads, looked at each other, whirled and headed for the door.

It was about nine at night. The place was filled. The music playing now was a mix of rap and reggae, which added a more mellow feel to the club. A lean man with light brown hair and blue eyes, introduced himself to me as Andrew Noyes, the manager of a strip club in Rhode Island and a friend of Mark Deane's. He said that he and his friend Keith, co-owner of the Rhode Island club, came by to visit and see Amber Lynne's show.

I asked about some of her comments, and he confirmed what she said about the stereotype of strippers on drugs. "Club owners know the users right away. No one wants to work with them. They're not reliable. If you spend a couple of thousand dollars in advertising to draw people and then the dancers don't show up, you're stuck. You want people who come in, get the job done, act professional, and go on their way."

Spread out below, the two main stages were rocking. Joy and Crystal did a girl on girl wrestling act, then Crystal sat on the edge of the stage. She'd reach over and pull a customer to her, stretching out a shapely leg and hooking him by the waist or neck. She controlled the contact, and commanded a tip. Bouncers hovered within a few feet. In the past six years Andrew claimed that the atmosphere of strip clubs had changed. "You don't have jerks coming in as much anymore, trying to grab girls. You have to present an atmosphere to make people feel comfortable, not make it sleazy. Protect your dancers, have enough bouncers who watch what goes on . . . you start by controlling that and the rest falls into place."

I spoke with Steve, the DJ, who said that he loved his job. He was an unemployed beach bum and he first worked at Mark's as a bouncer. He said people don't judge him. "My parents are really religious, but I'm making good money so they respect it."

Across the floor, Xavier, the dancer with the punky hair cut and alabaster skin, was crawling on the floor. She slid up to the bars of the jungle gym and did a back flip, an amazing sight when the gymnast is bare-breasted, wearing only a few inches of lycra and high-heeled shoes.

Keith, the other owner of the Rhode Island club, was only thirty years old, a big, dark-haired, sweet fellow. He said he thought the women should use the business as a stepping stone to something else. "Put the money away and have another goal."

One problem was that the women make so much, the biggest lesson was to learn to plan, not blow it. The other problem that bothered him as a club owner is the misconception that all the clubs have back rooms.

Dianah found this out in New York. Clubs are different; each has customers that vary, depending on the place and who works there. Some have "Champagne Rooms," lounges where the customer pays to enter and sit with the dancer of his choice. The man pays $400 and believes the dancer is getting a hundred of that. Actually, she has to pay twenty back to the club. "Some women will do more," Dianah said. She'd been in situations where next to her another dancer was giving someone a blow job—"No condom!" She grabbed the girl by the arm when the customer got up to go to the men's room. 'You're a fool!' Things that go on in that back room, that's not a stripper."

Why?

"A stripper comes out and puts on a show, teases you," she said. "You don't give nothing up."

"They're *dancers*," emphasized Keith, the club owner. "Entertainers. They're not prostitutes. They're not whores. Don't misunderstand." He said that people constantly come in and ask him to hook them up. "If I wanted to be a pimp I could have an office with a lot of phones and credit card machines, girls with beepers, and I could just call them. I wouldn't need the overhead I have, the liability that comes with a liquor license and the responsibility that comes with being open six or seven days a week."

At 10:00, the DJ made an announcement over the loudspeaker, asking for an "attitude check," which rated an alternating "Fuck you!" and "Yaaaaay!" from the crowd.

"All the way from Los Angeles, just for you, so let's show her what Portland boys are all about!" The crowd roared. "Are you ready? Our leading lady, our superstar, of stage, screen, and magazine! Recently inducted into the Adult Film Hall of Fame as the only triple X star ever to receive a lifetime achievement award in Paris, France. Join us in welcoming to the stage a young lady most men just fantasize about ever seeing in person, our triple X superstar, for the ultimate experience, gentlemen, this *is* Amber Lynne!"

A deafening wall of sound: screams, yells, claps, calls . . . you couldn't even hear the music. Amber Lynne marched on, dressed in a red military jacket with gold piping, stars, and military braid, black satin hot pants, high black pumps, and a very elaborate hat with a visor, out of which her hair spilled beautifully. Her music was very 1940's.

Amber Lynne strutted, swinging her hips. The place erupted with people screaming and throwing money. She gave her jacket to a guy on the side. Now she was in a black bra with deep cleavage, gold eagles on her patent leather belt. Her long legs carried her around the stage. She shimmied and showed her body, waving dainty little white gloves. Holding her arms out straight to the sides, she stood on the stage as if to illustrate what a perfect body looked like. Then, losing not another stitch, she walked off.

"Do you guys like it so far?" asks the DJ over the booming loudspeaker. "How many of you have seen her in a movie?" "Waa waaaa waaaa woooooeeeeeee!" was the considered response of the crowd.

Amber Lynne returned, strutting to the "Boogie Woogie Bugle

Boy." She moved lightly on her high black pumps, making lascivious faces, and waving a Mark's Showplace T-shirt over her head. She held it in front of her hot pants, then slipped them off, showing a black G-string that left her curvy ass bare, the mobility of which she illustrated by doing a split, then rolling one leg over the other, showing off her long supple limbs and flinging her hair. The bra parted company with her body and her full perfect breasts were displayed. The acoustic effect was like finding oneself next to concert speakers and wondering what percentage of your hearing you're losing.

She teased the crowd by draping the T-shirt across her breasts, then plucked her black G-string, her last vestige of clothing. The audience never ceased to cheer, they just whooped and hollered louder for each new move. By the time Amber Lynne strutted her lovely body off the stage, everyone seemed weak.

She returned to the slow pump and grind of "You Can Leave Your Hat On," the national anthem of stripping. She threw a full-length coyote coat on the stage and slid onto it. This act was a slow tease of peeling off outer layers, a black thong lycra suit, down to a tinier black string bikini that eventually flew out to the audience.

The next reappearance had her in a tangerine-colored bikini top connected to the bottom tiny triangle by strips. She crawled on the stage, did splits, twists, and then lay on her back with her arms spread and her legs in a V, moving as if experiencing sex with all the spectators. She sat up and closed her breasts around some guy's face and plucked his glasses off, then gave them back and sashayed teasingly away.

*   *   *

The hardest job in a strip club is being the act that follows a feature. "They've spent all their money. They're tired. And you're not her," Crystal said.

The lights were dimmed. Dry ice made a foggy cloud rise around the stage. Crystal came out wearing a monk's robe that covered her face. She had a laser light in each hand, and Gregorian chants filled the air. She lifted her lights to the sky, and twisted the robe to make it flow dreamily.

As the robe moved, you could see that underneath she wore black leather straps and a silver face mask. She whirled her arms, shooting rays of light around the stage, and the white flesh of her buttocks made a striking contrast under black leather straps. She threw the mask away, whipping her blond curls, and the tempo of the music went from slow chants to hard rock and roll. She emerged from her priestly robe. Her bodice was covered with a leather breast plate, layers of criss-crossing leather straps and chains everywhere.

Tough in her leather, soft with her angel head of blond curls, she strode over to the side and pulled a man's head to her crotch. He slid a tip into her G-string, and she strutted off, bare breasted under the S&M gear. She did a split, moving the V of her legs around in a circle. As the music intensified, the strobe lights winked off her silver chains. Her layers came off, until she wore only the bottom of a leather string bikini. She planted her legs and ran her hand up the cheek of her butt, whipping her head fiercely. The stage started filling with dollars.

"What she's doing is the biggest challenge, because it's not what they expect." Xavier, her punky styled friend came over to the rail to watch. She says that in San Francisco or New York, there would be more appreciation for an act like this, but even so, Crystal's enthusiastic reception was impressive, especially five minutes after Amber Lynne.

Back in the dressing room, the women teased their hair and switched into different colored bras and thongs. Pamela said the one bad thing about the business is a decrease in sex drive. Everyone agreed. "I used to love men, say hello to everyone. Since I've been doing this if some guy looks at me in public I want to snarl, 'What are *you* looking at?' If I wasn't married, I probably wouldn't even date."

Kirk and Dianah had told me how difficult this was for them. She said that most men would ask if she'd go out with them. When she said no, the idea was to dance for a living, they'd say, well, I'll spend my money somewhere else. When Kirk would hug her or touch her, she'd recoil. "I get touched so much it makes me sick." She usually needed a day or so after work to get over the feeling. Kirk called it the "I Hate Men" phase. Many female strippers report that when they're working, they want companionship and friendship, not sex.

A topless woman with major hair skidded into the dressing room, and dashed for the stall, "I have to pee so bad and I'm on in a minute!" Xavier, Pamela, Joy, Crystal, and about three other women scrubbed at makeup and changed into different outfits. Rakelle and Crystal talked about cosmetic surgery, ". . . yours look good, too." A moment later Rakelle stepped outside.

"She hates me and I hate her," Crystal said. "We came *this* close to fist fighting, so now she only says things about me behind my back. She knows I'd hit her in the face. I said, 'Pushin' it! Shut up!' We'd get fired if we did fight. Well, fuck her and the horse she rode in on."

It's nearing 1:00 A.M. and the club was winding down. Only a couple of dozen people sat around. Crystal yelled, "Whooo! Whooo!" high stepping on the stage. The place looks like the end of a party.

Her favorite house mom, Wendy, stood watching her. Wendy was a pretty woman in her late thirties who claimed she never would have dreamed she'd be doing this six months ago. She was divorced with two kids, age ten and twelve. To her surprise, she found she loved the job. She said it's all hard work, for everyone.

"What bothers me is that when these girls go out, even to a grocery store, you see people react . . . oooooh, there's so and so, from Mark's, and they treat them like they're dirt. These girls are intelligent, sensitive . . . they're actresses."

"Almost done," said Crystal, looking at the dressing room clock. She studied her arms and legs. There were fresh bruises from hitting the stage. "It's worse than my burn marks." She lifted her arms and shows deep white welts burned permanently into her skin. She showed me a twisted knot on her hand. "Factory," she said. "I worked in a hot molding factory, and I'd clean the machines I worked on. You touch them, you get burned. When I first started to do it, I had to take out bolts that hold thirty pounds of force. You do that when you weigh eighty-nine pounds, that's how you burn yourself up. Three years. I did my time."

She pointed to a vodka bottle peeking out of Rakelle's trunk. "This is what I told Miss Priss Bitch to cover up. I try to get along with her, but when I first came here she told people Kirk was queer and I had AIDS, that he gave it to me."

One of her friends said that it seems weird people in this business would say such things, when the worst problem they face is being judged, being called denigrating terms like "slut" or "whore", never mind homophobic insults.

Crystal nodded affirmatively. "I'll call Rakelle a bitch, but I'd never call her a slut or a whore."

*   *   *

It was not exactly morning when Dianah and Joy sat at the kitchen table, drinking coffee and talking about how things worked the night before. In T-shirt and leggings, they looked like two very pretty young women in their early twenties, miles away from the sex goddesses of the night before. Dianah said she loves being domestic. Her home was freshly painted, with new couches and pretty curtains. When she first moved in, it was a typical bachelor pad; now it was a home. Kirk had been spending more time in Florida and wanted Dianah to join him, but she was not eager to leave. She thought he moved too quickly. He spoke of getting financing to run a gym down there, of setting up his dance troop. He sounded confused.

Dianah and Joy talked about featuring. Joy has featured after appearing in a number of layouts. Dianah tells her about having posed for a good photographer in New York, but she wasn't sure what happened to the pictures. He could rip her off, sell them without telling her. The whole thing could be a waste.

Getting as much control as possible is a career goal. Dianah nodded when Joy said she opts not to lap dance. "If you're doing lap dances, the guy can come. They sell condoms in the bathrooms just for that. I don't like it."

"Just the way you present yourself tells a man what he can get away with," Joy added. "The best thing about the job is freedom. If you're good, you can always work. You have that security."

"To say no has become so much easier. I used to be so afraid someone would get mad at me," Dianah said. "Now it's, go ahead and get mad at me if you want."

Still, both Joy and Dianah pointed out that although they feel in control when they're dancing, they have to work at it. Both commented on a generational split in their audience, and said it had a strong influence on what men will pay to see.

"With young guys you can get away with almost anything," Joy stated, going on to explain that she thought younger guys have grown up in a more progressive age, and they react to women more as equals. "You can be more rock and roll, tough, strong, hard core," she said.

"Older men want you to be all delicate and feminine, all sexy and soft and silky, like, 'I could be hurt! I cry! I like diamonds and pearls,'" Dianah said, simpering in soft tones suggestive of satin sheets and bon bons. When asked how old are the older men she speaks of, she and Joy looked at each other and say, "Oh, in their mid-thirties and up." But it's more a matter of the type, Dianah clarified. "I don't like working for older business men who want you to be all girlish." She learned early that when these men asked what she thought, the worst thing she could do was to come up with an opinion of any sort. "They want a woman to be an ornament, not someone who thinks."

She wouldn't suffer fools. She told a story of three obnoxious young guys who came in and sat on the stage of a new girl and turned their backs. "I walked up to hand her a buck and give her that little boost of support I give to the new girls. And I see these guys sitting, backs turned, laughing."

" 'Hey, guy, how come you're lookin' down there when you have this pretty girl up here?' 'Oh, we don't have money to spend.' 'Well, why don't you get your ass off her stage?' That's all I said. That's not rude."

The guy told her she couldn't talk to him that way, he owned a Mercedes and came in here and spent all kinds of money. She found herself screaming mad, yelling, "Oh, my goodness! You bought one beer! Two dollars and . . . wait . . . fifty cents!"

"I did get in trouble for that," she sighed. "You can't be rude to customers. I'm not a bad-tempered person, but when I get mad, I get mad. They never came back. One of 'em is friends with a girl who works there and he said he'd never come back because of this smart ass blond girl. I think the customer is always right, but I'm sorry, I will throw every fit in the world but you will respect me. If you don't, you'll wish you had."

THE WORK SHE DID BEFORE

"If it wasn't for the Renfro Valley Music Festival ("We're hot kickin' country!" says the flier), Mount Vernon, Kentucky, would be a rural hick town,' said the lady in the Chamber of Commerce. "The Main Street has a little dollar general store, a cafe, a clothing store, and the funeral home."

The biggest industry is Mount Vernon Plastics, which employs 400 people. In nearby Somerset, Hartco, another factory, employs 200. Factory jobs are the best steady work. The Renfro Valley Music Festival runs from March to December, and even if you can find a job in one of the motels or restaurants, it's not year-round income.

Darlene King could tell you that, because she'd found all the jobs you could find. Dianah's mother drove a truck, learned how to drive a D9 bulldozer, and then went to those factories to work. The day Dianah turned eighteen her mother helped her get a job at Mount Vernon Plastics where she was a press operator. At age 38, Darlene's had triple bypass heart surgery and has been out of work since June 1993 due to a nerve damage injury.

Darlene had Dianah when she was sixteen. She went with Dianah's father ever since she was eleven years old. "I was fifteen before I ever knew what town was. We lived up the mountain. The kids never went to town and Mommy and Daddy went only once a month."

Until she was thirteen, Dianah lived with her grandparents. "I couldn't raise her. Her daddy was an alcoholic and he beat me all the time. I was afraid for me and her both." Darlene split up with her husband for good when she was pregnant with her son.

But when Dianah was two, Darlene tried to take her daughter back from her parents. It was a struggle. "Many times she had just plain tater soup and a piece of cornbread for supper. When it hit below zero weather, to keep her warm I built a fire in the bathtub. I didn't have money for fuel, and I knew if I asked my father he'd take Dianah."

Four years later Darlene's brother stole Dianah out of the yard, took her to their father and claimed Darlene had sent her back. "When I came to get her, Daddy run me out and got a restraining order." He dropped it when he talked her into having weekend and summer break visitation, which he reneged on. The courts supported his decision and Darlene's father and his second wife, Charlotte, kept Dianah.

Years later, Charlotte beat Dianah so badly that local authorities got involved, and Darlene took her own father to court, something a good daughter didn't do in those parts, but she didn't let that stop her. At age thirteen, Dianah came home to live with her mother.

"You don't have a choice around here. At least Dianah has the guts to do what Dianah wants to do, and the hell with what people think."

AFTER WORK IN MAINE

We were at Dianah's apartment in Maine, and she pulled out photo albums, letters, and mementos to help illustrate her life's history. She was filling in the gaps of her childhood story.

In the South, Dianah told me, women raise girls and men raise boys, so each sex can teach their successors how to act like a male or a female. She knew her stepgrandmother, Charlotte, shouldn't have beaten her, but "that was how she thought I should be raised" and with her high spirits, she wasn't always the perfect little girl. She remembered wanting her mother, wanting to go home, how the man Darlene was with had a big smile you could see for miles and that she'd dream of his smile, thinking that she was going to be back with her mother one of these days.

At age eighteen she did what everyone in her home town did, went to the plastics factory. It was a good place to work, and she liked it until they told her they wouldn't pay her the full rate for her job because she was a woman.

"I tried to do a man's job, and I did a man's job. I was the janitor there for over a year, worked third shift because I was a night owl." She mopped the factory floor, took the trash out, cleaned machines down on her hands and knees. That's where she got her scars.

After the first factory job she went to Hardco Hardwood Flooring in Somerset, one of the other factories nearby. She pointed to the paneled walls of the restaurant next to our table and said they made these. She worked on a conveyor belt where the pieces of wood came together. "There wasn't another woman on my line. I gained a lot of respect for myself. June, the lady who ran the place, thought I was the most intelligent young lady she'd ever met. I ran my line, and I ran it good. If my machine broke down, I got it *fixed*. I didn't wait around for three hours for someone to decide they'd do it. It was my business to get it done. If the company isn't making money, I don't get my raise, and you don't get your new car. If everyone looked at it that way it would all be so simple. I loved it. It was my job and I was proud to work there. At the time there was no other kind of life for me until I got married."

Dianah's wedding photos weren't professionally done. They're little square prints from someone's instamatic camera. She looked timeless, lovely with her hair piled high, her wedding dress white satin. Scott, her husband, was a handsome young man, which was what she'd noticed that first day he came into the factory and she chased him down the hall, saying, "Whew! Look at you! Why don't you come work with me?"

"I was extremely serious about my marriage," she said. "I was a good wife. I know he still loves me and I still love him and always will."

Dianah didn't understand why things changed after they got married. "If I wasn't allowed to go dancing on weekends, he shouldn't have been allowed to play ball every night of the week."

The whole time they dated, they played baseball together. "Same field, same league. I loved going to the baseball fields where they have the automatic machine that throws the ball at you to hit. It was my favorite thing to do. Then we got married. He decided he didn't have to play ball with me anymore. I'm a wife now. Not a companion. Not a friend. We didn't sit around and talk and joke and rent movies anymore. It all changed."

"I loved him," she sighed, "but that's the way it goes in the south. You stay at home and your husband does what he wants to." She was close to his mother and to her horror, witnessed Scott's father take up with a younger woman, which Dianah pictured happening to she and Scott in the future, so strong was her identification with the scenario. "I always said if he left me, that would be how he was going to leave me, and I couldn't see it happening. It ate me up."

Her father-in-law's affair devastated her. "You don't find too many good women in this world, and she was a *good* woman. Oh, hard-headed she could be, but a good woman. I'd listen to them fight and she'd convince herself she'd done something wrong. I'd think, "Patty! What are you doing! Don't cry! Don't cry anymore!"

One day Dianah went over to her father-in-law's house, two doors down. "Little bitch was over there. I knock on the door. Larry hides her in the closet. I said, 'I just got off the phone with Patty and she's crying her eyes out and I want to know why. Twenty-three years and you can't call her up and have the slightest bit of respect, if nothing but for the fact she's the mother of your children?' "

Later, when he found out Dianah was stripping, Larry tried to tell Patty she was no good, but Patty and Dianah remain friends. Dianah said he's jealous, because he'll never have the same type of friendship with his own son. Relationships between men, well, they're a casualty by the nature of the rules.

Dianah didn't know if she'd have the strength to leave Scott, but Patty finally convinced her that she should. It was quite a commentary that a mother would tell her son's wife that she would have a better life without him.

"She said, 'I don't want you to go through what I went through. Just go. Get yourself out of it. You can come here and live, you don't have to pay rent. Just take care of yourself and be happy, you don't deserve this.' "

She went to her grandfather, the preacher, for advice about her marriage. He told her you couldn't hang on to something you didn't have anymore. "He was a good guy," she said, responding to my comment that her grandfather sounded kind. "That was never the problem. The only thing that caused all the grief was that thing of men raising boys and women raising girls."

She made a big leap after she and Scott broke up. She went to Pure Gold to see, just to see. She had trouble remembering the first audition because she drank a lot of courage. But they offered her a job weekends. She made more money on Friday nights than she did all week at the factory job.

Gradually the opportunity to get away dawned on her. Even when she related the story, I could hear the wonder in her voice of how her life changed. When she first told me her story, it had only been a little more than a year since she worked in the factory. Her voice was a singsong of liberation.

"I could go lay on the beach. I could take two weeks off and still have money. I worked so hard for so long to have nothing." A few weeks after she started dancing, one of the men from the factory came to Pure Gold. He had someone snap a picture of Dianah and took it to work to embarrass her. Shortly after, she left to dance full time. Two months later, she met Kirk.

At this point in the story, Dianah hesitantly mentioned that Kirk had gone down to Florida to live. She planned to stay in Maine.

*   *   *

It was nearly 1:00 A.M. and soon she had to go to the club to pick up Joy, who was staying with her. She reached into her pocket and pulled out two dollar bills, folded into intertwined hearts. They were a gift from Perverts R Us, who gave these to her every night. She showed me dollar bills folded in the shape of elephants, frogs, and rings.

Dianah gave me the bills in the shape of the hearts. I still have them. Whenever I thought I couldn't keep writing a book about working sex I'd pull them out and look at them.

"I want to play you my favorite song," she said suddenly, putting on a CD. "It's by Travis Tritt. I used to hear this song when I was working in the factory and I'd cry and cry."

She started singing with the music.

Bobby played his guitar, on the harsh side of town.
Where it's hard for a poor boy to find the money.
He had dedication, he had the heart and soul.
He knew somehow he was born to play.

"That's me!" she cried.

People said, get a real job, support your family,
because there's no future in the road you're taking.
He never said a word, the dream just kept on.
Late at night you could hear him say

   I'm going to be somebody.
   One of these days I'm going to break these chains.
   I'm going to be somebody, someday.
   You can bet your hard-earned dollar I will.

The road was a struggle, it took him ten years to the top.
Now he's number one on the stage and the radio.
Still he can't believe how people come from miles around.
It seems like only yesterday, he'd say . . .

> *I'm going to be somebody.*
> *One of these days I'm going to break these chains.*
> *I'm going to be somebody, someday.*
> *You can bet your hard-earned dollar I will.*
> *Oh, yeah, you can bet your hard-earned dollar. I will."*

"That song is me. It's about what I used to go through, what I didn't have. And I don't cry when I hear this song now. I've struggled, and I'm number one at what I do. People *do* come miles to see me. Last year I was nobody. I was someone in Mount Vernon, Kentucky who was going to work at that plastic factory my whole life."

"I did cry the first time I heard the song. I thought, 'Am I *ever* going to be somebody and not struggle to make the dollar for my cup of coffee in the morning?' When I was married, to pay my bills and be able to afford to go out to eat was a task. And now, if I want a cup of coffee I can go get a cappuccino and give three dollars for it, and it's nothing. But then? To give three dollars for coffee? No, sir. And I know that sounds so stupid and childish, but that's how I lived. And I don't live that way anymore."

She put away her photo album and strode up and down, restlessly. "The song says, 'there's no future in the road you're taking' and they're just talking about him playing the gi-tar. They'll tell any entertainer, actress, anybody who's trying to express themself through something they do, get a real job, you're living in a dream. Well, *my* dream is just as good as any doctor's dream, any lawyer's dream, any secretary's dream, any nurse's dream. My dream is just to be free. And express myself."

"My whole life is reflected in this past year when I started dancing. Before I worked so hard, and I tried so hard to be a good wife. I was trying so hard to please so many people. And I wasn't anything to myself. I was miserable, I'd lay in my bed and cry every night. Just like my mother-in-law, someone I was telling, 'Don't cry anymore!' And now, when I hear the song, it's . . . halleluja! I will cheer that song! I've made it. I am somebody. And ain't nobody who can tell me different or make me feel bad about myself anymore."

* * *

Dianah has started doing more photo layouts in magazines in order to be known well enough to be one of the highly paid feature dancers. She finally found out what happened to those pictures that photographer in New York took, the ones she'd worried had been used without her getting paid. When she got the magazine, the pictures were beautiful. They were full nudity, front and back, and she looked lovely, page after page. She wasn't the girl on the factory line with glue in her hair, she was a fantasy woman. And then the magazine fell wide open and there she was. Crystal was a centerfold. You could be like Amber Lynne if you got more of those. She was on her way.

* * *

Right before he moved to Florida, Kirk was again on *The Robin Byrd Show*. People who knew Jesse waited for him to come ripping out, flexing his muscles and dancing to the fast party rock and roll songs he liked. I watched at midnight in my apartment, with everyone else in New York who would always have Robin Byrd for company.

But instead he danced to a slow, sad Melissa Etheridge song. He stood there, and his clothes began to slip off the body that had refused to die.

"So you walked with me for a while
Bared your naked soul . . . "

His hand moved slowly, opening the shirt.

"And you told me of your plan.
How you would never let them know
In the morning of the night
You cried a long lost child.
And I tried oh I tried to hold you
But you were young
And you were wild."

He stood with his head dropped down to his chest. The ridges of muscles seemed cut out of his stomach. He wrapped his arms around his body and closed his eyes.

"And you swore that you were bound for glory
And for wanting you had no shame.

But I loved you.
And then I lost you.
And I will never be the same."

He stretched his arm slowly in an arc, his hand held out entreatingly, fingers open wide. It was not a power move, not a muscle pose. It was almost ballet, as if he learned an old dance in an unfamiliar way. As if he was trying to touch something that was still beyond his reach.

5

Sex and D&S (Why I Can't Write About Domination and Submission)

THE WORK OF POLITICAL PHILOSOPHERS

"But what about the moral?"

"The moral is that woman, as Nature created her and as man up to now has found her attractive, is man's enemy; she can be his slave or his mistress but never his companion. This she can only be when she has the same rights as he and is his equal in education and work."

—Leopold von Sacher-Masoch, author of *Venus in Furs* written in 1870.

I've been trying to write about domination and submission since September 5, 1991. That's the date on my contract. It's significant that my involvement with domination and submission started with a contract. When a client goes to a dominatrix, the first thing they do is sit down and work out a verbal contract detailing what they'll do in the session. The French philosopher Gilles Deleuze wrote about contracts and sadomasochism, or domination and submission, the term we'll use. I prefer it. D&S lacks the distance of the medicalized "sadomasochism."

In, "Coldness & Cruelty," his essay on domination and submission, Deleuze explored Plato's idea that the law could be considered either in light of its underlying principles or of its consequences. "If men knew what good was . . . they would not need laws," he said. He proceeded to write about how D&S practitioners endeavored to use contracts governing their behavior: "I'll submit here, you'll dominate here. . . ."

What I came to see while writing about this topic is that when it comes to love and sex, it is difficult for many people to see where power enters the picture. Power is really what domination and submission is all about, a conscious enactment of power roles.

Power is tolerable only if it masks a substantial part of itself, as French philosopher Michel Foucault, wrote. "Its success is proportional to its ability to hide its own mechanisms."

The syndrome named "Sadomasochism" was derived from the writings of the Marquis de Sade and Leopold von Sacher-Masoch. The Marquis de Sade's novels involve elaborate torture and cruelty. The term "sadism" came from him, as "masochism" came from Leopold von Sacher-Masoch. Masoch, a historian and German novelist, wrote *Venus in Furs* as a metaphor for the human condition, part of a trilogy about love, war, and death. It's a dreamlike book about two lovers, Wanda and Severin.

When they meet, Severin believes Wanda is a dream come true, the statue of a goddess he worships come to life. She too, believes he may be what she seeks, saying, "I have always wanted to meet a true romantic, someone really different, and I suspect you are even wilder than I thought." They agree to an experiment. He wants Wanda to be his goddess, someone he can worship. She loves him and is reluctant at first. She finds herself repelled, then drawn to the idea, and warns him that they should stop before it's too late. "You have so corrupted my imagination and inflamed my blood that I am beginning to find all this enjoyable."

Severin insists that she take the role of the tyrant Venus in Furs, that she dominate him completely, allowing him to be a slave to love. It comes to a terrible, timeless, question-provoking end, as the fantasy turns out to be far less desirable than the reality. "It is too idealistic . . . and therefore cruel," the philosopher Gilles Deleuze borrowed from Doestoevsky, when trying to explain the meaning of the novel.

Sadism and masochism are not opposites but integral parts of each other. In degrees along a continuum, they are part of our sexuality. My job would be to write about it and make that point. My work started with a contract, a fitting irony the philosophers would have appreciated.

Regarding the law, de Sade wrote, "I have infinitely less reason to fear my neighbor's passions than the law's injustice, for my neighbor's passions are contained by mine, whereas nothing stops or contains the injustices of the law."

Masochists, Gilles Deleuze added, also challenged the law. A masochist was a humorist. "The masochist regards the law as a punitive process and therefore begins by having the punishment inflicted upon himself," Deleuze wrote. This way, he could experience the pleasure that the law was supposed to forbid. The contract in a masochistic rite ended up being a demonstration of the law's absurdity.

When one is first exposed to the world of professional practitioners of domination and submission, it seems weird, and the storm of media coverage in the early 1990s didn't clarify the fact that what was going on were interesting performances of sex roles. It's easy to become familiar with the vernacular and equipment, but each piece that was observed, the high heels, whips, dildos, served as a fetishized object that meant something.

Freud thought that fetishism was the substitute for the female penis. Modern psychologists such as Louise J. Kaplan have suggested that this explanation is misleading. The fetish object's purpose might be to disavow the difference between the sexes, which could compensate for anxiety. "The adult fetishist can assert his masculinity only with a fantasy that there are no differences between the sexes," Kaplan wrote, pointing out that while some fetish objects were phallic, like high heels and whips, others weren't. Even parts of the body could be fetishized.

D&S practitioners sexualized their fetish objects for use in a scenario that turned them on, a scenario full of mythological characters and sexual prototypes: punishing Mommy, bitch goddess, tantalizing torturer. It involved power, and each person had their script. The more I observed the sessions, the more I saw that it was the paraphernalia as well as the roles that were erotized. People could be aroused by actual things that were imbued with other sexual identification for them, things such as high heels, rubber diapers, underwear. It could be something completely innocuous that had been sexualized in the person's history, like frilly white anklet socks. The fetish object was integral in arousing the person in the session. This was particularly interesting, because it was a real enactment, the performance part of sexuality, as opposed to more subtle levels of what was supposed to be masculine or feminine. Everything I'd seen regarding sex roles was now being dramatized. "When you first start to work as a dominatrix," Ava Taurel, one of New York's most famous told me, "never use a whip or an implement. You must use your gaze, your manner, your entire being."

The clients knew what their scenarios were. Men and women could switch roles, but the performance was specific and significant. All the players had a part.

Where did they come from? Individual psychology, Hollywood, fairy tales, adolescent and childhood fantasy? A mix of all the above? Where do anyone's dreams come from? The line between what the psychological community had dubbed "paraphilia" and "normal" love had enough crossover to warrant serious consideration and decoding. Robert Stoller, M.D., a leading expert on gender identity and erotica, didn't think there was any such thing as sexual normalcy. He called "normal sexuality" a "lesser aberration." So someone who was good at sex work would aim to identify the individual sexual fantasy.

If I could succeed at writing the story, I could help to put sex and power roles as practiced by D&S practitioners and non-D&S practitioners into context, to make the link in considering tradeoffs of power in sexual and human relationships. I was excited about having this assignment. The only thing I didn't know was that the classic definition of a perversion is that it's a thing that hides from itself. I was about to enter a perverse situation, but the real perverts would be the hidden ones, the ones in power. As Foucault had said, their success was proportional to their ability to hide their own mechanisms.

First, I would witness the contract part. The best dominatrixes sat down with the client before each session and agreed what the fantasy was and what they would do together—did the client like bondage, genital torture, being suspended from the ceiling? What was the story line in their mind? Leopold von Sacher-Masoch and his wife, who took the name Wanda from his novel, signed contracts specifying the terms under which he would submit to her: "You shall renounce your identity completely. You shall submit totally to my will . . . Your honor belongs to me, as does your blood, your mind and your ability to work."

On September 5, 1991, I signed my contract. I thought at the time it was just another contract with a magazine. You never know.

This award-winning director's service has been featured as the top and most reputable Escort Service by USA & international news media including radio & TV.

When The Occasion Is Special, So Is Our Escort.

Our extraordinary escorts are known worldwide for their excellence in appearance, elegance, sophistication, charm, friendliness and social refinement.

These "Beautiful People" are models, beauty queens, actresses, dancers, airline hostesses, college students, young designers and other glamorous types. They are multilingual and available as your personal companions, the perfect complement for any social or promotional occasion. Hourly, daily, weekends or longer.

"**Give an Escort,**" a unique gift idea--for your friends, associates, out-of-town clients or guests. **Professional male and female escorts available. All transactions are confidential**

Phone: **(212) 765-7896**

• Major credit cards accepted
• Personnel's video tapes & photo catalogues available to view & make your selection in our office

You Have Just Discovered The Fabulous World Of

international
ESC❂RTS℠
Worldwide
Established Since 1973

The Most Exclusive Social recreational Service for Les Bon Vivants
Headquarters:
1841 Broadway
New York, NY 10023-7603
By appointment only

© Copyright 1997 International Escorts. All Rights Reserved.

Inquire About Our Other Entertainment & Hospitality Services Designed For Business & Tourism

Nerissa Braimbridge of International Escorts created the image of a glamorous couple in front of a luxury car, about to go on a date. Numerous escort agencies now have phone book ads with the car-couple-date theme.

SHE-MALE ESCORTS

The Alternative to the Routine

TV/TS: People of Cross Genders

Exquisitely Beautiful She-Males

Discreet Billing Assured

889-7349

NYNEX, the New York phone service, advertises by saying, "If It's Out There, It's In Here." This Yellow Page ad shows where escort services and sexual dysphoria meet.

Betty Dodson has been teaching women how to masturbate since the 1970s. "In my wildest nightmares, I never thought we'd still be living in a sex-negative culture coming up on the year 2000," she said.

Candida Royalle today.   Photo by Arthur Cohen

Candida on directing:
"I keep the camera moving in a *cinema verité* style,
sort of, 'Go over there, lie down, try what feels good.'"

Photo by Barbara Nitke

Dianah King and Kirk Hill,
Maine, 1994.
His recollection:
"When we met I blushed
and smiled and said,
'I do the same damned thing
as you for a living.'"

Dianah King.
Strippers can build their careers to being featured acts
by appearing in magazines and porn films.
The top acts can make up to $200,000 a year.

Talking about job interviews, Kirk says, "Clubs have pretty strict rules against birthmarks and tatoos, but when they see my body, the attitude is, 'Well, I guess we can put up with a few tatoos.'"

Eva Norvind
was a movie star in
Mexico in the 1960s
and …

…Eva as Ava Taurel,
a famous name in
D&S circles.

Mistress Suzi
in Her Office.
She lived right
across the street
from me in Chelsea.
The first time
I saw her place
all I could say was,
"I work at home, too."

Sue, ready for a night out.

AUGUST 1991

"When I said I'd retired, it wasn't the whole truth," Susan told me over the phone. "I've been working as a dominatrix for the past year. I wondered if you'd be interested in writing about it for *New York* magazine."

Maybe it's all timing. Six months later, the pop star Madonna had mainstreamed D&S, documenting her club forays and latex adventures in her skillfully marketed book, *Sex*. A year after our magazine misadventure, it seemed as if every dominatrix in America had appeared on *Geraldo* or *Phil Donahue* or some version of talk TV. I actually don't think that's a bad thing, although they always cast it as a freak show. I saw one where members of the audience stood up screaming, "You people are sick! Sick!"

When I did the original work on this subject with Susan, I spoke with Howard Ruppell, the president of the Society for the Scientific Study of Sex, a forty-year-old professional international organization of sexual scientists. We talked about the fact that there are all sorts of D&S practitioners across the entire sexual spectrum, gay through heterosexual, and the conventional take in the mainstream media didn't suggest complexity but rather gave us pat answers. He said he'd never seen a study of, say, 2,500 men who were involved with being dominated. "We hear often that it's movers and shakers who want to be relieved of their societal roles," he offered. "But besides bank presidents and supervisors, I've met bricklayers and assembly line people who want to be dominated. There haven't been enough studies and that's wrong."

"Why aren't more studies done?" I'd asked.

"It's hard to get tenure when you walk into the dean's office and say, 'I want to study bondage and discipline.'" He went on to tell me that two major studies, one of which concerned adolescent sexual behavior that put teenagers at risk for sexually transmitted disease, unwanted pregnancy, and HIV infection, had been cut by the federal government under the Bush administration. "If we can't get research by the top people in the field into the most awful health crisis we've faced, how can we get research into other aspects of sexuality?" he asked. "So we rely on anecdotal evidence. Anecdotal evidence in an age of science is ridiculous."

This was in 1991. In the next few years I would see people I'd interviewed, like Susan and professional dominatrix Ava Taurel, appear before graduate programs in human sexuality and sexological and psychological conferences, amazing progress. In many cases people in the field were having their first personal exposure to things they had previously only read about in textbooks. Human sexuality was such a suspect academic discipline that even some professionals had largely received arms-length training. One telling incident: Ava spoke at a presentation at one of the nation's top psychological associations and offered the people in the front row the opportunity to feel "a nice soft caressing whip" that she had brought along. The people in the front row shrank from touching it. If that was how they reacted at a conference, what would they do with a patient?

*   *   *

Susan had called after seeing a couple of articles I'd done in *New York* magazine. She said she'd worked as an escort and was interested in what I'd written on the subject. We agreed to meet and talk.

I visited her at her spacious loft in lower midtown. We talked for a long time, and she'd told me she'd retired from escorting, that a former client had purchased this loft for her and now she was in the design business. In those days, I didn't know exactly what a dominatrix was, and yet . . . there was something about her place. . . .

It was modern, stark white, and beautifully furnished. But in addition to the fact that her answering machine clicked on and off every two minutes (she has a lot of friends?), the decor was a little austere. A headless dress dummy stood forbiddingly on one side. Boots with spurs leaned against the walls next to crops and riding whips. Medieval-looking pokers were scattered about. There were holes in the walls, the sort pictures are sometimes used to cover, only they were really big holes. A heavy steel chain hung from the ceiling. If nothing else, she had intense taste.

Months later, she called me. She thought she had a story I'd be interested in. . . .

WORKING MAGAZINES

NEW YORK
Magazine

September 5, 1991

To: Marianne Macy
(Herein "Author")

This will confirm the agreement between Author and K-III Magazine Corporation concerning an article to be written by author for *New York* Magazine (the "Article") and the acquisition by K-III Magazine Corporation of rights in the article.

(1) The description of the Article is as follows: "Diary of a Dominatrix."

"You know, Marianne," remarked my editor. "I don't think we've ever done a story with you where we didn't have to add special legal provisions."

This time they were under Point 5: "Author understands that the activities contemplated by this contract, including but not limited to being present when the dominatrix performs her job, listening to client tapes and phone calls, and reading client letters, may be risky, and she hereby assumes such risks . . . ."

* * *

"Ready? You can't move after I let him in," Susan said. "You should be able to see everything on the floor." She took a couple of steps back to the rail where the raised bedroom part of her loft formed a duplex overlooking the sweeping main room.

I was crammed between the wall and her bed, in shadow, with a perfect bird's-eye view of the elegant space six feet below. I looked down on the main room—leather couches, her throne chair, the riding whips and crops, antique mirrors. I could see everything. Could I be seen in the shadows?

As if having the same thought, Susan quickly walked down the stairs, stood in the middle of the floor, and looked up carefully, then nodded. She went to the mirror to check her appearance as the client came up the elevator.

She was Mistress Sonya now, not Susan. Mistress Sonya wore black stiletto-heeled pumps, making her stand over six feet tall. She lifted weights every day in the gym, and had powerful shoulders and bearing. Her outfit was a silk bustier and fishnet stockings, accented by studded metal jewelry. She'd put her blond hair up in a French twist, and her makeup was a slash of red lipstick and deeply defined eyes.

The doorbell rang. She drew herself up even taller, assuming impervious posture. Sometimes, before an important appointment, people look nervous. I could see the face that reflected back in the mirror. Whoever was on the other side of the door should be nervous.

I'd never thought about whether or not I breathed audibly. Suddenly it was an important consideration. I flattened myself down like a hunted woodland creature, listening, watching. . . .

They walked to the center of the floor. He accepted her offer of a glass of wine. They moved to the couch to discuss the contract terms of the session before starting.

The client was a businessman in his mid-thirties. He was beautifully dressed, in a well-tailored suit with wonderful accessories. I could tell how expensive his clothing was even from my vantage point. "He's actually gorgeous," I thought, somewhat stunned, as I'd expected that a man who would pay for his sexual fantasies wouldn't, or maybe shouldn't, be handsome. He had deep blue eyes, reddish brown hair, was tall, well built, and had a soft Scottish accent, which she asked him about. He replied that he had come to the United States from Europe a year ago, to run a major division of a Wall Street firm. Susan, like a gracious hostess, asked about his job. He supervised forty people in his department. It was demanding, and tense, but he found it interesting. They were doing very well. No, he was not married.

"Where did your interest in domination come from?" she asked, raising her eyes over her glass of wine. He answered that he'd become interested as an adolescent, after realizing that certain scenes in films aroused him. He had been to a number of people in New York, every few weeks or so. This was the nicest place he'd been, he added admiringly.

"And what do you like?" she asked. He answered in a low voice, and I could only hear a few phrases: suspense, sensuous domination . . . he specified a few particulars, but I couldn't make them out.

"What I don't understand about the attraction of S&M, or D&S, or whatever you call it," Lance Bird, a filmmaker in New York told me, "is that it's always portrayed foolishly. All that high camp stuff, whips, chains, over the top outfits. During your research, did you ever see anything that seemed sexy to you?"

Below me in the loft, I remember registering all this . . . it was 3:30 in the afternoon. This man had told his office he had to leave for an appointment. Here he was, nude, stretched out with his hands cuffed over his head, while she used her fingers to tease his body.

Her ad specified she did "Sensuous Domination," and I could see what she meant. Every part was an agonizingly slow, deliberate prolongation of pleasure.

They were six feet below my shadowed hiding spot. I could see her painted fingernails run up his naked white arm when she put the silver handcuffs above his head, then attached them by chain to the wall. She let him strain against the metal, then slid her fingers from his wrist to inner arm, past his elbow, running back and forth, rubbing delicate circles all the way to his armpits, which she tickled until he tried to move away, but couldn't. She tickled him until he almost wept for her to stop, then she changed direction and commandingly placed her hands on his inner thighs. She spread her fingers out like talons, and waited.

Forcing him to focus on her was cunning. The philosopher Deleuze wrote that masochism involved "moments of suspense that are the climactic moments." Mistress Sonya stood still, towering over her naked prisoner. He'd given the keys to his handcuffs to a total stranger. She could as easily castrate him as make him climax. She whispered something enigmatic and taunting. Her nails were blood red, high up on his thighs.

Finally, Mistress Sonya moved her hands. The fingers dipped lower, encasing the sides of his thighs as if to trace the long bands of muscles to see where they lead. They felt their way up the inside, closer and closer to where his legs met at the crotch. Then she stopped, right before. She laughed as he begged her to touch his genitals.

It went on with her hands teasing up the thighs, down his belly, even in the air inches above him. He arched his back and strained to try to reach her, but she stayed just beyond where he could. She imprisoned him while stimulating him, to the point where he begged and begged futilely for release. He was writhing and pleading, and she continued to caress his inner thighs, his belly, his flanks, tormenting him to levels that were almost too much to bear. He moaned, and the leathery notes of his aftershave mixed with the sharp smell of his sweat, all so close it surrounded me with an unexpected, almost obscene-feeling intimacy. "Did I ever see anything where D&S seemed sexy?" was what I'd been asked.

Yes. I certainly did.

*   *   *

I spent time with Susan observing, talking about her life, her work, her thoughts for almost three months.

She was an amazing woman. She was smart, bold, funny, darkly sardonic, and creative. One of her signature statements was a pair of enlarged photographs that stood next to each other on an antique piece of furniture. They were headshots of two women at the height of their beauty. It took a moment to realize that one was Susan. The other was her mother, photographed while a dancer at the Copacobana. She had married a professional football player. Susan still had his team contract.

The story I wanted was how she'd come to her work in sex.

"The first job I had in New York was as a garment center model. I remember going to a showroom looking for a job. I can still see this guy sitting at a desk, saying, 'A lot of girls want this job. What will you do to get it?' and he pointed to his crotch. I did what I thought I had to do, and then he didn't give it to me. I was devastated. I kept thinking, 'How could this guy betray me?' That's how naive I was."

"Later I had regular work modeling in the garment center. I made good money for seven years, but there were things you did to keep your job. And let's not forget that bonus for helping to sell the fall line when buyers are in town . . . ."

Some women say that they'd rather sling hash in a restaurant than make a living through sex. "It sounds noble when you're saying it, but it's a tough rule to live by."

Susan first thought of becoming a dominatrix when she realized that her regal bearing and strong manner drew many people to her with unusual requests. A friend suggested apprenticing with Ava Taurel.

Susan went to Ava's and met a man who introduced her to the aesthetics of bondage. "He was discoursing about this thing he called The Nine Knots, while wrapping a rope around his genitals. You systematically tie the nine knots as tight as you can. He kept saying, 'Tighter, tighter,' until he was turning purple. I thought he was insane."

Ava Taurel did not hire Susan, but the introduction to domination inspired Susan to explore further. Four months later she placed her first ad in *New York* magazine. She got six phone calls the day it appeared from clients willing to pay $300 an hour. Between appointments, she taxied to an S&M boutique and bought latex breast plates and other fetish clothing and toys. She became Mistress Sonya.

"I'm sure some people will read this and see me as a vindictive bitch who wants to get back at men," she said thoughtfully. "But that's not the case. I like men. I've been married, and fallen in love more than once. I had a woman call me who asked if she could apprentice with me. She said she'd been abused and this would be an outlet for her hostility. I said, 'What you need is a good therapist, not to work as a dominatrix. Displaced anger has no place here.'"

She laughed, packing up her ropes and toys from that day's sessions. "I admit, the eroticism of power is a factor that makes this work very appealing to me."

WORKING TO DECODE

"I am dreadfully in love." I fell on my knees and hid my burning face in her lap.

"I really believe," said Wanda thoughtfully, "that your madness is nothing but an unsatisfied, diabolical sensuality. Such afflictions are a product of our monstrous side. If you were less virtuous you would be perfectly sane."

Leopold von Sacher-Masoch, *Venus in Furs*

"The dream of reason breeds monsters."

—Goya, quoted by Leslie Fiedler, discussing the novel's arrival in the age of rationalism

I read the psychological, philosophical, sexological, literary texts, all the interdisciplinary material relating to domination and submission I could find. To try and understand domination and submission involved thinking about a spectrum, or continuum. These aspects of sex are not two opposite and contradictory ideas. They're missing parts of each other.

A perversion is a thing that hides itself from itself, the psychologist Louise J. Kaplan wrote. If true that may mean that society is perverse, in that it wants to hide what we are. Your gender is your sex. Your gender role is what society tells you that sexual identity should mean.

The mind is a wonderful thing, though, and we seek our lost parts. What is called perversion is a psychological strategy to balance things out.

"Whether you look at sexual, political, or professional aspects, it's all different variations on the same theme," psychologist and author Thomas Szaz told me. "This is the most fundamental feature of human behavior." He pointed out that compared to other creatures, humans need exceptionally long periods of childhood and socialization, "during which we become used to being dominated, which connotes security and love. At the same time, most people develop an inordinate desire to no longer be dominated. We have both of these passions to an extraordinary degree."

It's remarkable what goes into the formation of people's sexual psychology, or love maps, as sexologist John Money calls them. This is the definition of paraphilia:

"a condition occurring in men and women of being compulsively responsive to and dependant upon an unusual and personally or socially unacceptable stimulus, perceived or in the imagery of fantasy, for optimal initiation and maintenance of erotosexual arousal and the facilitation or attainment of orgasm (from Greek *para* + *philia*.) Paraphiliac imagery may be replayed in fantasy during solo masturbation or intercourse with a partner. In legal terminology, a paraphilia is a perversion or deviancy, and in the vernacular it is kinky or bizarre sex."

But kinky in whose eyes? And to what degree did these traits show up in all of us? That was what sexologists meant by a continuum.

Susanne Schad-Somers, Ph.D., explained factors that influenced the formation of lovemaps. "The starting point is the first love object, mother. Although most people outgrow their childlike vulnerability, some do not, and therefore must cruelly dominate in order just to keep things even. The single most injurious piece of child rearing is to shame the child for wanting love. That is a central dynamic in sado-masochism, shame. Perversions are so literal, unimaginative. It's bedroom, bathroom, watersports. The script is what happened."

I was starting to understand the theory, but later came to realize that everyone got different pages of the script or different amounts. Outside ritualized D&S we all had roles and reenactments. It was this mix of how we incorporated our fantasy life and understanding of roles that formed individual sexuality.

Our minds create reparative fantasy to resist being overwhelmed by our developing sexualization. Robert Stoller wrote about how sexuality formed like the oyster's pearl around a grain of sand. Schad-Somers helped me see how the D&S scenarios fit into that process. I'd meet D&S clients who obsessively demanded the same scenario in their sessions. Every time they went they'd act out the exact same thing. Why? Schad-Somers said it was "a definite script that has to be repeated exactly. A fairy tale has to be told in the exact same way. Children become very upset if you get creative with the retelling of 'Little Red Riding Hood.' They want it repeated, the danger and the triumph, those are the two basic elements. Overcoming danger and triumphing in the end." By specifying what would happen in the session, the client was the one in control, unlike in childhood where the parent is in charge.

"The daydream" (in this case, the session) "guarantees a happy ending, saying that this time one has not only surmounted the trauma but even thwarted the original attackers. Finally, when the daydream becomes attached to genital excitement, especially to orgasm, the 'rightness' of the daydream is reinforced and the person motivated to repeat the experience . . ." wrote Stoller.

This was the mechanism of fantasy in D&S. But it would be a mistake to think these mechanisms function only in D&S.

In the *New York* magazine story I would describe a clientele that was male, white, and upscale. What troubled Susan and I was the oversimplification. D&S practitioners could switch roles. There could be different enactments than the ones we covered. There was a straight and gay S&M community, which writers like John Rechy had described in the 1970s, in books like *The Sexual Outlaw*. In a book called *Urban Aboriginals*, Geoff Mans wrote about leather sexuality, exploring the idea of transcendence through the D&S leather scene. He wrote about alternative sexuality challenging conventional thinking about sex. He portrayed gay men and lesbian women together, doing D&S scenes that proved eroticism could involve sex that was mental and physical without being genital. He quoted lesbian writer Pat Califia as saying that the experience had made her realize limitations in her thinking that were homophobic and sexist. "The most painful thing I learned was how the war of sexes looked from the other side." Switching roles and watching gay men switch roles made her realize that sexual power issues could transcend whether or not the person was a man or a woman.

The word consensual was vital. There was consensual and nonconsensual D&S.

Domestic violence represents the latter. It reveals a great deal about sex roles. Marsha Sheinberg of the Ackerman Institute worked with a group that studied case histories over extended periods of time. She spoke about rigid gender identities contributing to this extreme manifestation of domination. The Ackerman group learned that most often, the moment of violence followed a period when the man felt closest to his wife. "Closeness, gentleness, and tenderness are not what being a man is about in this culture," she says. These things make the man feel "too feminized, a way he believes he is not supposed to feel, and so these men develop compensatory behaviors, namely, violence."

Working with the men in therapy, they asked how their fathers were raised, if they could show fear or vulnerability, discussions that lead to self-discovery and possibly change.

"If your father felt being macho or assertive, the things that define masculinity, were important, if you're the son he selected to taunt or hit, then you develop a part of you that longs for his affection and to be like him. Another part of you feels differently. The discrepancy between your feelings is too great. Then you are at risk for developing symptoms of compensatory behavior."

"In a relationship with a woman, these men are a risk, because when they feel intimate and let their guard down and are soft and gentle, the woman feels very connected. She sees that other side of him, the vulnerable boy."

Why do women stay in these relationships? "Economics can be a factor," Sheinberg said, but many women in these situations are not poor.

"Part of it is that women feel responsible for maintaining these connections. It's their fault if a relationship comes apart no matter what the objective evidence is, they've failed the gender's expectations, so they're less womanly, just as men think they're less manly if they express sensitivity. Women feel that their own anger is bad and wrong. If we look at it in a simple way, we see that women have to claim their "masculine" parts and men their "feminine" parts, and that in society we have a bifurcation of gender which denies us our full range of experience and feeling."

"It seems we are not encouraged to recognize these things," I said.

"Right," she answered. "So we have to find the other half of ourselves in that partner, which essentially is a false promise, from which a lot of these difficulties develop."

"What you've said about alienation from these parts of ourselves, can we apply it not only to couples experiencing violence, but relationships in general?"

Sheinberg responded that what's been paid less attention to is the way schools, families, churches, synagogues, and other community organizations make distinctions between boys and girls. "No matter how we progress we don't change that much. There's the argument, boys and girls are just different, and in fact there's a fear of treating them equally and similarly. That prevents us as a culture from allowing everyone their full potential and range. I think this is such a larger problem than has been recognized, the bifurcation of gender roles, that men and women each experience secret feelings of gender failure when they don't achieve a cultural norm that they hold in their minds. It varies from person to person. It's like two broken halfs, the feelings that are attributed to the other gender. What we attribute to the other sex are disavowed parts of our own."

I would spent months working on domination and submission and in the end, I couldn't write about it for *New York*. Domination and submission was about role play. Maybe it was too much to hope that it could be fairly discussed in a mainstream magazine. The same publication would later portray how hilarious a man in a dress was, how weird a woman with a whip was. They could not see that hiding from perversity was itself perverse. Why couldn't we look at what is in front of us? It was back to what the critic Leslie Fiedler had said: we needed the freaks to disavow parts of ourselves.

SCENARIOS, FAIRY TALES, AND MAGIC TRICKS

"She's beautiful, isn't she?" Frances breathed, looking at Susan. He was a regular client. Today Susan was in an elaborate equestrian outfit, with breaches and high heeled riding boots.

We sat on the couch. Susan commanded him to tell her mistress in training, which was the explanation for my presence, how he had come to D&S. He was reared in a reserved Swiss family. While in school, he rented a room in a large apartment from friends of his family who were often away. There was an attractive housekeeper, some years older.

One day he fell ill, and became delirious with fever. The housekeeper nursed him, and to break his fever, she suggested cooling his body temperature by giving him an enema in the bath. "My skin was burning. She stripped me, and took the hose, and slowly the cold water . . . the shock of it." He described every moment of that day from forty years ago, the woman taking charge of him, the physical sensations, the texture of the hose. He replayed it in obsessive detail.

When they became lovers, Frances and the housekeeper would replay the enema ritual as part of their sexual repertoire. His sense of wonder as he told the tale made it as vivid that day in Susan's loft as it must have been four decades ago in Switzerland. The almost hypnotic way in which he repeated the story, down to the details of the stained chrome on the faucet, the manufacture of the hose, the water temperature. . . . Every aspect was immortalized. Frances finished his story and said that his pursuit of D&S had been lifelong.

"Are you wearing what I told you to?" Mistress Sonya asked sternly when he was finished.

"Yes, mistress," he responded.

"Then take off that suit and show her your ballet act," she commanded.

The perverse scenarios worked like magic tricks, Louise J. Kaplan, Ph.D., explained in her book *Female Perversions*. Prior to her book psychoanalytic literature dealt almost exclusively with male perversions, as they were defined. Kaplan thought women were just as perverse, but the "codes" of how the sexes could evidence perversion were determined by societally-defined behavior for the two sexes. This was *not* to say that men and women didn't share characteristics, or that men and women didn't engage in the same sexual behavior, even in D&S scenarios. But men were always statistically reported on as more active participants in such things as patronizing dominatrixes.

The more interesting questions might be about how the sexes acted out sex roles in perverse and contradictory ways. Kaplan thought a "female perversion" was less visible because it blended into things that were societally-sanctioned female behavior, such as submissiveness, compulsive shopping, and dieting disorders. Kaplan saw these as outlets for women's aggression, denied them by traditional sex roles, which required men to be the more aggressive sex.

Men's perversions were more visible, according to Kaplan. Engaging in "kinky sex" such as D&S scenarios, males feel elated and energized while conforming to a social stereotype of masculinity. Perversion worked like a magic trick. Kaplan explained: "It is the special strategy of male perversion to permit a person to express his forbidden and shameful feminine wishes by disguising them in an ideal of masculinity." The ideal was something a man could feel dangerous and triumphant about. Underneath the performance, he could reach his hidden submissive "female" side.

With the bifurcation of gender roles, he could only reach his hidden side this way. "The audience is meant to keep their eyes focused on one piece of risky business so that they will not notice that something else is being sneaked in from up the magician's sleeve," Kaplan wrote. If it was a trick mirror, one side reflected: "I am a kinky man doing something sexual and vaguely dangerous." The other side of the mirror illustrated: "I am identifying with my hidden female self."

As we watched, this elegant grey-haired man took off his expensive watch, cufflinks, tie, and tailored suit to reveal his mature body. He kept himself in good shape for a man in his sixties. He had rippling stomach muscles, which we could see when he removed his shirt and pants to reveal frilly pink women's string underwear. He stood proudly in the panties, his dress socks still on. Susan barked, "Dance!"

Instantly, Frances began to leap across the floor in ballerina-like paces while she shouted instructions. "Hold your arms more gracefully! Spread your legs more! Point your toes!" She ordered him around the room until he was panting. Only when he was exhausted did she permit him to rest. The session ended with a glass of wine and him encouraging me to open myself up to this world. After he left, she said, "I've heard him tell that exact same story in the exact same words half a dozen times."

Susan, as well as other dominatrixes I would later speak to, had many phone clients. Men who were at their summer homes in the Hamptons on a family weekend would sneak into the bathroom and call for a phone session. The dominatrix's job was to be creative with punishment fantasies promised at some future date.

Susanne Schad-Somers talked about the difference between people who experiment with D&S and someone who practices it in a desperate, repetitive way. Again, the idea was to see sexuality on a continuum. People could experiment with D&S or occasionally incorporate it into their sex lives. That was different from someone who was compulsive about it.

But as for what was going on with these phone clients . . . "They need this to make the marriage possible," Schad-Somers explained. "The marriage can work because the panic-ridden part that needs to make a woman safe is taken care of." His vulnerability to his wife, and women in general, could be diffused by the controlled scenario with the dominatrix.

I knew people who thought S&M was sick. But these same people had affairs outside their marriage which they described as giving them a sense of freedom. The affairs made them feel "not trapped." It was a form of domination and submission, even if people didn't view it that way.

There were many different scenarios. Susan described one session with a client who was a "nondescript, birdlike, quiet fellow. He wanted a totally regressive scene. He brought diapers, complete with pinking sheered edges, folded in triangles. He even had little blue plastic elephant safety pins. He got into a fetal position, crawled into my lap, sucking his thumb, talked baby talk, and had me comb his hair. If I didn't pay enough attention to him he'd wail, 'Waaaaah!' I found the whole thing very unnerving."

Denigrated female, helpless infant. The clients got to claim their disavowed sides. The sessions were therapeutic. The psychiatrists I talked to argued that it served the purpose of fulfilling needs that allowed them to keep functioning. One argument was that it was only a temporary measure, to ward off panic. Others vehemently disagreed with this, saying it wasn't just a stopgap measure, that with love and consciousness added to the sessions, the person could reach a higher level in their development. Others wanted it pointed out that there was an important difference between someone who experimented with D&S and those who were compulsive about it. "But that's true about golfers," Howard Ruppell, a sexologist reminded me.

Like most sex, there were all different levels and applications of D&S. Different levels of sensitivity meant that what would traumatize one person in childhood would not affect another. Some people just wanted to experiment with D&S for the hell of it. You couldn't make pat statements. I began to worry about people who did.

There comes a point in reporting when you have to call it quits and write. I spoke to my editors at *New York* every week and they were fascinated to hear what I had discovered. In our last week, Susan showed me a videotape that one of her clients liked.

It was a film on cross-gender roles and childhood punishment. A rebellious adolescent boy, a tattletale sister, and an aunt, the spanker, who looked like the Dustin Hoffman character in *Tootsie*. The drama was to build suspense on the way to a spanking: "We're very upset with your insolence! Take your pants off!"

"Anticipation is very important," Susan observed, adding that she and her client would watch this video then do their own playlet where she was the governess. "He said that his parents weren't affectionate or demonstrative. The only time he was touched growing up was when the governess would spank him. In his later life, a psychiatrist told him not to worry about his attraction. If he wanted to act it out, he should, because it was harmless."

"Where do you get the tapes?" I asked.

"From a local video store. Come on, it's a nice day. Let's visit some choice S&M shops."

As we were leaving, her answering machine went off, and a lively young woman's voice asked, "Mistress Sonya? Are you home?"

"My sister. I'll call her later." Susan nodded. She put on her sunglasses, and anticipated the next question. "My whole family knows. We're very close."

We went to an S&M boutique down the street from Barney's department store. We looked at the selection of harnesses, handcuffs, and collars. Susan showed me the suspension equipment. "People spend a lot of money for particular fantasies," she said. "They have a costume workshop in the back. I've come here with clients who order outfits."

The back wall displayed head-to-toe latex body suits. Some had inflatable pouches to put pressure on genitals. Some lacked arms; these held the wearer's arms against the body, encasing them and preventing any movement. Some had head coverings with no eye or mouth holes.

I didn't understand the attraction of being trapped in these suits, but later Ava Taurel told me that it worked to create a womblike submission. Her clients used them to attain a state of meditation similar to religious rituals. Some of the sessions would go on for hours. I remembered the popularity of isolation tanks, warm water with a high concentration of salt for buoyancy that made people float effortlessly. The tanks closed, leaving the person suspended in a state of darkness. Ex-Beatle John Lennon had used them. It seemed similar.

My first reaction to the latex suits had much in common with how the mainstream media views domination and submission practices: they seemed weird, foreign, and frightening. But once I understood its purpose, I thought it would be an intense, intriguing experience to try the sensory deprivation of latex suits. It would challenge you on a range of mental levels—fear, disorientation, patience, alternative perceptions. The terms domination and submission apply here. We're so accustomed to controlling our own perception. Wearing one of these would mean relinquishing that. I also began to realize the degree of trust that must be involved among people who participated in these activities. This would be the measure of a relationship. No wonder people feared the idea of it.

Our next stop was a Times Square specialty store. We went to the S&M section, which was divided into categories: Bondage, Spanking, Gay, Straight, Transsexual, Suspension, numerous choices.

We were the only women in the store. One young man in a grey business suit glanced at us as he was leaving. He was attractive, with brown hair cut short, nice face, very tall. He seemed surprised to see us.

Susan grabbed a card by the counter and pushed me out. When we got back on the street, she bounded ahead and I had to hurry to catch up to her. "There's the guy from the store," she whispered, accelerating until she caught up to him.

"Hi," she smiled. He nodded uncertainly.

"I saw you in the store," she said. "Are you into this? Because I'm a dominatrix and this is my apprentice."

For a moment, the sky seemed to be overly blue. My brain froze. It squeezed out pieces of thoughts: Susan. What. Are. You. Doing.

The young man just stood there, squinting to see if we were for real. She spoke crisply, telling him she was a professional. She did light sensuous domination, and had her own business. "Are you into this scene?" He nodded, and she asked what he liked.

"Bondage, being dominated," he told her. They stood on the sidewalk, chatting, comparing notes, then she got to the point.

"Listen, we wondered if you'd be interested in working with us? My place is beautiful and private. Usually I charge $300 an hour, but we would give you a free session. I'm training her in domination, and we're looking for a subject. You seem healthy, a good specimen." She turned to me. "He looks like a fitting subject for us, doesn't he?" Seeing my face, she rushed on. "I'm Elsa, and this is . . . Erica. And you?"

Struck dumb, I could not meet his eyes. I could see his controlled excitement as he cautiously listened. I looked at the size of his shoulders, his height, thought about what she was saying, and realized if we hit him with all the hardware in her apartment we couldn't take him in a fight. People walked around our cluster on the sidewalk, paying no attention, which seemed odd to me. I was so paranoid it felt as if their conversation were being broadcast through concert speakers.

". . . Rob," he introduced his name, after a baptismal pause.

"Rob. Very good. Here's my card, and we'll see you after the weekend. Nice meeting you." She ran me down the street, and jumped into a cab, telling me to meet her Monday. "And next time, try to be more cool!"

*   *   *

"I have to ask you something," I said to my magazine editor over the phone an hour later. I told her the whole story. I didn't know what to do. This was going to be *their* call.

I didn't know if this was crossing the line from being a reporter to a participant. With undercover assignments, the idea was, you entered another world. My role was usually that of the observer. This sounded a little more hands on. I wanted my editors at *New York* to be responsible for the decision of how to proceed.

My editor wisely deferred to the boss, Ed Kosner, Editor-In-Chief. She instructed me to put all this in a fax, detailing what had already happened with Susan, and what she'd proposed for Monday. Should I do it or not? Did it fit in the parameters of responsible reporting?

By the end of the day, she called back. "In for a penny, in for a pound," Ed Kosner had directed. "Go ahead."

WORKING DOMINATION

"It'll be good for you to see that two women like us can dominate a man his size," she said, checking her image in the mirror. Fishnet stockings, high pumps, makeup, and the black bustier again. "Okay, you know what to do. Turn on the kitchen light. It scares the hell out of them to walk into a dark space." She had me greet him at the door. "The Mistress will see you now." My only line.

Rob entered the loft to find Mistress Sonya seated regally in her large thronelike chair. She instructed him to put his briefcase by the wall and stand by the couch. "What are your limits and interests?" He answered that he was into body worship, bondage, not extreme pain, but he could "take a spanking."

She lounged imperially. "Very good, Rob. We will maintain your limits. Now you will strip for our amusement." Obediently, he removed jacket, tie, shirt, and kept on until he was standing there completely nude. Mistress Sonya stretched slowly and dropped a long fishnetted leg to the floor, like a signal. She rose from her throne and circled him, noting his various good points as if he were a horse she might buy at auction. Her scrutiny was more academic than sexual. She ordered him to kneel and worship her. He prostrated himself, forehead to the floor.

"Mistress Erica, I want you to take that whip and stand by in case he does anything that doesn't please me." Then to Rob: "Spread your legs, slave!" And coolly, to me: "Make sure you hit him right between his thighs if I instruct you to."

She lead him through foot worship, instructing him to kiss her shoes while on his knees, eventually letting him kiss her ankle. "You've done that in a satisfactory fashion," she told him. "Now you may do the other one . . . carefully! Show me the proper amount of veneration." He kissed her other ankle as if she were a pagan goddess.

"You may rise," she told him finally. He kept his head bowed. She walked around him, pivoting, crop in her hand. She asked him his height (6'3") weight (210) and age (24). She picked up an object from her table and lifted it, addressing me. "As you see, Mistress Erica, our subject is a very nice specimen. He is large, and healthy. But he is totally ours, to do with him as we wish."

She fit a dog collar around his neck and fastened it, leaving a length of chain dangling down his chest. "Rob, this collar is a symbol of your total subservience. Do you understand?"

He bowed his head. "Yes, Mistress Sonya," he said in a low voice. "Good." She opened an antique copper container filled with props. "Mistress Erica, use your whip to keep him in line." I gingerly struck the floor five feet away from him, dominating a dustball into moving an eighth of an inch.

She came forward, moving ceremonially, and holding something out. "Have you ever used nipple clamps?" He shook his head, and she fastened what looked like giant binder clamps to his chest. He winced but stood straight. "Is there pain, Mistress?" I asked quickly. She darted a warning look at me and I backed off. "Of *course* there's pain!" Her voiced seemed to have blown off an iceberg. I looked at him. He was taking it. I shrank back. When she had him nipple-clamped and hand-cuffed, she pushed him back against the wall, raised his arms above his head, and attached his cuffs to a hook on the wall.

She ran a hand through his hair, then grabbed a fistful as if about to dash his head against the wall. I shut my eyes. She relaxed the fist, opened her fingers, and stroked his head, tracing down his neck to the front of his chest. "That's a good boy," she murmured. Then, with another unpredictable movement, she raised her hands to both sides of his face, taking his head in her hands. "You know you are totally in my power, don't you?" she whispered. "Yes, Mistress," he whispered back.

Then she asked him if he knew about the Nine Knots. He responded no, sounding worried. As she tied each knot with a nylon cord, pausing between yanks, I remembered the words of French philosopher Gilles DeLeuze: "The real dominant in the D&S situation is the submissive."

I looked at Rob. His eyes were shut as if in prayer. I watched Susan, as she calculated the amount of pain, subtly adjusting as she went along. Before she freed him, she took my hand and put my fingers on his chest, so I could feel the beat of his heart.

The session ended with her commanding him to masturbate himself to climax. It was utterly legal for a man to stand nude masturbating in front of two women after an hour of his sexual specifications. If one of us had masturbated him, we could have been hauled off to jail.

We had a glass of wine together afterward. He had put on his jacket and tie. Mistress Sonya lounged on her throne, a relaxed goddess. She asked him why he decided to accept her invitation. He answered with what appeared to be considered honesty. "You looked like a confident woman who knew what she wanted out of the world."

We asked him about his life. He was of German and Polish extraction, raised Catholic, a former alter boy. (He smiled, appreciating the irony.) He said he had a steady girlfriend. We asked if she knew about his interest. He shook his head. He told us he'd been pursuing domination for almost two years, that he'd only been to a few places in New York.

When Susan asked if he and his girlfriend had experimented with play at all, he told her they had tied each other up, but nothing more. He was afraid to tell her. "I might lose her." "Are you going to get married?" Susan asked, and he said yes. She nodded, and we looked away. He waited, with an anticipation and trust.

"Listen, I believe you should think about this," Susan said earnestly. "The person you marry should be the closest person to you in the world. If you can't tell her, or share it . . . obviously this is important to you. You've sought it out more than once. As you become more successful you'll have even more need to relieve the stress."

"What were you planning on?" I asked, curious. "Were you going to maintain a secret life?" He looked troubled. He didn't know. He repeated that he was afraid of losing his girlfriend. Timidly, he asked Susan if he could ask me a question. "Why did you want to find out about this yourself?" I told him I've always wanted to know about things people keep secret from each other.

"What would you do if you found out your girlfriend was exploring domination and not telling you about it?" The idea seemed a fresh one to him. He thought for a moment, then said he guessed he couldn't be upset with her. Innocently, he told us he didn't know that there were other people who shared his fantasies and needs. "More than you know," Susan said wryly from the throne. "I really hope you talk to your girlfriend before you get married. Secret lives catch up to you one way or another."

*   *   *

Curiosity took me to Eva Norvind, whose professional name was Ava Taurel, the mistress who introduced Susan to domination. I'd heard a lot about her and wanted to meet her. She spoke seven languages, and was a journalist who covered film and fashion for international magazines. She'd interviewed Steve Martin, Jeremy Irons, Harrison Ford, Goldie Hawn, and Robert Redford, among others. She had a stable of dominatrixes working for her. Clients could select from a book of photographs.

Ava was passionate about her work, unlike Susan, who found D&S a job, not an adventure. But Ava extended her profession in her personal life. "One former client is now my personal pleasure slave," she told me. "He sees this as an art form. I'm not interested in someone who can take 1,000 strokes. I'm interested in fewer strokes with someone who can feel it."

She claimed that most of the women who work for her similarly extended their interest in D&S. "I don't hire if someone is just in it for economic reasons. I hire if there's a psychological connection, if it's in their lives and relationships." The clients are "mostly lawyers, white-collar professionals."

Ava had her own answers to the question that most often came up in debates about domination. Was it, as practitioners claimed, consensual and loving, or an unhealthy reenactment of childhood trauma? In our first conversation, she discussed gradations of emotions in the sessions that people who argue about this stuff don't include in their thinking.

"When you give pain to a person, you must also give a lot of love and tenderness to compensate," Taurel believed. "If you don't, something is wrong. It indicates deep psychological problems. I stay away from that kind of session. People who want only pain have often been abused when they were young. They never learned what love was. They got attention through pain and humiliation. So you provide warmth and positiveness to bring them to a different place now. That can slowly educate them. It's not good for business, but it's important for people."

She told me a story of a man who had a desire to be a dog. She put a collar on him, put him on all fours, and as she commanded him to eat the dog food he was overcome with memories that his father, a veterinarian, gave more attention and love to the animals in his care than his son. The man never came again, but she believes she helped him.

As we talked, we make our way to her waiting room. A slender young woman in a red leather suit smiled shyly at us. Ava introduced her as Carrie, another slave, and sighed, "Unfortunately she is madly in love with me." The young woman smiled and blushed. "She loves to have me slap her. " Carrie knelt before her and Ava smacked her hard across one side of the face. A pause, then she smacked the other side. The two women put their arms around each other and hugged, Ava cuddling and stroking her slave. Carrie insisted she likes such treatment very much. She'd been working for Ava for eight years. She was a math teacher with a masters in psychology.

Ava, who had been an actor, a well-known dominatrix, and a media personality, knew how to play to the crowd to get attention. But I would find out that her theatrical side could work against her. She did care about people's psychological and spiritual health, and had remarkable energy and intellect. But the promoter Ava could undercut the deeper Eva. She told me she thought she'd destroyed something very precious by exploiting it. It was a complex problem. Ava Taurel and Eva Norvind were a lot of different people.

GETTING WORKED BY MAGAZINES

I stopped by Susan's loft to let her read a copy of the story I'd turned into *New York* magazine. She liked it, and asked when I thought it would run.

"They told me in a few weeks," I said. "I came over as soon as I heard. My editor told me that Ed Kosner came out of the office, put a fist in the air, and said, 'We've got another bestselling cover.' He said to ask if you'd pose."

We were both thrilled, and exhausted. Susan mentioned that she hadn't slept well the entire time we'd worked on the story. Neither had I.

"I didn't want to worry you, but my worst fear was something going wrong. Like when you were hiding, if someone discovered you and got angry."

"God, what would we have done?" I asked. Susan walked over to her basket of ropes and fished around, then turned to show me. "I had this."

She was holding a large, shiny hunting knife that had been hidden under the ropes. It glinted. I felt sick. "That was there the whole time?" I finally asked.

"I've always had it," she said. "People have this idea that if you make a living in sex, you're having a great time and getting paid for it." She looked at the knife. "If they only knew that you're never without fear."

*   *   *

"There's a problem." My editor sounded very nervous. It was the third day of the week after they'd told me they were running "Diary of a Dominatrix." Now they thought they should get some expert opinions on domination and submission from psychologists and sexologists.

"I've read a lot of material," I said. "Those people are accessible. I can talk to Ron Moglia. He's the head of New York University's Human Sexuality graduate program, the biggest in the country. And Louise Kaplan, a psychiatrist, just wrote a book published by Knopf that's been reviewed in the *Times*, called *Female Perversions*. The head of the psychology department at Columbia thought it was significant. I can get to a lot of people."

"Do that," she said.

"Any other problems?" I asked.

"No. He said to get expert opinions explaining what's wrong with these people."

WORKING HUMAN SEXUALITY

For the next three weeks, I consulted with writers, psychiatrists, educators, sexologists. The head of Columbia University's psychology department referred me to Kaplan. I interviewed Dr. Ronald Moglia, at New York University. I spoke to Howard Ruppell, head of the Society for the Scientific Study of Sex. I spoke to Susanne Schad-Somers and a lawyer named Robert Fogelnest who explained to me the standards in New York law that made D&S legal. I read the formulative writers on this subject, John Money, Richard Green, Robert Stoller. I spoke with an editor and Columbia University philosophy professor named Jonathan Crary at ZONE books, which were reprinting classics in the political and philosophical literature that dealt with sexuality.

I had a major problem.

FURTHER ADVENTURES IN FREELANCE WRITING

"It's too simple, it's ignorant, and it's *wrong* to present it as 'what's wrong with these people.' Human sexuality is much more complex than that . . ." I was on the phone with my editor at *New York* magazine.

She called a couple of days later. When she first said the words, "It's not going to run," I didn't believe it.

"But he already accepted it! What am I going to tell this woman?" I said, feeling betrayed. "Ed had me ask her if she'd pose for the cover! She told her family! She told everyone she knows! She gave us three months of her time and then you sent me out for another three weeks after *that!* You had me interview all those experts! What do you mean you're not going to run it? WHY?"

She was upset. "Ed said . . . he decided it wasn't suitable material for our readers. He said he's sorry, and he specifically said, 'Tell Marianne we still love her.' He just couldn't imagine his little daughter picking up the magazine from the coffee table and saying, 'What's this?' "

"Shouldn't he have thought about that before? We've been speaking all along! He had a very descriptive, in-depth proposal that said exactly what this was about. He approved me participating in that session." The more I thought about it, the angrier I became. "What did he think?" I asked, my voice shaking.

"I'm sorry," said my editor.

* * *

I don't remember what Susan's first words were. I've blocked it out. I do remember that she screamed, and kept screaming. And then she asked me the best question I heard in all my years of reporting:

" 'It doesn't belong in the magazine'? I don't belong in the magazine?! I'm already in the goddamn magazine!" she shouted. "I'm in the magazine every week in the back pages with all those other ads for 'Role Play' and 'Psychodramatists' or whatever euphemism your hypocrites prefer to hide behind! I spend ten thousand dollars a year on my ads in his magazine! They have 35 to 50 ads a week for D&S at that rate! He makes money from me doing what he says will offend his tender readers! I get my clients from *New York* magazine!" She stopped, and there was a long silence.

"Why is it okay for me to be in it that way, but I 'don't belong' in the magazine this way?" she asked me. I couldn't answer.

WORKING ON

In the next couple of years, Ed Kosner left *New York* magazine and went on to edit *Esquire*. Kurt Anderson, one of the trio who'd started *Spy* magazine, took over the editorship, not an unimpressive feat, especially to those of us who'd been at the opening party for *Spy* and had seen the mocking life-size cutout figures of Ed Kosner and *Vanity Fair*'s editor Tina Brown (who Graydon Carter, another part of the *Spy* trio, replaced when she decamped to the *New Yorker*). The secret of New York magazine publishing appeared to be: Create cardboard cutouts and aim for them.

In the weeks after the "Diary of a Dominatrix" fiasco, I sent Susan the tapes of our weeks of interviews. In retrospect, I think that was a mistake. It was my work too, but at the same time I felt she was owed something.

I decided I'd had enough of magazines and wanted to write books, which seemed to have more space to stretch out in and might be harder to kill. I came to know Ava Taurel better, and she agreed to be the subject of a chapter on domination and submission. I found out later I had writer's block on the subject.

One day I was walking in Manhattan and ran into Susan. Both of us were working on books. We had a short, comforting conversation about what a long, strange trip it had been. We wished each other luck.

It was about a year later that I was in Barnes & Noble and I saw a book about being a dominatrix, with Susan's byline. I bought it. "How did she do this so fast?" I wondered, and then realized, she'd had the tapes transcribed. I read page after page, and remembered a friend I'd talked to about sending the tapes to Susan. "Don't worry, your karma is clean," she'd said.

I read her book and it was good. It sounded like her, funny, smart, world weary, lively, with a heart underneath. I had a flashback to sitting in her loft when we'd first met. "Every day I see the most amazing things. I want to tell my story," she'd said. She did it and did it well.

WORKING WITH AVA

I had a book contract, and Ava Taurel, dominatrix, agreed to be interviewed for the D&S chapter. Eva Norvind had become tired of being Ava Taurel. She felt that commercializing her interest in D&S had destroyed it for her. She became interested in going to graduate school in Human Sexuality at New York University. One thing about Eva, she was a fearless critic of her own life. She never stopped pursuing what was important to her, even if it meant taking new risks.

She taught me to enlarge my thinking. Every time I thought I would lose patience with her (testing limits was almost an involuntary reaction with her) there would be some way in which she would force me to examine the interaction that took place. I'd always learn something about subtleties of human nature. Domination and submission, was, as she'd always said, a deep part of her. But so was consciousness, love, and feeling.

Once we went to see the film version of Shakespeare's *Much Ado About Nothing*.

The love story, shot in a villa in the hills of Tuscany, darkened via the evil intervention of the jealous Don John who tricked the young lover Claudio into thinking his fiancée had betrayed him with another man, or as Shakespeare put it, "She knows the heat of a luxurious bed." At a beautiful outdoor wedding the bride was struck across the face and knocked down by the grieved, outraged Claudio. Innocent and so stunned, she wept hysterically, staring at her would-be husband leaving her in disgrace.

There was the flinch of a visceral reaction at my side. Tears started streaming down Eva's face, tears of grief and pain. She shrank in her seat, her shoulders shaking quietly. The raw betrayal and shock on the screen seemed to overwhelm her. She sat, sobbing. Later, after the lovers reunited and it all ended happily, Eva was just not sure.

"There she was, loving him with all her heart after that betrayal!" she declared, her voice still a bit shaky. We walked down the street, where a soft rain had fallen. She looked exhausted, her eye makeup smeared, searching for a telephone on the street. "I would have a very hard time forgiving him!" She found change in her purse and called her office to see if the scheduled domination sessions were going smoothly.

We talked at all hours on the phone. I'd visit the midtown hotel where she lived. In the course of observing her, I would see her tremendous creativity and her wild spending.

I noticed a disregard for other people's time. The pattern became clear one day when she told me I could meet her at 1:00 o'clock in the afternoon. She called and asked if it could be later. At two, no Ava, so I called her. No, she wasn't free yet.

I tried to be accommodating because I know an hour of sexual sessions could mean a few hundred dollars. But Ava had people she could delegate her sessions to. Finally at 4:00 o'clock I called and she said she'd be right down. Politely but impatiently, I said we'd arranged to meet three hours earlier, and by the time she got here it would be another half hour, so we should reschedule.

A few days later, I'd waited nearly an hour in a Soho restaurant before she showed up. Enough.

"Ava," I said firmly, running through the past few incidents, "I'm here to report on domination and submission with you. Not to act out the dynamics. I won't do this anymore."

Across the table, her face lit up with joy and pride. "Marianne!" she exclaimed with delight. "You sound so dominant! It's wonderful!"

I started to say something and she cut me off, truly enthusiastic. "You can be so polite and accommodating, I thought, here is a submissive woman. I admit, if someone gives me that opportunity I will take it. But no! Listen to you! It's fantastic!" She was never late again.

She struggled to avoid being "nonconsensual" in her personal life. For most practitioners D&S was an act of consent between people who wanted to be conscious of their power exchange. But in her personal life, Eva most often went off track. Sometimes it seemed to be part of her social commerce.

The cat thing told me a lot.

I have two gentle, shy, loving cats that I raised from kittens. During one visit, I returned to my living room to find her "playing" with them. "Scratch me, scratch me. Come on!" she urged, waving her fingers in their face to irritate them.

The little female cat jumped down from the counter and hid. Ava backed the male against the wall. "Scratch me!" Ava continued to wave her fingers closer. I moved to stop her. As I did, I saw the tormented, confused cat who'd never scratched anyone in his life tentatively raise his paw. . . .

He looked over, caught my eye, and howled in dismay. He couldn't do it. I snatched him away and comforted him, asking her what on earth she was doing.

"You're denying them a fundamental right of their existence!" she exclaimed. "Their aggression!" I responded that if she won the lottery she would not feel deprived of her right to earn a living, and if my cats didn't have to fight their way through life it was fine. We discussed this incident later, and she added that a man I'd referred her to on a business matter also hadn't liked it when she tried to get his cat to exercise fundamental rights in the same fashion.

"What happened?" I asked, thinking, uh, oh.

"Oh, he asked me not to do that," she responded lightly. "I think he might have been displeased."

On a hunch, I called the man to check. "Touch my cat one more time and I throw you the fuck out of my apartment," had been his exact words. Ava added the cat thing to the nonconsensuals she had to watch out for.

It was during the domination class that our relationship was clarified.

"My agency represents women and men who enjoy enacting a variety of erotic fetishes and fantasies as well as pursuing spiritual and intellectual interests. I take pride in finding bright, attractive people from the art and business worlds who are not jaded and who take true interest in fantasy role play. . . ."

This was part of the recording a new client would get upon reaching the Taurel Institute. She'd suggested that I might find it interesting to attend a training session with some of the people who were starting to work for her. Accordingly, I found myself there one afternoon with half a dozen attractive young women. We sat and listened to Ava discuss how the sessions worked, what might happen, what they would be expected to do.

She'd kept records for seven years. The Taurel Institute had seen 2,650 men, ninety-five percent of whom wanted to submit to women. Only one percent wanted to dominate. The other four percent would switch roles. She discussed imagination and creativity, that it was important to be able to improvise. Blindfold a man and tell him if he was very good, he might touch your shoulder. Never dominate in a degrading way, such as "You fat slob. I want to spit on you."

"No, it's more important to stretch parameters. Tell him you want him to pose as a *Playboy* centerfold. Force him to come up with more graceful or lascivious poses. Tell him you want to see his legs spread, his mouth held in a more feminine way. These things are embarrassing but the man will feel sexy because you're changing his identity."

Ava spoke of good friends of hers in Europe, a married couple that enjoyed D&S. "They take turns, physically controlling and binding each other. But they always respect the partner. In America you see imagery of S&M where people are vilified and degraded. They don't know the difference."

She challenged preconceptions about D&S. I was intrigued to see the success of Ava's mainstream business workshops on domination and submission throughout the country. She was profiled in *Redbook*, after which more average American housewives came to her workshops. She was offering a mechanism of communication over power roles in relationships that attracted ordinary suburban couples. They were experimenting with sex and power roles in their marriages. Ava was on to something.

At one point I interviewed a psychologist who used D&S exercises for couples who were fighting. "For the next week," he urged them, "if you do anything that involves power, practice it consciously and ritualistically. Be conscious of everything from economics to who takes out the garbage to who defers in conversation." Would they end up communicating more about the use of power in their relationships?

My thoughts were interrupted by a half hour's exercise in bondage. While Ava demonstrated ways to quickly and efficiently tie knots, "It is most important to *look* as if you know what you are doing, to be in charge," we broke up into pairs and took turns practicing tying each other up. Occasionally I'd have the out-of-body experience of seeing myself as an observer might. The office suite across the hall housed a dentist.

Ava had introduced us all when we arrived. Most of the women were actors. There was one student, and one Dutch translator. Ava had told the group I was a writer. We got on well together.

"And now, to give you some hands-on experience," Ava announced toward the end of the afternoon, "one of our regular clients will come in and you can see what an actual session might involve."

So, a bonus. The client is pleased because he has a number of beautiful young women paying attention to his wishes. The agency gets paid. Ava Taurel gets to scope out the talent of her new group. The group gets to "practice," a chance to gauge their interest. It's a practical trade-off.

"Everyone, I would like you to say hello to Frances," Ava introduced as he came in.

The last time I'd seen Frances he was doing ballet leaps in his pink underwear at Susan's loft, a year ago. She'd introduced me as her slave in training. Ava was introducing me as a writer. This was not going to be good.

"Writer?" Frances repeated, his brows raised above an unpleasant expression. No, it was not going to be good.

"Frances has been interested in D&S for many years," Ava continued. He is one of our regular clients, and he will tell you how he first came to this." Everyone sat down. Frances crossed an immaculately trousered leg and began his tale.

"I was going to school in a city in Switzerland, and renting a room in an apartment from friends of my family," he started. "They often traveled. It was a lovely apartment and the only other person was an attractive housekeeper, some years older than I was at the time."

"One day I fell ill, and became nearly delirious with fever. The housekeeper came to nurse me, and to break my fever, she suggested cooling down my body temperature by giving me an enema in the bath. . . ."

The story was exactly, virtually word for word, the same. It was amazing. Talk about not getting creative with "Little Red Riding Hood." He went through the same sentences, same details, same chrome faucet, same hose. The sexualization of this scenario had been captured for eternity.

When he had finished his story, he smiled at the dark-haired woman closest to him. "Would you like to be the nurse?"

She smiled back. "Certainly I would." Ava opened a closet and beckoned for help while wheeling out a doctor's examination table. Frances stripped off his clothes.

"I will go into the other office and continue instruction with Monique and Avril," Ava said. "The rest of you will continue here."

The dark-haired woman and another assistant presided over the preparation and execution of his enema. Frances managed to give them instructions and me grief about being a writer at the same time. Why hadn't I mentioned it previously? Did I think spying on people was a good thing to do? Despite my respect for people's rights to pursue their fantasies, I was discovering enemas weren't on my lovemap. But more upseting was the hostility he was managing to create with people I'd hoped to report on. Talk about the true dominant being the submissive.

"Is your name Carol? Carol, I'd like you to come over here and touch my penis," he instructed, and she did.

"Now, Marianne, I'd like you to come over here and touch my penis," he said, pausing. "Well?"

"I don't feel like it, Frances."

"Carol just did. Do you consider yourself superior to Carol because you're a writer?"

"No, Frances, but it's time for me to leave."

Thoroughly shaken, I stuck my head in Ava's office. She was instructing the two women on the permutations of spanking. One of them was over her lap while the other observed.

"I'm sorry, I have to leave." She demanded to know why. I said I'd run into her client before and he was being aggressive about it.

"You can't leave! Get back in there!" she barked. "Get back in there and do what he tells you! You have to do what I say when you are in my place!"

I felt completely, utterly foolish and upset. Upset because I wanted to write about all this, foolish from what had happened with Frances.

"Get back in there!" she shouted.

"I'm sorry, Ava." Over my shoulder, I saw her raise her hand and spank the woman bent over her knee hard, her face contorted with fury. I got out fast.

*　　*　　*

"Why? Why did you want to write about domination and submission?" I asked myself the next morning. I'd thought I would learn something about life, something usually hidden. But maybe there was another reason, a dark one. I thought of the people I respected, even loved, who thought that the things I chose to explore in my work were things best left alone. Maybe they were right.

I thought of Ava's face. Oh, well, it didn't matter now. That was that. My phone rang.

It was Ava. I listened, numb, as she told me that she'd called her therapist last night, to tell her what had happened.

"We discussed that . . . I can't control you," she said in a deep, soft voice. "You are beyond my control and if I work with you I have to accept that."

We were both silent. "Well," she said, and I could hear resignation in her voice. "I accept it. When do you want to meet with me again?"

*　　*　　*

One of Ava's spiritual beliefs was that things should be respected for the truth of what they are. She never lied about her life. She'd show me any part of it, however unflattering.

John was a former client of Ava's who had been personally involved with her. He says Ava was unrealistic about money. She would have an especially good month and calculate that every month's income would be as much. "She got an apartment, then a studio, then the dungeon, then another studio, then another. She thought she would fill them with girls but you couldn't advertise enough to make that pay. She has tremendous drive and is exceedingly bright, but she's not a realist."

Ava pulled in energy from everyone around her. Carrie, her slave, worked in the Taurel Institute even after Ava broke her heart by taking a new lover. Carrie was frustrated by their business practice.

"I'm supposed to be the slave girl. I don't know anything, okay, but I kept telling her and she won't listen. I may have my fantasy about her, but she lives in one herself. She destroyed our business. Now we don't even have a proper dungeon!"

"She can drive you crazy," Carrie added. "She's the most disorganized person in the world." John, the longtime client, told me a story of trying to get Ava to a plane. "We kept telling her, get packed, let's get going, and she'd dawdled, talking on the phone, doing anything but getting ready. Finally we got in the car and halfway there, I said, 'Forget it, Ava! It's too late! We'll never make the plane now. We should just turn around.' Well, she was like a little girl. Got tears in her eyes and became real quiet. Then she said, 'Can we call and ask them to have the plane wait for us?'"

COWORKERS

Work was tough for Carrie that year. She would go to Ava's apartment with office work she had prepared on the computer, correspondence needing to be signed, bills for equipment, advertising copy to be approved.

The door would open with the chain still on. Ava's hand would come out, or she'd give an order to slide the papers through the few available inches. Then the door would slam shut. This went on for weeks. "Once she let me touch her hand," Carrie told me.

It had been a circuitous route to the Taurel Institute. In the early 1980s, Carrie knew she had to meet Xaviera Hollander. A shy math tutor in New Jersey, her fascination began after reading *The Happy Hooker*.

Persistence and detective work paid off, and finally Carrie found herself in Europe, typing manuscripts, and becoming Xaviera's pleasure slave. "Zav was the first person to put a label to the stuff that was going on in my head."

"You must be a masochist," Hollander informed Carrie early in the relationship.

"How do you know?"

"Because of the way I treat you."

Carrie described her background as "middle class and normal." She doesn't remember an undue amount of family discipline and claims she never got hit, although she had an older brother she idolized and hated, who always teased her. She thought maybe her D&S came from that. Either way, her ideas of sex roles determined the pattern of her role playing. "Most men want to be superior. My major S&M relationships have been with women. That way, I feel more equal and I can decide to make someone superior. My fantasies started when I was eight or ten, seeing movies like *The Ten Commandments*, *Spartacus*, or *Patch of Blue*. When I saw someone get whipped or yelled at it excited me."

Xaviera Hollander was the first person to whip her. It didn't match her fantasies and was mostly painful. Later she would learn there were different ways of whipping people. "Ava is so good, because she goes vertical. Horizontally along the spine hurts. Sometimes I want to be hit really severely, and other times just as a stimulant. Afterwards I like to have the marks to look at. Maybe that sounds sick but it's like enjoying having a hicky."

What I didn't understand about the pain experience was that when people are sexually aroused they can absorb a greater amount of sensation. For practitioners, this is the sexual physical exchange, in the way kissing or intercourse would be for others. Carrie's analogy was a good one.

Carrie saw Xaviera Hollander on and off for ten years. "Zav would say she loved me, then get involved with a guy and not need me." One day, she showed Carrie a letter from a dominatrix friend who was coming to visit, along with a photograph of Ava Taurel.

Carrie and Ava met at a party Zav threw. "She came into the kitchen and said, 'Oh, you're Xaviera's slave girl,' and it was neat, she started talking to me." A month later, Carrie sought Ava out in New York City.

"Zav had said I was a nuisance, but Ava invited me over." They went to Ava's apartment, where Ava ordered Carrie to strip to her underwear and walk around in high heels, and then promptly became engrossed in watching *Dallas*, forgetting Carrie was there. Carrie wondered how she could love such a person, but when it was time to leave, Ava yanked Carrie's hair back and slapped her face.

"I had a tingling sensation in my stomach. It was so fantastic. That's all it took, I was in love," Carrie said. "Later when I did my first session with her and a client she put heavy-duty nipple clamps on me and she beat me really hard. I was crying and told her I wouldn't see her anymore, and she said, 'You'll be back.'

I said, 'How do you know?'

She said, 'I know.'"

Over time, Carrie became indispensable. "I'd call and say I was in the neighborhood, could I drop over and have you whip me?" and she would. If there was a client it might inspire him to see both of us." Between doing sessions and hanging out with Ava's daughter waiting for Ava to finish a session so they could all get a bite to eat, Carrie managed to patiently work her way into being a necessary part of Ava's life and work.

"Zav came to visit and it was the greatest thing, the two of them were fighting over me."

* * *

"Servants have enormous power over people, you become dependant and needy for them," Ava Taurel told me later, sitting on the same couch where Carrie had told her story. "My mother always wanted to protect me, to pick up after me. It made me an invalid and I had to learn to be responsible for my actions. My mother was my maid. I've created similar situations with female figures in my life coming to my rescue and I become involved in a horrendous dependency relationship."

Encouraged by Ava to find someone else, Carrie placed ads looking for a relationship that included D&S, but she was unsuccessful. She didn't pursue it with enthusiasm. "It's hard for me to find someone else when I'm emotionally attached," she explained. She said part of the excitement for her is not having what she wants, namely Ava.

Ava claimed that she met Carrie at a point in her life when she was hungry for somebody there, but she claims to have no feelings for Carrie. "Absolutely not, never, never had a romantic feeling for her, never a sexual feeling."

"Even though you have sex with each other?"

"Yes. Because I would dream about guys that would rape me while she would do sexual things to tantalize me. She's the only woman who ever brought me to orgasm, but I've never been with her in my mind. I never thought of her. Years ago Xaviera had told me about this slave girl and how unbearable she was, how truly masochistic and how very submissive. I thought, 'My God, what a sick girl. I never want to meet her,' and then unfortunately she came and worked for me."

And here Eva was characteristically honest. "I guess Carrie and I are both people with serious self-esteem problems."

"What about the time Xaviera Hollander came to New York and the two of you were competing for Carrie?"

She sat back on her couch. "She said that? I guess she likes to feel important. Neither Xaviera or I are interested in the poor girl. But we are both possessive creatures. We are in a sense looking at her as our property of convenience!" She laughed heartily. "God, I can imagine how this will look on the page!" She laughed again, even harder. "I don't give a damn!"

EVA IN LOVE

Gerard and Eva met through the personal ads. They took time together before they slept together or she introduced him to D&S. Within a few weeks, though, something had changed in Eva's life. For a woman who had never lived with anyone, she found she was only happy when he was there. Carrie went on vacation. When she returned she discovered he was spending nights with Ava. She promptly named him "Geraldine" and declared he was no intellectual equal for Ava and they would soon split.

"What is your lover like?" I asked Eva.

"He is a very tall, well-built black man. He works in a library, has two years of college, stutters, and is twenty-six years old. He doesn't have social skills like making eye contact. He is very respectful to other human beings but has communication problems and has struggled with learning disabilities. But he's very honest and pure. We seem to be an impossible couple and I sound sentimental. But he is starting to mean a great deal to me."

They shared increasing amounts of time together. It was all new for her. "It was revealing to spend three days with a man when everything wasn't exciting and wonderful. We watched movies on the VCR, and worked in the office." They became friends as well as lovers. She pushed him to get a better job.

"When did you decide you wanted to be with her?" I asked him months later.

"On the third date, we started putting our cards on the table," said Gerard. "She confessed she was a professional dominatrix, a mistress, and said if she didn't get to know me, she'd take me to her place, have sexual pleasure, and that would be it. I said it wouldn't be that way because I wouldn't be happy if that happened." He had the stereotypical view of D&S. "Whips, chains, all that. But after stepping inside Ava's world and seeing the people I realize they're just like everyone else. They just have different ideas and philosophies about sex."

Words were difficult for Gerard. He concentrates and slowly forms and releases sentences, struggling for clarity before he speaks. What he says has a sense of being from deep inside, considered.

They both believed the relationship has been good for them. "Ava's helped me a great deal," he said. He always addressed her by her professional name, never Eva. "I told my uncle the only way I can get myself focused is if I can find someone to knock some sense into me. That's what Ava is doing by being hard on me."

As for Eva, Gerard forced her to consider the complications of a different kind of involvement. "I feel I'm dominant in the relationship, sometimes in a nasty sense," she said. "Once he was helping me clean the bathroom and I saw this bare torso and I was, mmmmm. It was such an inspiring back to whip. If he didn't clean it well he deserved a whipping. In the dominatrix role I would have played at the situation. But for our relationship, I thought it wouldn't have been good. I've had to learn to see his side."

Sensitivity to the relationship was something Eva had to work at. Once she had him bathe and wait for her to finish a session. Instead she went to dinner with the client and returned hours later. "Eventually I did call and he was so nice about it. I knew he was hurt. I freaked out when I realized how mean I'd been. I'm mean to people I care about, I can be so mean!"

Sitting on the couch, she started crying as she related the incident. "He doesn't deserve to have me be so mean!" She sobbed and Gerard hugged her. He checked to see if she was okay. They held hands as she explained she was trying to be more aware of his feelings.

"I never felt invaded by Gerard," she said. "I feel I have my life alone and I have him at the same time, and they can go together." The differences in their backgrounds, ages, and worlds don't phase them, both claim. "He is a thinking person, very intelligent. His handicap has only added to his personality, made him richer in a sense because it gave him the opportunity to experience pain and made him into a fuller person. I don't think I could have a relationship with someone who's never experienced pain because half is missing of life. Life is happiness and pain."

Eva and Gerard are still together. They have traveled throughout

Europe and on to India on a spiritual retreat, as well as the Middle East to study sexuality in other cultures.

DIFFERING OPINIONS ON D&S

When two professional sexologists, Wendy Maltz and Marty Klein, got into a debate over Ava Taurel being interviewed in a professional journal, I spoke with each of them. Both were mainstream authors who disagreed with each other over something a lot of people didn't understand, the idea of consensuality in sexual practices.

Maltz and her husband Larry, both licensed clinical social workers, run Maltz Counseling Associates in Eugene. Her book, *The Sexual Healing Journey, A Guide For Survivors of Sexual Abuse* was published by HarperCollins in 1991.

"I want to share with you something I read on a plane when I was coming here from Oregon," Wendy Maltz said from the podium. The conference was in Washington, D.C., in November 1993. The subject was "Advances In Treating Survivors of Sexual Abuse, Empowering The Healing Process."

"It ruffled my feathers," said Wendy Maltz, speaking of what she read on the plane. "Perhaps it will ruffle some of yours. This was a great example of addictive sexuality and the way sexuality can be bent."

She asked if the audience knew what she was talking about, indicating an issue of *Contemporary Sexuality*. "If you're a certified sex therapist or belong to AASECT (American Association of Sex Educators, Counselors, and Therapists) you get this for free every month. This issue has an article called "An Interview With A Dominatrix.""

"There are good examples here of the addictive," Wendy Maltz declared to her Washington audience. "See if you agree." She read from the magazine. " 'This is member Ava Taurel, owner of Taurel Enterprises, a company that provides talent, wardrobes, and locations for people to engage in fantasy role play. While the fantasies are erotically charged, the participants do not engage in oral, anal or genital sex during these interactions.' "

Maltz added, "Masturbation is very common, of course, and painful touch is part of it, too."

She resumed reading. Ava was asked in the interview, "Where do you take your clients?" " 'If they want me to I can take them to the edge. You can do this in very different ways . . . in a physical way, through pain, or it can be through restriction, being bound on the outside, but giving the person a sense of inner freedom.' OH-KAY!"

The audience laughed. Maltz continued, this time reading about sessions of public embarrassment " 'in a place far from family, friends, coworkers and associates.' Okay!" More laughs from the audience. She quoted Ava saying that to overcome limits in an erotic situation made some individuals feel they can do it in other areas of their life. "She goes on to talk about taking up skydiving." The audience chortled.

Maltz referred to her model of unhealthy sex. "Draws on fear for excitement, and on shameful and embarrassing situations."

She finished by comparing Ava talking about using affection in her sessions to cult ritual indoctrination. "I couldn't help making a little bit of a connection between these cult behaviors and doing this sort of behavior, bondage and whipping, to the victim."

"To me," Maltz concluded, "It is such a blatant example of reenactment of early trauma. I feel sorry for this woman."

Later, during a phone interview, Wendy Maltz maintained her belief that what goes on in Ava's sessions is a reenactment of early trauma. When I asked if she saw the possibility of different kinds of enactment, whether or not she'd consider the possibility that with love and warmth, the sessions could be something other than abusive, the answer was no.

"It's a restriction of the sexual energy," she responded. "You don't have to pollute the air for people to realize the need for clean air. It's just a re-creation of childhood trauma. The dominatrix is being abusive and humiliating. They're not caring for the soul of the individual or respectful of the body. They're doing the sorts of things done in abuse."

"When you're healing, you go into the issue of human betrayal, the need to be protected and loved," Wendy Maltz declared. "Healing does not happen by reenacting sexual pain."

"But practitioners claim the sessions are not necessarily abusive and humiliating," I said. "Could you allow for the possibility that the sessions involve understanding aspects of power?"

She responded no, because "the people are being sexually objectified and their inner experience is being ignored." She attributed this to disassociation, and says that each time a person acts out sexually in a way that's humiliating to them it damages their inner sense of integrity, which to her means "it generates shame and self-loathing and damages their self-esteem."

And what about the fact that many D&S practitioners don't see it this way at all, and believe they have a right to their own sexual choice?

And that many maintain they were never traumatized but rather enjoy adding D&S to their range of adult sexual expression? "They're blind to their inner reality," Maltz responded. "They're cut off from their inner child that's hurting."

"Do you think that we should say, 'This is the way you should have sex?' or 'These are the emotions you should have?' "

There was a long, thoughtful pause. "I see it in terms of people developing a higher consciousness about what their inner experience is. It is important to ask 'what is this behavior doing for me? Is it increasing my self-esteem, bringing me closer to other people, making me feel more connected to my world, universe, life? Does it increase a sense of connection and contentment?' "

I asked her how she accounts for the fact that D&S practitioners feel very close to their partners because they are honest and open about their shared sexuality together.

"I think they have close mutual fantasies," she responded, "but how can you genuinely care for someone and whip them or cut them at the same time. It does not compute for me."

"Would you consider the possibility that these sessions could incorporate love and tenderness, communication and getting in touch with feelings?"

"No!" she said firmly. "You have disrobing, masturbation. . . . I'm not opposed to them in certain contexts, but you have strangers in a separate world, compartmentalized, which is what a lot of sexual compulsives do. They're meeting with someone with whom they have no real ongoing relationship, who has their own psychological agenda of getting paid for acting out their own stuff. The dominatrix has a psychological agenda for herself, so she can't be a healer."

And close married couples, or long-term sweethearts who practice D&S, what about them?

"Does it increase their capacity for intimacy, affection, and a sense of belonging? " she asked. "They might say yes. You might have a couple enjoy fantasy, and they do some fanny pinching or spanking during sex. But again, is it enhancing and increasing self-esteem and a sense of belonging? Is it life-affirming? Maybe one of them goes to a place of shame or wants to be punished by the partner as an act of self-loathing."

Maltz continued, "And as for married couples who've done D&S for years, I would ask them, 'Do you feel your partner would love you if you suddenly decided you had to stop doing this for good?' "

*   *   *

"I totally agree! Ask them! If they say they couldn't have their marriage without D&S, she's right, there's a problem," said Marty Klein, another AASECT member who is a practicing therapist and author of *Your Sexual Secrets* and *Ask Me Anything: A Sex Therapist Answers the Most Important Questions for the '90's.* "And then ask them if you took away their piano would the marriage last? Or their summer house in the Hamptons?"

Marty Klein declared that many people who participate in D&S role-play do it because it's enjoyable. "A lot of people who do it have not had any childhood trauma," he said.

Perhaps they're blind to their inner experience. Perhaps they've disassociated from their childhood trauma.

"There are those who will tell you there are only two kinds of people, the ones who remember their trauma and the ones who don't. Which is to say everyone has been traumatized. I don't believe that."

The other major point he found salient is that all sexuality involves power relationships. "And it's not a bad thing, or it only is if we're afraid of power dynamics. You're naked, inviting a part of someone's body into your body. You're entering a very primitive part of the human mind."

Being conscious of power is more the issue than whether or not there are power dynamics in sex, stated Marty Klein. "What D&S is about is simply the recognition and conscious manipulation of power dynamics in society."

"But Wendy Maltz believes that people in D&S are being sexually objectified and that their inner experience is being ignored. How do you respond?"

"That is a religious discussion," Klein answered. "It's not about science and not about sex. I don't know how she thinks she has access to people's 'inner experience.' If you talk to people about D&S, they say they like the intensity and they like the surrender. In other cultures there are aspects of sexuality that are highlighted that aren't in our culture."

As far as the idea of a "trauma bond" between practitioners he claimed to have "no idea what that means. You could say anything is a trauma bond, even someone not wanting to go away to college." If the only way a person could have sex is with D&S, there's a problem. "But I would say that's also true if the only way a person could have sex was while listening to country & western music."

"What about D&S desensitizing people, damaging their integrity, and generating shame and self-loathing?"

After "Oh, please!" he said, "D&S is about trust, not violence." He thought being conscious of power in sex is something our society can't handle. "Some people in D&S *are* acting out hostility and unresolved trauma, but that's also true of some people's marital or career choices."

And what about the range of sessions? "Wendy Maltz said D&S was 'going to a contrived place, meeting with a stranger or someone with whom they have no real ongoing relationship, and that the dominatrix has a psychological agenda for herself so she can't be a healer.'"

"Bullshit! Every psychotherapist has a psychological agenda! Every professional has reasons for doing what they do! It sounds like people who make these arguments are against casual sex also. If you are against casual sex, come out and say it. I have no problems with it, as long as both people know it's casual sex. Having sex with a stranger isn't necessarily a dehumanizing experience. People who have been married for twenty years can have dehumanizing sex."

"These objections aren't really about D&S," Marty Klein concluded. "They're about much deeper philosophical issues, that have to do with what is sex for, what is the meaning of sex, is sex dangerous or not, is it appropriate to use sex as a vehicle for self-exploration or pleasure or transcendence? These are fundamental questions about sexuality that D&S raises for people."

EVA JOINS THE ACADEMICS

In 1994, Eva entered New York University's graduate program in Human Sexuality. She excelled in her coursework, and concentrated on nonconsensual domination, namely, sex offenders. She met Wendy Maltz at a conference, and the two of them decided to talk and further explore their areas of mutual concern.

I spoke to Wendy Maltz in April 1996 to learn how she and Eva got along. Her appreciation of consensual domination and submission had not significantly changed, although when I read her previous comments back to her, she wanted it clarified that while she wouldn't recommend it, she didn't want to cause shame or say someone was wrong. "I can't know what someone else's experience is," she said.

Maltz concentrated on what she considered a source of trauma, Eva's background. "She had early arousal patterns that established the lure of dominance, lack of protection and appropriateness, the message that a man wanted sex the woman has to give it. The cumulative effect of it was traumatic." Maltz referred to things Eva had told her about hearing her parents having sex, concluding that her father was dominant sexually over her mother. When I'd interviewed Eva on this subject, she'd told me her mother had encouraged her father to have lovers because she'd felt she was more sexually experienced. It may not have been a conventional marriage but it was consensual. Maltz believed that this background was responsible for Eva's need to dominate. Eva believed this to be an oversimplification.

As for her exposure to D&S, Wendy Maltz concentrated on the examples of heavy domination, examples of people she'd interviewed who did sessions with sewing needles and meathooks. "Excuse me if I don't applaud that. Just because people say 'I'm getting kissed or stroked while we do this,' or 'I'm chosing the power permuations now,' doesn't make it a good solution to their pain," she declared. When I asked her how she felt hearing the D&S practitioners say it was their conscious choice and they felt closer to their partners because of it, she answered, "People feel close to people they do drugs and alcohol with as well."

Ava Taurel led her clients through sessions that involved pain mixed with pleasure, pain sexualized to be attractive to them. Wendy Maltz led her patients, who came for treatment for incest and abuse, through sessions where they learned to trust touching their own and their partner's body to regain a sense of mastery and boundaries.

Maltz told of a wife who abhored kissing because the person who had abused her in childhood had insisted on kissing her. To master her fear, she sculpted a pair of lips and practiced touching them. She had control over the lips this time. Eventually she was able to enjoy kissing her husband.

Wendy Maltz wouldn't agree, but there seemed to be common ground between the sessions she did and the sessions Ava Taurel did. Ron Moglia, the head of the Human Sexuality program at New York University, called Taurel a "working, functioning therapist." Maltz told me that she admired Ava's guts in expressing a desire to address a sexology convention together with Maltz.

It was an interesting issue. What was legitimate sex work? Eva Norvind had a quality only possessed by the best people who worked in the field. It was the idea behind one of the basic training of therapists. One had to enter the fantasy world of the person they were working with, as sensitively and acutely as possible. To witness Eva's work as

Ava, the dominatrix, was to know someone who was utterly comfortable with entering another's sexual world.

A medical expert dismissively said, "You can't take a person's word if she earns a living from her sexuality." I'd asked what she meant. She said that such a person couldn't possibly be objective.

Was that the dividing line in working sex? A line the leading therapists as well as the professors and sexologists running the graduate program didn't draw? These ideals of nonpartiality and nonparticipation might be misleading. John Money, author of some of the seminal work on paraphilia, had written over 300 scientific papers and several books. He had a Ph.D.from Harvard, and received the American Psychological Association's Distinguished Scientific Award for the Applications of Psychology. He had served as president of the Society for the Scientific Study of Sex.

In his book, *Lovemaps*, Money traced the formation of lovemaps of our sexual desires on a continuum, from what we call "normal" to paraphilia. The most courageous thing this expert did was to write of his own lifelong fantasy, Acrotomophilia, otherwise known as attraction to amputees. When Money was a child, he was lonely. His parents had divorced and he and his mother lived with grandparents who'd disapproved of his parents' marriage. The grandfather died when he was six. The atmosphere was critical and without a male role model, he felt inadequate. He tried hard to excel in school. One day he heard pity being expressed for an amputee, and he thought that if he was an amputee, they would care about him.

Soon a pretty girl amputee became sexualized in his imagination, and a lifelong fantasy (Acrotomophilia is not uncommon) was created. *Lovemaps* is well worth reading to see how delicate people's psyche and sexuality are, how complex the formulation. John Money had the courage to be honest about his own sexuality. He didn't separate "work" and "sex." He wrote about his personal relationship to his sex work. It was bold humanization from one of the country's top experts.

*   *   *

Many times I'd observed while Ava worked on the phone with clients. I witnessed some of her more unusual sessions.

One client wanted a woman who was my type, classic looking, tall, someone who could project a mixture of intelligence with authority and still be accessible. He wanted to be dominated by this woman, and Ava, having established (to her dismay) that my wardrobe didn't have latex and leather, thought at least this was someone my business suits and high heels could work with. We came up with a name, Stephanie, and borrowed from part of my background to create an archivist who catalogued rare manuscript collections.

Then she told me his fantasy was to be smothered by the woman in the business suit, having her cover his face with her skirt. "But," she assured me, "you will be wearing panties and stockings, and although he wants to put his face against you while you're sitting on him, he will not be able to reach you with his mouth while you are smothering him."

"*No*," I thought immediately. A few days later I expressed my concern about the principles of reporting, of "objective journalism." I thought it best not to do the sessions, I told her.

Given the subject matter, concern over how to report was always an issue. But also an excuse. I couldn't do it. My inability revealed to me how flexible Eva needed to be. There is a gap between what professionals can accommodate intellectually and what they can actually *do*. Writers, academics, therapists . . . how many of us, I wondered, could handle both the intellectual analysis and the reality of dealing hands on with these people? The ability to do both gave Eva Norvind a huge edge in insight over the rest of the field.

"Are you being honest with yourself?" she asked me later when we discussed this separation. No, not entirely, I knew. Concentrating on maintaining my "professional" standards (distance) had kept me from the heart of the matter, what it actually took to partake.

I'd responded negatively to the idea of smothering a man with a woman's crotch, the ultimate vagina dentata enactment, man's fear of being devoured or smothered by woman. This was ancient, mythology and psychology.

I had come far enough in my understanding of D&S now to appreciate this man's sexual need. I knew that Ava would be able to act on that understanding. But I couldn't. It upset and repelled me. That was an alarm bell for me, the same way it was for Wendy Maltz. Which meant until we could meet the client (patient) on the ground they needed, we would be of little use to them. Wendy Maltz's practice was predicated on what they "should" do. Ava dealt with them on the ground of what they could and would do.

She could find love, was comfortable with even the unusual sessions to give emotional validity to the clients. She could *see* it in a way most people weren't capable of.

She also respected paraphiliac intelligence.

She read a book called *Perfume*, a bestselling novel from the late '80s.

It impressed her deeply. It's about a man from a severely impoverished background in 18th-century France who develops an ability to create perfumes that speak to any human instinct. He becomes rich and famous, but his desire to create the ultimate perfume drives him to kill a beautiful young virgin whose essence he thinks he can capture in the most perfect scent ever made.

"I related to the book," said Eva. And killing the young woman? I'd asked.

"It's horrendous," she responded, "but although he happened to kill people I would never call him a murderer. He was an artist, pursuing the essence, a soul. The body was just a carcass, an externalization. He got rid of bodies to get rid of the barrier to the soul."

"Eva, if I killed you for the same reason, would you excuse me?"

"If I go outside myself I couldn't objectively blame you," she responded. "I understand the motivation. I wonder how many killers are like that. I think it's different for a man to be searching for an essence. It's a moral judgment. Animals don't think of sin. Since I read *Perfume* I have a different view of cannibalism, and reasons for killing. In his mind, he was pure."

When I became upset with Eva it was usually because she did not make the connection between her actions and people's reaction to them, much the same as in this novel. It seemed to be the far end of the continuum, nonconsensual paraphilia, involving people who do not see the link between cause and effect in terms of moral responsibility.

She told me of a client who was into cannibal fantasies, to try to get me to see the scope of what we were discussing. "He's a very lovely old European man who likes to envision that he will roast a young woman on a spit and then eat her alive. He has a beautiful spirit. The session doesn't involve cruelty to women because he is is only talking. He wants to be lead by a dominant woman in fantasizing how to capture his prey. I would act the part of the young virgin girl by pointing to areas of my body and discussing where we would cut, and which morsels would be given at the dinner table," she explained.

She had the capacity to relate sympathetically to his decidedly odd interest. "By wanting to eat this woman's flesh, the man is sublimating the woman. He really wants to lick a woman's genitals but is much too afraid of that. Because he doesn't dare to go that far in his real life he only allows his imagination to eat the safe flesh," she said.

I asked about the devouring vagina dentata, and she concurred. "He is afraid of being devoured by women, and cannot deal with his attraction to the vagina." Her work in forensic psychology would be different, she declared. "In regular psychology you trust your client's word. Working with criminals, it's a whole other ballgame. There is so much malingering. I'll have to learn new skills."

Eva also learned that some offenders had unusual abilities. She told me that most of the offenders she worked with in prison were gifted, near genius. They were mechanical, or artistic, or they had photographic memories. Was is possible they were graced as well as cursed?

And what about herself? Eva had a mind like a vacuum. She spoke seven languages and in the past four years studied Arabic, Japanese, Swahili, and Hindi. She got her Masters in Human Sexuality and Health Education at New York University, and was pursuing another Masters in Forensic Psychology.

It seemed to me that Eva's talent and compartmentalization was similar to that of sex offenders. "I don't mean to hurt people!" she would say when she did, and I believed her by virtue of her genuine anguish upon realizing she had. I came to know another man, a gymnetophile, someone whose fantasy was the lady with a penis, or chicks-with-dicks. He was funny and creative and bright, but when he told stories, he often lost the thread. He lacked sequencing ability. "How did I get to this point?" he would ask, mystified, in the middle of a conversation.

In the early spring of 1996 Eva called, sobbing. "I've been asked to leave my internship!" she said. She read me a letter that had been written by her supervisor, a professional sexologist contracted by an East Coast prison to run their program for sex offenders. Someone had sent him a magazine article in which Eva had allowed herself to be photographed as Ava Taurel, sitting on top of a slave.

She had informed her supervisor that she had been involved in therapeutic work involving domination and submission fantasies. However, he did not know about Ava Taurel and company. I flinched hearing the anger in his letter, but I couldn't blame the man, I told her. Getting public support for in-house residency counseling programs for sex offenders was difficult enough.

Sex offenders such as pedophiles, wife beaters, and rapists do not elicit much sympathy. Lock 'em up and keep them there, is the common response. But as a corrections counselor in the New York prison system told me, eventually, the offender will be back on the street, and with nothing but jail time, likely to repeat the crime. "It's a disease," said the counselor, "the same as alcoholism or any other substance abuse." The disease is treatable, and the few prisons in the United

States that have programs for sex offenders have shown a dramatic drop in the recidivism rate of the offenses.

William Prenderghast, a psychologist and certified sex counselor, worked with sex offenders for thirty-five years. He developed and ran the first center in the country for treating sex offenders in the penal system. It became a model for other programs. His books, *Treating Sex Offenders in Corrections Centers, Not My Child,* and *The Merry-Go-Round of Sexual Abuse* are important reference works. He also works in a private practice to help victims of sex offenders. "I believe it's important to go back and forth from the abuser to the abused, so as not to become an advocate for one and lose the perspective of the other," he told me. I'd come to believe this was the blind spot in Wendy Maltz's approach. She concentrated only on the victims.

"A therapeutic community means that the offenders are in the program 24 hours a day, living, sleeping, and breathing sex offense counseling, therapy, and education," a senior corrections counselor, who supervises a similar program in a New York prison told me. "The concept is that they catch each other, assist each other in being honest, and when they do break through the denial and are crying and upset they get positive support and re-enforcement from their peers. It's a very important part of treatment, where they have to admit about their behavior to others."

After the six-week assessment and education phase the prisoners were transferred to another facility where they attended vocational classes, drug treatment, and at night had follow-up counseling, which is voluntary. New York State's corrections department studied programs from Minnesota, New Jersey, Washington, and Vermont, compiling statistics from their mandatory residential programs for sex offenders. Minnesota showed that of the people who've gone through this program, the recidivism rate (repeated sexual offenses) dropped to nine percent. Without the program, the rate is thirty-two percent. In New York state, without programs, the recidivism rate for sex offenders has been over forty percent.

"The public has such strong emotional opinions and misinformation on this subject," the corrections counselor told me. When Eva was reading me the letter, I thought of all this. Her university professors encouraged her to finish her coursework. But the issue was whether a dominatrix should be allowed to work with sex offenders. If society deemed that she shouldn't be allowed, Eva could try to hide Ava Taurel for the rest of her life. Talk about perverse.

WORKING LAW

"Did they pay you the full amount for the story you did?" Larry Levine asked me over the phone. My first New York job was during college, as a summer receptionist at his firm, Beldock, Levine, and Hoffman. They were an entertainment law firm, with clients ranging from movie stars to rock stars. Besides the entertainment and business work, the three partners were politically active, with high profile death row cases and social causes, many of which they'd supported for decades.

We'd been friends for fifteen years, and he remembered "Diary of a Dominatrix." So when he picked up his copy of *New York* magazine to find "Mean Sex," a cover story on S&M, he called.

"They paid you $2,000 out of a contract for $4,500? Why didn't you sue them for the rest?" he asked.

"Sue them?" I tried to explain to him that there aren't that many magazines, it's a small community, and suing probably would be a great way to not get work.

I remembered running into Ed Kosner on the sidewalk outside the magazine, a couple of weeks after the story I'd done for them on D&S had been killed. It was coming up on the holiday season. I was exhausted, and sick. I'd lost ten pounds working on the piece and, I was broke. Having a story killed when you make a living as a freelance writer is a blow. What I couldn't shake, because of the nature of this story, was the unpleasant feeling I'd done something weird or wrong.

Kosner and I had a hurried conversation that last day. I know he felt awkward. I remember standing there on the sidewalk, with a cold sleety snow falling.

"Let's just get this straight," Larry Levine said. "They told you they accepted it. They even asked if the woman would pose for the cover. Then they sent you out for another three weeks?"

"To interview experts. I have another 200 pages of those interviews. Then they said they couldn't run a story on this topic in the magazine."

"Well, they've come a long way, baby. How about this, from the pages of *New York*: 'A man in black leather pants whispers in her ear, whips her, and shoves a funnel-like instrument in her vagina.' And here's a reference to 'sleazy weenie-wackers,' very nice. I'll call them for you."

"They'll say they paid more than the kill fee, which would have been just a tenth of the entire fee."

"That indicates that they did something wrong. It's a partial payment. When they sent you out again, you were three-quarters of the way up the flagpole. They told you to go the rest of the way. And then after a contract exactly describing what you'd be doing, with specific legal provisions denying their responsibility if you got hurt, they claim they can't run an article dealing with what those provisions spelled out? Come on. And now they run their own article on it? I'm calling them."

I read the piece, "Mean Sex." The language was crude, they were trying to shock. They took the freak show, 'let's make fun' approach. I thought, great, this is what they finally run and even this superficial stupidity is a year and a half behind the daytime talk shows.

KIII, the parent company of *New York* and I would end up in court. It went on for the better part of a year.

"Does lawyer-client privilege mean I can tell you something I was told off the record as a journalist?" I asked Larry one day after months of thought.

"Yes. What is it?"

"Well, I'm sure Ava got a major kick out of this. She had me interview this man who was her client for five years before becoming her personal slave. He was retired, and he'd call me from phone booths. He loved to talk about his fetishes, because his wife despised them and it was the only outlet he had."

"So?"

"He was an executive at *New York* for many years. He also was interviewed for the 'Mean Sex' piece." I pulled out transcripts and tapes and showed Larry. I hadn't told anyone all this time. But in the piece they ran, he was interviewed again, with quotes that matched the ones he'd given me, and while they'd changed his retirement location, he was described as a former publishing executive.

We went over to his stereo console under Larry's fabulous collection of contemporary art, and slipped the tape in. A deep voice filled the room. While we listened, I vividly remembered my conversations with the man. He was "John," the man who'd been Eva's personal pleasure slave as well as her client, but he had left New York and Ava to retire. My heart had gone out to him. He was quite miserable hiding his sexuality, and he told me that at night his dreams of Ava haunted him. He'd said that he had not had sex with his wife in ten years. I remembered Ava's words: "It is risky to show someone who you really are. But the pain of not doing so will be greater in the end."

"I came out of the publishing business, magazine publishing in New York, forty-two years of it," the deep voice said.

On tape, I'd asked: "Did you, at one point, say, I'm going to follow my interest in this?"

"I'll tell you how it began," the voice from the stereo speakers responded, reverberating from wall to wall of the office of this senior partner of a Park Avenue law firm.

"It came out of *New York* magazine. When Murdoch bought *New York* magazine he also bought the *Village Voice*, and every week we got a copy of the *Voice*, which I'd never read. But in there, there were ads constantly for mistresses and domination. I got more and more interested in it. One day in 1980 or so, I stayed in town. I thought, I'm going down to one of these places, the one on West 19th Street. This was Club O, and the two mistresses were a couple of lesbian gals. They had quite a setup, a stage and stocks, where you put your arms and heads in, and some cross-dressing was going on. The first time I sat and observed. Next time I went down, several weeks later, I came prepared to get dressed. I wore a red rubber dress, red panties, stockings . . . ."

"Had you tried cross-dressing on your own before this?" I'd asked.

"Yes, I'd get hotel rooms and cross-dress all the time. But it wasn't satisfying because I didn't share it with anybody. I needed somebody who would not be judgmental to share it with."

"Your wife? How did she feel?"

"She knows I have a fetish and stuff like that, but she hated it. I don't blame her. So I kept it very much away from her. She's caught me a couple of times with clothing and stuff on . . . there was a scene. " He went on to speak of getting involved with Ava.

"She is the most interesting dominatrix that I've ever met, and the one I got the closest to and had the most fun with, and enjoyed being her complete . . . let's face it, I was her slave, and I mean slave, in every possible way. I got my last whipping in June 1989, when I retired."

"How often would you see Ava?" I'd asked.

"Nearly every day. I brought my car in because she ordered me to. She wanted to go here, and there. . . . She's a very demanding person, very cruel, very sadistic. She admits it. But she has a very soft, loving side, too. She's a hell of a woman. She's not like anybody you're ever going to meet again the rest of your life."

While Larry and I listened, "John" detailed how he would handle his job at *New York* while seeing Ava. Larry raised his eyebrows. "Why do I get the feeling this wasn't the best-kept secret in town?" he asked.

"Hang on," I said, fast-forwarding to later in the interview.

His voice resumed: "I appeared on *The Morton Downy, Jr. Show* with Ava."

I asked if he was concerned about being recognized at his job.

"Myself and another fellow were behind a screen, so they never even saw us, I was Mr. Y and he'd ask questions . . . I brought Eva into the office one day and introduced her to a couple of people and a secretary, an assistant to our promotion director, nice little gal. A week or two later she said, 'Were you ever on television? *The Morton Downey Show?*' I asked, 'Why do you say that?' She said, 'I recognized your friend who was here the other day. And I thought that was you.' "

"I said, 'Listen, do you think you can keep your mouth shut?' and she said yes, so I said, 'All right, listen, I was there, just to have some fun.' She said, 'Okay. Holy cow.' "

"I'll bet she didn't tell a soul," Larry said.

"Secretary to the promotion director? Of course not."

"Okay, here's what we do," said Larry, scribbling notes on a brief. "We subpoena Kurt Anderson, Ed Kosner, your editor who worked on the story, their editor who worked on this story. You tell your story, just as it happened, play that tape, and let the judge decide."

"But you can sit in court for hours, for weeks and months, before getting to see the judge," I said.

Larry looked up from his writing. "Good."

*   *   *

New York magazine and I came to a settlement. I got money. And satisfaction after all.

I had a lot of time to think in court about domination and submission. How do you explore subjects as complex and loaded as these, in the limited space provided by magazines, newspapers, and broadcast outlets? And yet, if we don't try, will we keep having the same pseudo debates about castration for rapists, or comforting illusions like Megan's law? Megan's Law, named after a little girl who was murdered by a sex offender, concerns the registration and notification to a community in which offenders move in to. I could well understand the emotion in the public's demand for such laws. Solutions like this were considerably more popular than the confusing questions about working with sex offenders in the prison system. But what would be more effective, and more protection, ultimately? Complex problems called for complex analysis and discussion. It had to start somewhere.

I didn't care if I lost the case. I just wanted to hear myself tell a judge that is was more important to try to tell a complex story then simplify it into a freak show.

Robert Stoller, M.D., was one of the writers about sex I learned the most from. He believed that society needed perversion. What he wrote about families reminded me of how the people I worked with at magazines, who made money from sex, couldn't see their connection to the people involved in D&S, who also made money from sex.

"Scapegoating helps many families, who choose one member to serve as the 'sick' or 'evil' one, allowing projection to protect the other members as individuals as well as the whole family as a unit. Once this is done, parents can live out some of their perverse wishes in the chosen child."

"A constant threat to perversion's smooth functions is the perverse person and his paranoia. He who breaks the rules by refusing to play the part of pervert as written in society's mores and sanctions—who rebels against his assignment and will not help his neighbor by being clown and victim—may in time force social change, if not downright revolution."

WORKING TO MAKE SENSE

Eva and I continued to talk through the winter and spring of 1996, when she got her degree. The issue of whether or not the former Ava Taurel would be permitted to work with sex offenders continued to haunt her. The issue of writing a letter in support of her continued to confound me.

"Eva, I think you are one of the smartest women I have ever met. I believe you know more about paraphilia than anyone in psychological and sexological fields. But every time I come to believe in you, something happens where I find myself doubting you. It's basic human conduct where you lose me."

She asked what I meant, and I went over the numerous times where her need for dominance resulted in crossing over the boundaries of everyday social interaction. In our relationship, as in many of her relationships, it had continued to the present day, and it filled me with trepidation. I also knew she was one of the most unconventional people that most of those working in her field would meet. Her honesty about her life and things she did would work against her. I knew, as did her academic advisors, that her understanding of unusual sexuality was deeper and more complex than most people in the field. Unlike the majority of professionals, her understanding didn't come from mere analysis, but from embracing a much larger sexual spectrum.

I told her, "I want to stand behind you in getting support for your work. But I hesitate when I think of writing a letter to all the top experts in your field when I realize if I was to tell the truth, I'd be saying, 'She's one of the most knowledgeable people in this area. Never mind the way she acts.' Eva, what can I do? You are the most disturbing person in my book."

If I'd said it to anyone else they wouldn't speak to me. They'd get upset. They'd hang up. They'd deny it. Not her.

"Oh, Marianne, you are so right," she sighed soberly. "It's like that time in the restaurant when you spoke to me for making you wait. You were so right then. It is me."

"You want me to recommend you to work with sex offenders. People who have trouble with impulse control. Lack of impulse control is your middle name. What do I do?"

"I've thought of this a great deal. I do not want to be a therapist. I want to work as a team with a therapist," Eva said. "My insight with the supervision of a trained psychologist would work. But I don't want to do it on my own, for many reasons, among them what you said. But what I have to offer is invaluable."

"I believe you. But you make it so hard to vouch for you. Eva, I know you're the best person to do this work, but you come with all the problems of the very people that only you can reach. How can I write a recommendation for you when I know this is true?"

"You could write it just the way you said it," she suggested.

*   *   *

In May 1996, Eva graduated with her Masters from New York University's Human Sexuality Department. She is pursuing a second Masters in Forensic Psychology, which she should have in 1998. After that she plans to go to Europe to study clinical psychology. She has been invited to speak at a number of international conferences on sexuality. She wants to publish on related topics, especially consensual and non-consensual paraphilias, as well as eventually starting a non-profit clinic.

Her slave, Carrie, is still working at the Taurel Institute and doing sessions with clients. D., Eva's longtime friend, the person who introduced her to D&S, is there as well. Eva and Gerard are still together. "Peace and cooperation are the most important things to me now," Eva says.

6

Sex and Transsexualism: Sexual Dysphoria and Societal Dysphoria

WORKING THE PROGRAM

"What a good-looking guy," was the first thought that occurred to me. Handsome, in his thirties, his neatly tapered brown hair accentuated classic bone structure. He looked very Metro North, a fellow you'd see in an expensive raincoat over a business suit in Grand Central Station, reading the *Wall Street Journal* on the way to a home cooled by emerald trees and lawn, Connecticut Cheever style. He moved his newspaper to make room for me, giving a slight smile. His presence was a mix of Waspy coolness and a physical energy warm as musk.

I was in a Seattle-style coffee shop in New York City, reading about a Sexual Attitude Reassessment weekend being offered by a sexologist. The material described SARs as valuable for people who worked in fields related to sexuality. The workshop would be a forum for people to understand their hidden preconceptions and biases related to sex. If one planned to do work involving sex, those attitudes would limit comprehension and empathy. A SAR is when you consider how you consider sex.

My life had turned into a little SAR this particular week. A short while ago, I'd met my neighbor, Sue. Every day for the past year, I'd see from a distance this same woman leaning over a Chevy van engine, tinkering. She was tall, with long thick hair nearly to her waist, big breasts, slender, with muscular legs. She looked like an outdoors person, a kayaker or camper.

I'd gone to the store and for the first time, walked within a couple of feet from the van woman. I did a double take.

She was unusually attractive, her face smooth planes and pretty huge blue eyes. But there was something about her. I don't know what made me realize that the girl next door in Chelsea had once been a man. She smiled at me, and like a chimera, male/female flashed in both smiles. You could see she was a beautiful woman. You could see she'd been a sexy man. She had crackling energy, and walked down the street waving to neighbors. She straightened her short shorts with a provocative gesture and went inside.

That night Sam, one of the livelier elevatormen in my building, caught me. Sam was the one who answered questions like, yes, we have had jumpers from the roof of the building. This one guy found he had terminal cancer, and jumped from the seventeenth floor. Only he chose the garden courtyard so on the way down he hit the wall and was decapitated. Some poor guy on the second floor came home from work that night and turned on his lights and found the head staring at him from his windowsill. He ran out the door and never came back. Someone moved his stuff a couple of months later. "I don't know why the guy picked the courtyard side instead of the street," Sam sighed. "Some people just want to make a statement."

"Okay, now what are you doing?" he called, leaning against the doorway, catching a breeze from the Hudson. I'd nonchalantly tried to peer in my neighbor's windows and nonchalantly fallen off the curb. It was time to utilize other resources for neighborhood intelligence gathering.

"Sam, the woman across the street, with the long brown hair and the blue eyes, the one who fixes the van every day . . . is she . . . She seems. . . ."

"She's a transsexual," Sam nodded. "She's been on Howard Stern. I saw her on the show. Matter of fact, I think she was on a couple of times. Maybe she'd talk to you about it."

Later, Sue said that you have thirty seconds to decide when you meet someone if you like them or not. She was kind enough to shut off the motor the next day when I came up and introduced myself, lowered the hood of the van, and invited me to pull up a spot on the curb to chat. She agreed to discuss her life, and wanted to talk about things she thought the public didn't understand about gender dysphoria, which is what someone who is born as one genetic sex but goes through life feeling that he or she was meant to be the opposite sex, experiences. Sue had done interviews before, and believes that educating the public "is part of my life's mission." That afternoon we continued the mission. I realized from the beginning with her that I would have to try to sympathetically understand the process transsexuals underwent to change sex.

And now, some months later, I was in the coffee shop waiting to go to my first transsexual support group meeting. There are many such groups throughout the United States. "Support groups are important for a person who is considering transition. They can explore their options in a supportive atmosphere with people going through the same thing," Sue explained. Having talked to Sue and friends of hers for some time, I wondered what a support group would be like. Sue's group had established their new gender identities some ten years earlier. Support groups more often are for relative newcomers who need to deal with the problems posed by their changing lives.

I looked at the clock and saw the meeting would begin in five minutes. Crumpling the coffee cup, I took one more look at the handsome guy reading the *Wall Street Journal*. I wondered what he'd think if he knew where I was going. An hour later when it was his turn to speak and the first thing he said was, "Hi, I'm Alan, I'm a woman," I realized he probably wouldn't be too judgmental.

* * *

The clock hums on, twenty-five long minutes past the time the meeting was scheduled to start. Everyone has surreptitiously studied everyone by filing numerous quick glances. Right next to me is a big blond girl, maybe in her thirties, thick legs, and wide pink lips. She is pretty; her bangs and braids make her look Dutch. For the first few years, people who plan to make a sex change start living as the opposite sex. The term for this period is transition. Some of the women, like this one, look as if they'd always been the sex they are now. A pretty woman named Rosemary, with soft rounded baby doll cheeks and chin and a softer, fuller body, and another woman on my right, an exotic, sexy, dark Mediterranean beauty, both look like they were born women.

Others appear as if they were in the process. "It happens to all of us," Sue had told me. "You haven't learned to move, to act, to be. For the first few years, you look as if you're cross-dressing." About six or eight of the others still had that look.

"Is our monitor coming at all?" The question is from a pale, almost librarianish male-to-female transsexual, with a slender face. She is dressed in hose, flat shoes, conservative skirt, and white blouse. Kate, the Dutch-looking blond, rummages for her program notes. A friend next to her wears sheer stockings and high heels, but has a deep, recognizably male voice that makes it a little tough for her to pass. The two of them are funny. "Wrong notes, Kate," she says, looking at the paper she'd been handed.

"Oh, no. That's my Overeater's Anonymous card!" Kate laughs. "I'm on the circuit!"

After a few others come in, someone reads the group's statement of purpose, which is to function as a twelve-step support group to defeat shame over being transsexual. Silence falls again, then the meeting begins.

The first person to talk (or in the jargon to "share") is a Japanese male-to-female transsexual, who speaks in a monotone for a very long time. It seems she doesn't know where to end and might not. She talks for over thirty minutes nonstop, but no one hurries her. The people in the circle give sympathetic nods and encouraging smiles. She says she was born of German and Japanese parents in Japan during World War II. "Japanese culture makes my condition very unacceptable," she said, "I was born a hermaphrodite, but because I am very beautiful I decided to have surgery to be a woman." She goes on to speak of getting a Ph.D in mathematics, of coming to the United States and working at New York University where she fell in love, but the person she loved died six years ago, and now she only has her two cats. She says she is glad to be able to come here to speak to people who understand because she is depressed. She winds down rather than stops speaking.

Kate is next. She recalls her surgery a year ago, and the fight to not abuse alcohol, the loneliness of carving out a new life and the difficulty of finding acceptance.

"Sometimes I don't know if I'm a man or a woman. I know that sounds strange, but I feel both ways. I look at the world as if I'm both. Sometimes I don't think that's bad. It's as if the best of these two worlds are running in me all the time. My feelings want to burst out of me." Her voice is singsong, happy.

Kate sweeps her hair from her face and leans forward. "I feel as if . . . I feel as if I'm in love. I feel so much love that I feel pregnant with it. I want to have a baby. I can't believe it's impossible when I feel this strongly, when I want it this much. I can't believe I don't have ovaries. Until they do an autopsy on me and prove it, I won't believe it. I feel them. I feel as if I could be pregnant, and I know who I want to make me pregnant but that's another story. . . ." She blushes.

There is no doubting the intensity of her words. The sweetness of her expression, and the feelings of a woman in love and wanting to love come through. She means it. She feels it. The woman's magazines have made an industry of falling in love, marriage, babies. *Mademoiselle*, *Cosmopolitan*, *Bride* . . . . Kate, like most women, is not immune to the message.

"Sometimes I fantasize about stealing a baby," she murmurs. "But it would hurt the mother too much, so I'd never inflict that pain. But you know how in New York you hear about drug addicts trying to sell their babies? I'd do that. Buy one. I feel as if I have so much love I'm going to explode."

This meeting showed me the dichotomy faced by transsexuals. By observing what the people who want to change sex experience, you realize how many ways sexual identities affect us, both organically and as societal constructs. A male-to-female (m-t-f) transsexual named Kelly, who ran a support hotline in Atlantic City for people in transition, gave me poems written by Kara, a m-t-f transsexual friend of hers. The poems offered agonized laments over the lack of a menstrual cycle, over self-respect, of wishing to go shopping for lingerie and be accepted as a woman, about loving high-heeled shoes, about shaving her legs and chest hair, about envying girls who look great in jeans.

She wrote musingly about wanting to trust people who seem understanding, but she was afraid of being condemned. People say, I know you, she wrote. But if they *really* knew you, what would they do?

The people in the support group meeting understand the complexity they face. Kate's friend, who says her name is Robin, gives a long sigh before she speaks. "What intense things, Kate wanting a baby," she says sympathetically. She looks over at the Japanese transsexual. "What I really found amazing about your story wasn't that you were born a hermaphrodite, but that you're a math Ph.D."

She crosses one leg over another. There's something remarkable about her appearance, backed by her measured, determined speech. She's wearing an orange silk blouse and a dark wool work skirt, nylons, heels. Her hair and her makeup make her look like she's metamorphasizing, as if this moment is one frame in a strip of film recording her changing. You can still see edges of the man she was before. Watching her in this moment reenforces the individuality of human beings, the extent of each person's potential evolution.

Robin speaks of having a dysfunctional family out West that is in a moment of crisis. "I'm processing my anger at them. They don't know about me, the voice on the phone sounds the same, so when I say there's been a lot of changes in my life . . . !" She punctuates by crossing her nylon-sheathed legs. ". . . they're left with the illusion that I'm the same person!" She pauses and continues, saying her family was not there for her when she was in her sex-change crisis. Now, however, they need her support because a sibling is in trouble.

The language is the kind of pop-psychology speak people invariably adopt in these groups. Saying "processing anger" instead of "I'm mad," and "dysfunctional" instead of "fucked up," is a way of dealing with emotion by making it a separate entity. "I want to be further along," Robin says, firmly. "For them. And for myself. I want to be beyond anger and shame." She hesitates and her body telegraphs all she's holding in, the tension and pain. Then she relaxes. "That's all," she says.

"Thanks for sharing," the circle of people murmur.

"Getting beyond all the anger is important. I work at it all the time," says the slim, olive-skinned woman next to me.

"Last Saturday night my neighbor was waiting on the landing for me, drunk again, calling me names. He followed me and hit me. It all ended with the police being called," she relates. "They said to me, 'this isn't the first time. Why are these incidents happening to you?' I responded, 'Maybe it's because I'm a transsexual.'" She rolls her eyes. "Before I did a lot of growing I don't think I could have admitted it. I mean, the average man doesn't get the whole concept. You'd voluntarily cut your wee-wee off?! I'm past the point of caring about what they think. But it took a long time."

"And there's always some threat you'll get hit with prejudice from some angle you weren't expecting," says the slender, librarianish blond.

Her company had been sold, and they'd told her that her job wouldn't be threatened. She raises her eyebrows with a "We'll see!" gesture.

"Same in my personal life," she continues. "I'm dating this man who seems very sweet. I like him so much that I know it would really hurt if something went wrong with the relationship. We've been together for a few months. He knows about me, and he sees me as a woman. But I'm having trouble with something now. He's entered therapy to resolve some complications in his relationship with his family, and he's gone back in his past and is dealing now with all these things that he experienced as an adolescent boy. When he tells his stories, my heart goes out to him. But I've found myself biting my tongue to keep from blurting out, 'Oh, God, I know exactly how you feel! The same thing happened to me when I was that age!' I mean, I don't want to freak him out. He knows I had a sex change, but we relate to each other as man and woman. If I open the part of me that was a male to him, it might scare him off completely. It scares me, it's very complicated. I identify with his experiences so much, but it could be a tremendous problem. This is something I'm trying to sort out right now."

"Thanks for sharing," everyone says. People consider these stories silently for a few moments. Then the guy from the coffee shop introduces himself as "Hi, I'm Alan, I'm a woman."

Alan tells his story. He had a nervous breakdown four years ago when he realized that he was a female in a male body, but now he was ready to deal with his life change. "I know I have a heavy beard and a deep voice, but I'm a woman, I feel at peace with that now," he said. He speaks of admiring the younger people in the room, who could deal with their sex change ten years before he could face it. He spoke of getting ready to begin his process, of knowing what he would go through to change his sex. He thanked the group for their support and inspiration. "I'm hearing myself in everyone tonight."

One person, whose transition lies like two photo negatives laid on top of each other, introduces herself. Her evolving female identity is a very 1970s-looking woman, with low slung jeans over skinny hips and legs, a maroon V-necked sweater revealing large braless breasts, long straight hair, tweezed brows, and dark lipstick. She still looks like a male with cosmetic additions that haven't been smoothed over yet, and when she speaks, the voice is that of a guy from Brooklyn, which she says she's working on. "I was a cop, and I come from a family of cops," she says. "Believe me, in my family, this was a hard change to make. I don't have much to say, just that I feel for everyone here who's gone through the tough stuff. If it helps, the more you let parts of yourself out, the better it feels."

"I'm having a hard time right now, I have to say," says the person sitting next to the former cop. Her face and voice are still recognizable as those of a young man, not thirty years old. Her hair color doesn't match her sideburns and she has not yet begun electrolysis. She is not a person with a light beard.

"I was set off by a pronoun today, because someone at work called me 'he,'" she says unhappily. "I thought, what's the damned point of shaving and plucking my eyebrows, doing the makeup to fix my face, if someone takes one look and says, 'he.' It's only a pronoun, but it's really about the fact I see myself as a woman and the world doesn't. I'm very cerebral and I can keep my mind aloft, but it got me." There's a long silence. She finishes by saying in a noncommittal tone, "I'm not thinking of the 'S' word."

The expressions that are telegraphed across the room are instant and sensitive. Thinking about how you're not thinking about suicide means you're thinking about it, they know. Alan leans toward her and squeezes her shoulder. In a few minutes when the meeting breaks up, two people immediately come over and engage her in deep conversation.

Now nearly everyone in the room has spoken. Two people glance at me. Robin and Kate, acting as leaders, glance about the room. "Does anyone else want to share?" Robin asks. Now several people look at me. The silence goes on.

"Well, then, will the people who have not shared tonight please help us close the group with the Serenity Prayer?" Robin asks. The group rises to its feet and everyone looks to me.

I've drawn a blank. Serenity Prayer? "Oh, God," I mutter. My hands are clasped on each side as the circle forms, and then everyone is saying the next words, "Please give me the courage to change the things I can change, the strength to live with the things I can't, and the wisdom to know the difference." Next other hands take mine while another invocation fills the room, "Keep coming back, it works if you work it!" I slip out quietly. Over my shoulder, I see people hugging each other with caring expressions on their faces.

FORGING A NEW SCIENCE

When Christine Jorgensen died in 1989, her obituary in *The New York Times* ran with before and after photographs, captioned, "George Jorgensen, Jr., in 1943 and Christine Jorgensen in 1953, a year after undergoing the first sex-change operation." George's portrait was a straightforward solemn headshot of a fair-haired young man with fine features and big ears who looked a bit like Lee Harvey Oswald. Christine's was of a smiling glamorous woman, with a patterned scarf, fur hat, and glittering earrings. "Christine Jorgensen, 62, Is Dead; Was First to Have a Sex Change," observed the headline.

> "George Jorgensen shocked the world in 1952 by undergoing surgery in Denmark to become a woman," read the body of the obituary, after observing Jorgensen had died of cancer and that the actress Dorothy Lamour had sent her condolences. "The woman who left the Copenhagen operating room was an instant celebrity."
>
> "Her notoriety," the *Times* continued, "took her on the lecture and nightclub circuit. She met royalty and celebrities and ended up with enough money, jewels, and furs to live a comfortable life."

The New York Times restrained itself from adding that Christine Jorgensen had lived happily ever after.

When his work with transsexuals was just starting, Dr. Harry Benjamin, at age sixty-seven, was five years older than Christine Jorgenson was when she died. Harry Benjamin lived to be over 101 years old, and Christine Jorgensen was one of the people who spoke (albeit over the telephone) at his memorial service in 1986. At that same service, Dr. Leah Cahan Schaefer, who, with Dr. Connie Christine Wheeler, became the keeper and archivist of his 1,500 patient medical files, pointed out that Harry Benjamin had urged Christine Jorgensen to make herself available to those trying to provide information on transsexualism. "Benjamin realized even then the importance of networks and support systems," Schaefer said.

It wasn't through a directory that I found "the architect of hope" and "persistent pioneer," although it would have taken about thirty seconds in the Sexuality Information and Education Council of the United States (SIECUS) library, to locate Harry Benjamin's name. No, the people who called him mentor, Leah Schaefer and Dr. Charles

Ihlenfeld, were the doctors of transsexuals I met. The others who spoke when he died, like John Money, Richard Green, Ira Pauly, became important sexologists, researchers, and writers. All were colleagues of the man who first recognized and treated transsexuals. Benjamin was a man of science who had an ability to listen and the courage to experiment based on what he heard. His first patients, Renee Richards and Christine Jorgensen, became famous. The transsexuals I met all remembered hearing about these original cases and thinking that when they grew up, they too would get a sex change.

Albert Ellis and Harry Benjamin were the founding fathers of the oldest (est. 1954) sexological organization in the United States, the Society for the Scientific Study of Sex. Ellis credited Benjamin with being one of the first people in his field to defend the rights of prostitutes.

In 1966 Harry Benjamin coauthored the earliest serious book on transsexualism, *The Transsexual Phenomenon*. "The book gave patients their first ray of hope and taught many professionals their first lessons in gender identity," said psychiatrist Charles Ihlenfeld.

Renee Richards recounted at Benjamin's memorial in 1986 that she had been traveling every day to New York to be psychoanalyzed by "the most significant Freudian psychoanalyst in New York City . . . I'd lie on the couch and he sat behind me, blowing cigar smoke in my face. I became agitated, realizing I was not going to be helped by my analysis. I announced I was leaving to consult Dr. Harry Benjamin. Well, that was a bad word in Freudian circles in those days and I was warned that all kinds of terrible things would happen to me if I did so."

Richards was impressed with how respectfully the physician treated him. Dr. Benjamin sent Richards to his associate Wardell Pomeroy, who did tests using Kinsey's Scale of sexuality and found Richards ranked low on the homosexual scale. "It gave people a lot of pause to think of a transsexual whose previous history had been primarily heterosexual," recounted Richards.

"But it didn't put off Dr. Benjamin because he was beginning to understand that there did not have to be this link between the homosexual scale and true transsexualism."

Harry Benjamin formed a new comprehensive scale on which a transsexual or transgendered person could be measured. That scale allowed for complexities that aren't generally understood even today.

The Harry Benjamin scale listed a range of classifications of transsexual and transgendered behaviors. Benjamin distinguished between transsexualism and transvestism, which is to say, people who cross-dressed. He pointed out that even in this category, there was a wide range, with some people dressing for comfort, some for sexual arousal, some for relief of role anxiety. Benjamin recognized that characteristics were complex and did not necessarily remain static. "All kinds of combinations may exist and no two cases are ever alike," he wrote.

Benjamin came to see that transsexuals were people who wanted to change their sex, who believed their bodies were an accident. As Renee Richards had pointed out, their gender role and their sexual preference could be two very different things. Benjamin referred to Kinsey's landmark *Sexual Behavior of the Human Male*, saying that the term homosexuality was misleading when applied exclusively to transsexuals, "since only fifty percent of the population is exclusively heterosexual throughout its adult life, and since only four percent is exclusively homosexual throughout its life, it appears that nearly one half (forty-six percent) of the population engages in both heterosexual and homosexual activities or reacts to persons of both sexes in the course of their adult lives."

The point Benjamin made was that the term "bisexual" could be applied to the forty-six percent. Through his interviews, he knew that his patients had different sexual orientations and that those orientations could change, just like nontranssexual people.

"Harry Benjamin heard old voices giving new utterances to an ancient complaint," Leah Schaefer and Christine Wheeler wrote. It was "a condition that had prevailed throughout history but which had precious few tellers and no listeners, and no treatment. Harry Benjamin alone listened and was inspired and compelled to journey into a unique new discipline . . . gender dysphoria, that is, a discomfort with gender."

"It does seem crazy when you think about it first," Dr. Charles Ihlenfeld told me. From 1969 to 1975, Dr. Ihlenfeld worked with Harry Benjamin's practice, doing follow-ups on the endocrine systems of people who wanted sex changes. The experience made him interested in what motivated people to act as they do, so Dr. Ihlenfeld did a second medical residency in psychiatry. Twenty-six years later, he still sees some of the original patients from Benjamin's office.

He said, "I can understand why people feel threatened by the idea of the surgery, breasts and genitals removed. For me, the proof came with working with hundreds of people over years." Like Harry Benjamin, Charles Ihlenfeld discovered that for the most part after treatment, "People turned out to be happier and really functioned as more productive human beings and experienced less conflict."

"Benjamin's earliest patients came to him *self-diagnosed*," Drs. Schaefer and Wheeler wrote in a historical review of Harry Benjamin's first ten cases. Nobody had ever heard of "gender dysphoria," and yet, here were people who reported that since they were children, they thought they were born the wrong sex. The first ten patients reflected a wide range of patterns, from the intellectual transvestite Doris, whose years of correspondence with Benjamin provided tremendous insight into the condition and who had the sophistication to discuss related ideas with him, to the married couple Carol and Christian, sent by Alfred Kinsey to Harry Benjamin in 1949. They were both only children who married each other twice, the second time after they had sex change operations reversing their birth gender. "Carol and Christian had remarried each other by the time Benjamin had met them, and for both he remained the overseer of their hormone treatment for the rest of their lives; he was also their guide and advisor about all medical and psychological problems," reported Schaefer and Wheeler.

THE OPPOSITION

In 1979, the Harry Benjamin Association drew up Standards of Care that are, as Alice Webb, the current association president describes, "set up to protect the consumer against quackery and unethical behavior in treatment, such as price gouging and terrible surgery." The Standards' recommendations, Webb allows, are not legally binding but in the case of a lawsuit, it would be important to determine if they'd been used. The Standards call for a period of three months during which the patient lives full time as the opposite sex before commencing hormone therapy, six months before nongenital surgery (breasts, face, etc.) and twelve months before genital sex reassignment surgery. Letters of recommendation from a psychologist or psychiatrist who has known the patient for at least three months are suggested.

A number of people have written opposing sex reassignment surgery, among them Janice Raymond, whose 1979 book, *The Transsexual Empire: The Making of the She-Male* argued that the modern treatment of transsexualism through surgical alteration of gender was a creation of the medical-psychiatric empire that re-enforced sex roles. Vern and Connie Bullough, who wrote, *Cross Dressing, Sex, and Gender*, point out that Raymond's discussion of transsexual surgery as the consequence of a patriarchal society and her declaration that the surgical transformation is the ultimate step in continuing male domination over the female, "ignores entirely the growing number of female-to-male transsexuals."

Harold Leitenberg is director of the Ph.D. program in clinical psychology at the University of Vermont, as well as the director of the Behavior Therapy and Psychology Center there. Like Raymond, he also believes that gender identity confusion is a form of sex role stereotyping. The very title of Leitenberg's *Transsexuality: The Epitome of Sexism and Homosexual Denial*, provides a clear indication of his position on the issue.

Leitenberg argues that according to rigid definitions of appropriate masculine and feminine behavior, the child concludes he must be a girl, that his outward body appearance is a cruel mistake. "But is this conviction really anything more than a delusional rationalization of an extreme preference for one sex over another?" he asks.

"Furthermore, if transsexuals have homosexual urges (and they usually do) these are denied as being truly homosexual because the male-to-female transsexual wants to be loved not as a male by another male but as a female by a male (and vice versa)." "But once again," Leitenberg continues, "is this really anything more than another rationalization, a denial of homosexual feeling?"

Working on this book, I've found that the people who are actually involved in doing the things written, argued, and legislated about can illustrate complexities that the most dedicated academic, lawyer, or psychologist cannot. Theory is different than practice. I thought Leitenberg's arguments were compelling. And then I met Sue, Kim, and people involved with their work.

MISTRESS SUZI REFUTES LEITENBERG

"If you're attractive to people, you're attractive to people," Sue snorted impatiently. " 'Homosexual denial'?! Deny what?" I was reading her sections from Harold Leitenberg's work. "I've always had the luxury of being attractive to both sexes, no matter what sex I was," she continued. "I really couldn't care less. I make love to a *person*. I gave up those preconceptions a very long time ago."

Being in Sue's apartment across the street from mine had become a metaphor for expanding parameters, in much the way that she could instantly change the space by moving sheets of plywood and black drapes and blinking strings of tiny Christmas lights. She lived alone, except for a constant stream of clients, friends, and B.C. (Boat Cat), a fluffy white feline who was a kitten back when Sue had sold her film production company for a quarter of a million dollars, bought a sailboat, and sailed for several years.

When we'd first talked, I'd jotted down my phone number on a Salvador Dali postcard from the Metropolitan Museum of Art. A few hours later we ran into each other on our street and she handed me a documentary film about restoring Dali prints.

I watched it that night. The preservation work was revealed as artistry, and then the artist's works were used to show the inspiration driving the preservationists. There were melting objects at wave's edges in the desert, body parts floating like wild dreams. Seeing frame after frame of Salvador Dali, the surrealist who showed us that things weren't only what they seemed, was the perfect start to knowing Sue.

The next day, Sue showed me photographs of Bob, her incarnation as a male. One thing that never changed was the gorgeous blue eyes. One photograph showed Bob smiling, shirt open, his body muscular and lithe. Another shot captured him looking like a rock star with long hair and wearing bell bottoms. Robert M. was the son of a Canadian radiologist, and grew up well off. In the '60s, he was a silver medalist on the Canadian, then the United States ski team.

He studied photography at the Brooks Institute in Santa Barbara, California, where he married and lived for some years. In the mid-'70s, he was a commercial and architectural photographer in London, and a member of the Royal Photographic Society. He moved from there to Toronto, where he started the first company that offered slide-to-film or slide-to-video transfer.

"The whole '60s thing was very freeing," Sue said. "I was at Haight Ashbury in '67. I'd gone to art college in 1965, and in 1966 I'd done acid with Ram Dass and Richard Alpert at UCLA, when the LSD experiments were happening. I think it was there that my "male" sexuality and socialization took a beating. I was never the same again."

"How so?" I asked.

"If you talk to someone who knew me as a guy, my opinion of what I think of as lovemaking now is probably not that different. I was never penile oriented. The idea of 'bouncy bouncy and come' wasn't the highest thing on my mind. To me, making love to a person meant making love to a person. Sex as a male and sex as I am now is probably not that different."

"What does that mean?"

"What's the biggest part of sex?" she asked, shaking her long hair out. "Body contact and friction. Is the actual penetration the best or most significant part of sex? Yes, it feels good, but so does being held, being close. When you split the sensation of penetration out, it's not that big a deal."

"That bears out what people who are treating patients for sexual dysfunction say," I answered. "Practically the first thing therapists do is to stop the couple from having intercourse because they've become so goal and orgasm oriented that they're numb. They get them back to sensate focus, learning how to touch again, go slow, feel things."

"Exactly!" Sue exclaimed triumphantly. "Men lose all the fun in sex. They forget it's more than sticking their penis in a hole."

She noticed me looking at the picture of Bob and declared that she much prefers to be a woman, because she wouldn't trade the sexual experiences.

"I don't think the excitement as a woman is as high, but with a guy it goes up and BOOM and drops down flat. Whereas as a woman it lasts so much longer and is so much nicer. Men get cheated. You grow up around locker rooms and the superior person is the one with the big penis. Shucks, who really cares. I'd never want the sensation of male sex again. Male conditioning is why there are so many dissatisfied women out there. Men think sex is having an erection and coming. Speed and lack of sensitivity during penetration ruins sex for women more than any other thing."

I had many, many questions to ask about her transsexualism, but I found myself distracted by how she made a living. Sue was in the fantasy business. She advertised as "Mistress Suzi," and did sessions in her apartment as a therapist and fantasist for people exploring gender issues. Her apartment was a stage set, with curtains, blinking lights, lighted mirrors, and photographs of Sue as Suzi in many different erotic costumes, varying wigs, corsettes and garter belts and stockings, high heels, bustiers . . . there were a lot of Suzi personas to choose from.

She didn't do just domination and submission, and she didn't do plain transsexual prostitution. "I'll take you to the clubs and explain that whole scene to you," she offered, "but my clients are more interested in a specialty based on my experience." Mistress Suzi did unique sex work.

She was sexually and intellectually fascinated by role-playing and what she called psychodrama, because after all, huge parts of her life have consisted of living very different roles.

A lot of transsexual prostitution was fairly straightforward, Sue explained. The sexologist John Money had used the term gynemimetophile, to describe a person who enjoyed sex with a lady with a penis. "That's why if you open a copy of *Screw* magazine and check out the ads for chicks-with-dicks it gives you how many inches the length is and a picture of the pre-op transsexual prostitute. Aesthetics and size are important to the client."

"The last thing you want, if you're a true transsexual, is to go screw someone," Sue explained. "The idea of having a penis and having sex with someone while being in the masculine role and claiming you're a woman is bizarre to me. My head goes, whewwwwwwww!"

"But you're . . . ."

"I'm chemically castrated," Sue said. "I never had the surgery. I'm pre-op."

"You still have your. . . ."

"Yep."

"But you live as a woman."

"You got it." For years, having the surgery was a burning concern. Then as she'd relaxed with herself and her new identity, she started thinking. If she was enjoying sex the way things were, why spend $20,000 for another organ? She had male lovers, female lovers, and neither she nor they were overly concerned by Sue's genital construction. On the Harry Benjamin scale, she was in the mid range.

"Remember when you said that in the '60s you didn't have a strong sense of yourself as strictly male? Why couldn't you allow yourself the sexual range without having to change into a woman?"

Sue sighed. Her life's mission of enlightening the world wasn't going to be easy. "It wasn't a conscious thing," she said slowly. "I slipped into it from the time I was very young. My family was well-to-do and shipped me to a psychiatrist, and in those days, there was no knowledge. They'd say, 'Don't think about it. It'll go away.' Well, that doesn't work for someone who suffers from gender dysphoria. I identified with being a woman, do you see?"

"I've been on hormones for years. I had plastic surgery for the face, and I augmented the boobs, even though I had fairly decent ones from the hormones. But for any transsexual, once you get your identity and the satisfaction of the role, that's what it's about. The physical modifications are one part, but for me, the difference was changing the hormones in my body. Estrogen therapy made me happy with my mind, it made me feel what being a woman is."

For Sue, this brought a big change in how she thought. "It was the greatest education of my life. I was a terribly arrogant male. I constantly tried to prove myself. I was blind as sin until society started treating me the way I had treated women. I found out what it was like to think, 'He doesn't care about me! He's not even looking in my eyes, he's looking down my dress!' "

"This is still more of a consciousness thing, isn't it?"

"Yeeeesssss. But the hormones had a tremendous emotional effect on me. I felt at peace."

Charles Moser is a sexologist and internist. A lot of his medical practice involves hormonal treatment of transsexuals. He explained to me that his patients feel they were born into the wrong body, and no matter what they do, it doesn't feel right. "Now, something they desired occurs. We let them into a program where there's some feminization (in the case of male-to-female) of their bodies. These people are orgasmic over this. I mean that literally and figuratively. It's like a high school girl with her first evening gown; it's an orgasmic thing. A whole body orgasm."

I asked Dr. Moser how that worked. "Do hormones influence behavior and feeling?" he repeated. "Yes. The difficult question is, we don't know how. We don't know all that hormones do, or exactly how the changing of hormones affects people. It's obviously got a psychological component." He said that psychology was a young science. "We have a lot of questions and not enough data. And we're in a very repressed period in this country and the idea of spending money on sex research has been anathema to politicians."

However it worked, hormones made Sue feel more feminine, and one of her feminine personas was Suzi. Sue made a living from a lot of clients who wanted Suzi. It was their chance to explore their feminine sides. Many, if not most of her clients were married, and often their wives knew they came to her.

"How the wives were brought up has locked them up so that they can't handle seeing their husband in a feminine role," said Sue. "That's the feminine side of the gender wars."

Years ago, when I'd first started a project writing about people who made a living from sex, I was fascinated when escorts told me that men came to them to act out secret desires that they felt they couldn't request of their wives. What were those things? Acts the men and their wives considered unmasculine. Sometimes it was something as simple as anal play. Part of the explanation of transsexual prostitution was the appeal of having sex with a person who was a woman, but who still had a penis. The man could be penetrated, but it was still by a "woman," which eased his homophobic self-image. But Sue would show me that things were much more complex and interesting than that.

"You know what 90 percent of the sex business is? Men who want to be taken and used, men who want what their wives won't be (a slut), men who want to emulate the slut!" Sue declared. "They want what they do to women, to be penetrated, a distinct form of vulnerability. Americans have a super uptight attitude about the anus, but it's part of the body. It's very erotic, but any erogenous zone that they don't consider masculine, like nipples, forget it. This is the attraction of transvestites and transsexuals. The men can get screwed by someone who looks like a beautiful woman. That's a big part of the business."

"I'd say that 80 percent of the fetishes and the reason a happily married man goes outside the confines of a safe monogamous relationship is to get something he can't get at home. If wifey would pay more attention to erogenous zones, hubby would stay put."

"Right now," Sue added, "I'm more interested in sessions that are more like psychotherapy. The club scene can be very limited. I'm not a young puppy, and I'm much more interested in deeper connections to these gender issues. You still have to wake up every day and be a person. If you want to go out and put on the high glam drag queen stuff, I'm sorry, society is not going to accept you. I don't take Mistress Suzi out of the house. And speaking of which, let's resume tomorrow or the next day. I have to put on jeans and go work on my van!"

*　　*　　*

Sue would call me to come by after her sessions, and over weeks and months, we talked. I was fascinated by her work, and with the attention to fashion she and Renee, another transsexual she teamed up with, observed. Beautiful dresses, stockings with seams up the back, Italian shoes, handmade sandals. Often, I'd feel dowdy next to them, which I wasn't accustomed to.

I also had to learn to be sensitive to the subtleties of sexual identity. I made mistakes. Sex has very little to do with gender. After knowing Sue I realized it had little to do with genitals. What was inside the person, their feelings, was what mattered.

In the beginning, I screwed up with Sue because my mind couldn't absorb a fundamental tenet of transsexualism. Just because you have one sex's genitals doesn't mean you're that sex. You are what your heart and mind say you are.

But I had trouble absorbing the lessons. I wince to think of it now, but in the first few days I would fumble around, not knowing if I should refer to Sue as "he" or "she." It hurt her feelings.

Another time I upset her by noticing she was wearing a wig. I thought she looked great, but she thought I was being critical.

One day it came home to me. I was speaking to a man I knew, telling him of my research, of going to transsexual clubs and to support group meetings. "Do they think you're a transsexual?" he asked.

I was stunned. What did *that* mean?! Did he think I wasn't feminine? Why did he ask *that*? Would anyone mistake me for a former man? I was astounded, wounded. Maybe what upset me was that I couldn't always tell with so many of the people I met. Was my identity so apparent? This was all very unsettling.

And then, with a flash, I got it. I knew how Sue felt, I knew how I'd hurt her feelings now that it was *my* sexual identity that had been challenged. I called her, apologizing. She was very nice, but I noticed her grin when she next saw me!

It bothered me, to realize how insensitive I'd been. A few days later, I went to her apartment to continue our interviews. "Look," I said, turning so she could see. I'd cut off my hair.

"I like that boy look on you," Sue said.

SUZI AND SEXUAL FANTASY

Headspace was the word that Sue used in regards to her clientele. Each one had a particular headspace in which the sexual fantasy they wanted came from, and the headspace was what they created. The sexologist John Money thought of it as a lovemap, a mental template expressed in each individual's fantasies and practice. She always talked about her clients' headspace. I wondered about hers.

"Did you ever go through a stage when you were your own fetish object?" I asked Sue.

"Now that sounds like you're reading those books again," she teased. Sue forced me to see things on a continuum, to not accept simple answers. She hated it when I used shrink-talk, especially the sort that suggested it had the explanation for everything. It was okay by Sue for me to say that clients at Edelweiss, a club for transsexual prostitution, fetishized some of the transsexuals, that some of them fetishized themselves, as long as we allowed that the *Sports Illustrated* bathing suit issue and *Victoria's Secret* catalogue did the same in another way. Everything was by degrees, nothing was pure.

Seeing my face, she softened. "Okay . . . sure. We all have images that turn us on. What we need is a place for the sexes to join. A lot of men hire professional sex people because they can't explain to their mate what the image is, or worry they may find it offensive. This isn't gender oriented, it's ideology oriented. You want a blond with big tits?!"

She opened her closet and put away three strappy pairs of Manolo Blahnik high-heeled shoes. The light glimmered on her working clothes.

"A lot of transsexuals, people who've had surgery, can overstate an image of what a woman is. For someone whose headspace is totally transvestite, the song is so different. They're turned on by the clothes. I'll show you a trick. Come here."

She walked me to the mirror lining one wall. "You're a client. We put you in the pretty lingerie. And . . ." Sue took a black curtain and draped the top of the mirror, cutting off the reflection at the neck. "There you go, darling, welcome to the ballroom! Look at the body, not the face. It's especially good for guys with beards who want to dress up."

"For the transgendered person who has a problem with gender identity, which is why you get the narcissistic transsexual and transvestite, they want to dress up in woman's clothes, stand in a mirror, and masturbate. They want sex with that female image but they can't achieve that image because that human being doesn't exist. It's more narcissism than autoeroticism. Autoeroticism you have a relationship to your body. Narcissism is totally image oriented."

Sue surveys the pictures of herself on the wall in her Suzi shots. "It took me three or four years to get over my narcissism. It's part of the development. I'm not the most interesting lover I ever met! The curious puss in me said, 'Hey, why am I limiting myself? I'm just one more of my lovers, and I'm not my best!' "

*   *   *

'What's with the ankle socks?' I asked a few visits later as Sue checked her makeup in her lighted mirror, getting ready for a client.

'With a lot of cross-dressers I assume litttle girl personalities, because when they first try cross-dressing they want to go out as sluts or whores. It pisses me off, but often the older the man is, the more slutty his initial concept.' She adjusted her tiny jeweled belt. 'I want them to be normalized, and since they never went through puberty as women, we go back to the beginning, back to the sandbox if need be. I find that by using the persona of a playful young girl I can defuse their insecurity. Sue added that she was thirty years old when she had to go through puberty again, this time as a woman, so she understood.

'I don't like the clubs, like Edelweiss,' Sue said suddenly. 'It can bring out a lot of the worst behavior. The club scene is my pet peeve, because it makes it impossible for someone who wants to dress up as just a part of their life to have the world perceive of us as normal because the world sees these people.'

'What do they do that contributes to the prejudice?'

'Many of the chicks-with-dicks use the worst street behavior. They have an incredible look, but they think and act like a man in drag. Even though they look like women, they're missing what being a woman is all about. They are the worst nightmare of a woman.'

'I'm not putting down drugs,' Sue continued, 'But drugs used to get clients high so they can be ripped off bothers me. And drugs used to get some pretty little tv who just came to New York to live his fantasies and instead gets sucked in as a house whore and ends up dead in a year . . . that's a problem. Married men who go out and play with cross-dressing and become the woman their wife hates, a nasty little stoned, crude bitch . . . that's destructive. That's the worst of the scene, and I hate it.'

'You've seen me around the neighborhood. You didn't even know about me for a year, that's how low a profile I keep, right? I don't like the 'in your face' scene because it's the behavior society sees and judges all of us by. I was in Saks Fifth Avenue buying a purse and a well-known cross gender entertainer came in, wacked out, approached the counter, and said, 'Where's the crack department?' Ruins it for the rest of us. I have a great girlfriend who I've known for fifteen years. She said, 'I don't want to go to the club with all the mannequins.' That's what she thought of Edelweiss. Best description I ever heard."

KIM ON THE CONTINUUM: A DIFFERENT LIFE

After I'd known Sue for eight months, she arranged for me to meet her friend Kim, who she'd been in a support group with eight years earlier. Sue thought that Kim would give me a different representation of transsexualism. Kim lived an understated life in New Jersey, where no one at her work knew she had gone through transsexual surgery. Kim was getting her second Ph.D. The first one had been in history, and she'd taught at a college. But she wanted no one to connect the person she'd been and the person she was now. If that meant getting a second Ph.D., so be it.

A tall woman with a long ponytail, minimal makeup, and comfortable clothing came into my apartment. Kim was opinionated and thoughtful and humorous. She sent me the novels she wrote when she wasn't pursuing academic degrees. They were well written, riotously readable, and engagingly refreshing takes on familiar genres. One was a secret agent novel, only this time the superspies were two sexy, talented lesbian agents who had graduate degrees from seven sisters schools and went to romantic countries where they had fabulous adventures. I felt sure, reading it, that *Double-O Sappho* was the *Goldfinger* of the 90s. Then there was the historical horror thriller, *Vamps*, a sort of bisexual Stephen King meets Ann Rice. Forthcoming was a sports novel and screenplay.

The first thing we talked about was that Kim's second Ph.D. would be in psychology. She'd noticed that I had a copy of Janice Raymond's *The Transsexual Empire: The Making of the She-Male* on my desk. Raymond's 1979 book was a scathing inditement of transsexual surgery, saying that it was the male-dominated medical establishment's reenforcement of sex roles. Kim said she'd thought to call in the EPA upon reading it, as she'd considered it toxic waste.

I told Kim how a few nights before Sue had stopped by, kicking off her high heels to roll around with my cats, and we'd read sections of Raymond's book aloud. "We were surprised that Raymond was so critical of male-to-female transsexuals who became feminists," I said.

"As if they weren't before," Kim made a face. "In some cases it might be role-playing but the same goes for genetic women. I have to be so skeptical of anyone who talks about changes caused by surgery that have anything to do with something that the surgeon's scalpel doesn't touch. The surgery only rearranges the plumbing to conform with the person's inner vision of themselves, their conviction of what the core of their being is. If you use your own definition, there is no: 'a man or a woman is supposed to be . . .' It's yes or no. I am. I am not."

I asked what she thought of Harold Leitenberg's thesis: "The transsexual prefers to keep up their delusional preference for one sex over another and their delusional denial of the fact they are homosexual."

According to this line of thinking, she pointed out, Kim would have gone through years of her life and tens of thousands of dollars to delusionally deny the fact that Mike, who she was before, did all this to hide the fact he wanted to sleep with guys. Only now that Mike was Kim, she wanted to sleep with women. Kim was a lesbian. She wasn't denying anything, her life just didn't fit into the parameters Dr. Leitenberg had imagined.

Kim's earliest memories were of lying in bed, praying to God that she would wake up as a girl. "It wasn't until I was six or seven that I discovered divine intervention was not necessary. That's when Christine Jorgensen made all the news magazines."

"Did you think you might have the surgery when you grew up?"

"No. I thought, I WILL have the surgery. It's just a matter of time."

After this first meeting, Kim sent me her journal, which juxtaposed significant events:

"Tuesday, 16 October 1983: Heard an interesting news item on the radio. The organizers of the Miss America Pageant have rewritten their eligibility rules to 'tighten' the restrictions concerning moral turpitude but didn't specifically mention posing nude. They also decided to specifically ban transsexuals. Um! What are they going to do, give each contestant an Olympics-style chromosome test? How absurd. Well, we already knew they were firmly rooted in their thinking—in the 19th century (or is that the 16th?) Personally, I take it as a left-handed compliment. They're admitting that a TS could not only be selected as the most beautiful woman in one state, but perhaps even *win* their pageant! Can you understand what an admission that is for such neanderthals? That a former man might be able to go on stage before the entire country with fifty of the most beautiful women, and out-bathing suit, out-evening gown, out-talent, and out-interview them all. They're admitting their inability to identify a TS without medical checks and background investigations. Why, thank you!"

There was the parents-get-the-news entry. Kim wrote about her father being the successful son (an FBI crimefighter) of an alcoholic family:

". . . My father grew up as a straight-arrow bookworm who was tormented to distraction by the laughter of the neighbors at his father. And he vowed that nobody was *ever* going to laugh at *him* that way!

Such was part of the filter through which he saw my decision. People were going to laugh at him, call him a lousy parent, a weak role model. Geez, look what your kid did! Ha, ha, ha, what a jerk! And he simply could not bear it—not after half a lifetime of working his butt off to reach a point where he was almost universally respected and admired. He saw me as some demon taking an ax to the tree of his life.

. . . In too many ways I was almost a clone of my father, the 'New and Improved' model. As his firstborn I was automatically slated to 'carry on his name and family tradition.' How many men in this patriarchal society don't dream of a son who'll be bigger, stronger, faster, smarter, and more capable than they are? Our children are our immortality, and an offspring who has the potential for greatness is the best chance most of us will get.

. . . So you can see that the news that his eldest son, the repository of all his dreams, his hopes, his ambitions—was not going to be his *son* anymore was a crushing blow to him. Because he could not be equally proud of me as his daughter and because THE CHANGE would prevent any ego-identification by him, I was literally amputating his chances at immortality."

Sue and Kim wanted me to realize the differences among transgendered people. Individual transsexuals show up in different places on the continuum of the Harry Benjamin scale. They were good examples of this. Sue was "blissfully in the middle," as Kim put it. Only the extreme, of which she included herself, should go under the knife. "It's only the tip of the iceberg who are legitimate candidates for surgery. The rest have chosen another place on the fringe of the gender continuum."

"What's the vital distinction between someone who can make a complete sex change as opposed to someone who shouldn't?" I asked.

"Leah Schaefer was doctor to both Sue and I. Sue is incredibly fluid on the spectrum, and she's happy with that. Her range of sexual preference for partners is wide open, and she's comfortable with having gone through hormonal therapy and cosmetic changes to be a woman, but can live with being pre-op. What I swore to Leah was that if I were marooned on a desert island with no chance of ever seeing a human being again, which sex would I want to be? Female. That's the picture I have of myself. It's who I am. In my head I'd felt a mistake had happened and I'd been born deformed. It was a birth defect. I wanted my body to be such and such, which was not the same thing as saying, 'I want my *role* to be such and such.' "

For Kim, unlike Sue, there was no question. "As long as I had that piece of flesh on my body, I felt I was deformed. I felt it was disgusting. I would have cut it off myself if they didn't."

"How soon after the surgery did you feel better?"

"It was close to instantly. One thing I regret is not keeping the testicles to put swimming in a jar on the mantlepiece, like old Uncle Ralph in the urn. And I'm sorry I didn't store my sperm. It would have been kind of neat to have my own baby."

We laughed, and she said, "But really, it was like sailing out of a storm into a sudden light. I never was happier. It gave me peace of mind and a feeling I wasn't living a lie. For three or four years later I had nightmares that it was growing back. I'd wake up in a cold sweat, terrified. I still have them once in a while, and they upset me just as much, which gives you an idea of how I felt about it. I was a woman with a birth defect, never a man."

"How did it affect you sexually?" I asked. Kim explained that she lived largely androgenously. She took part in male rituals, like drinking and socializing, and had many women friends, which to the men she knew was "evidence of being a cocksman. But I never used the penis in sex. It was like having lesbian sex with an extra piece of meat along." After her surgery, many of the women she knew confessed, "We're not surprised." Kim believes women are more perceptive. "Men are socialized from an early age to shy away from deep emotion, inner thoughts," she said. "I may have seemed to be a man's man. I was popular. But it was a mask, a damned good one, but a mask."

I tell her we're on the subject the critics find dismaying about transsexualism, that it reinforces these roles rather than say, lets men be more emotional or women more assertive.

"The relationships I had with women were on an intensely personal psychosociological level where you opened your basic inner being. Men are trained to think, 'This is verboten. It leaves you more vulnerable than a man ever ought to be. It's evidence of latent homosexuality.' "

"That doesn't mean that men are incapable of going deeper. You're dividing this up in a limiting way."

"That's the way my existence as a man *was*," Kim insisted.

"So who *shouldn't* have transsexual surgery?" I asked.

"Anyone who is more caught up in what other people think about them than how they feel about themselves is not going to be happy with how other people deal with them after surgery. In a way, transsexuals are society in microcosm. They are every variation and shade between one extreme and the other. You have Sue, who has a broad range of sexual preference. And me, who is disgusted by the male body. I find men unattractive, unappealing, and if they take their clothes off, downright disgusting."

"Isn't that extreme?"

"Yes, I happen to fall at one end of the spectrum."

Kim speculated that one part of Leitenberg's writing had merit: there *were* some people who considered transsexual surgery to legitimize homosexual desires. "They don't hate their male genitals because they're not right for them, but because they label them: You have a penis and you like men and that makes you an outsider in society. In those cases the therapist must make them aware of the limitations of their thinking and weed them out as candidates for surgery."

"But whether on not this man has the surgery, if that was their attitude, it's a problem." I said.

"The surgery is just going to make that person even more unhappy and screwed up than they already are. Another problem type? Let me think. The transvestite who is trying to legitimize his feelings. He's actually going to have his penis cut off so he can wear dresses. It's his attraction to the fetish rather than his identity. We had one person like this in our group. He was a heterosexual tv who thought having his dick cut off would allow him to dress up in public."

"The point was to try and make him understand that cutting it off wouldn't change anything," Kim continued. "He could still go out in public, the only thing that would change was what was under his panties. When he's walking down the street in a dress no one knows what's under the panties anyway."

"I've read that a lot of transvestites want the reassurance they have their penis under their skirts."

"It's true, and you have to make them understand that. 'No, you don't want this cut off. You use this, and enjoy it, don't you?' There's a difference between fetishizing women's genitals and having them, especially if it means losing your male genitals. Maybe some would be happier being hermaphrodites, but transsexual surgery is not either/or. It's a one-way street. You can't say, " 'Oops, we made a mistake. Let's put it back on.' The diagnosis is crucial. Maybe they could use virtual reality in therapy. He looks down and sees nothing there. The sexy woman walks in and what does he do? How does he feel?"

Kim shared Sue's lack of affection for the commercial chicks-with-dicks scene. "The kind of transsexual I'm going to be happy with is the one now fitting into society the way they always wanted to. The club scene is not like that. I found it very uncomfortable because the majority of people were not gender people. They were people who prey on them. I got out real fast and never thought of going back."

SCIENCE AND PSYCHOLOGY / TREATING TRANSSEXUALS

"I met Harry Benjamin on April Fools Day, 1969." It's how Charles Ihlenfeld, psychiatrist, remembers what was to be a momentous date in his life. Charles Ihlenfeld is an original member of the Harry Benjamin Society, the association of medical and psychological professionals who treat transgendered patients, named after the founder of transsexual surgery. Twenty-six years later he still sees patients from Benjamin's practice. He was a good person with whom to discuss aspects of transsexualism that still confused me.

If, as Dr. Charles Moser said, doctors didn't completely understand how hormones influenced behavior and feeling, why do some would transsexuals want hormones so much?

Charles Ihlenfeld explains that for people in sexual transition, the hormones helped a biological adaption and were an affirmation of their choice. "If you are a man who identifies with females, estrogen will effect chemical castration. The testicles will atrophy and testosterone levels drop. Losing erections in sexually stimulating situations is a big plus. They feel like themselves. They're coming together. It's psychologically soothing, reaffirming."

Alice Webb is the acting head of the Harry Benjamin Society.

Her Ph.D. research is on orgasm and sexual function in female-to-male transsexuals, who, she believes, are seldom studied because of the greater visibility of male-to-female in our society. Webb stresses that the people she's interviewed are fully orgasmic, and says that Dr. Marianne Schroeder did a presentation at the Institute for the Advanced Study of Human Sexuality about her work interviewing seventeen post-operative female-to-male transsexuals, all of whom were also fully orgasmic.

I mention to Dr. Ihlenfeld that I'd found people get upset by the idea of transsexualism. I've been asked questions like, "How can you reassign someone's sex?? Their DNA is still the same!"

"If I see myself as a woman, even if I'm able to function as a man,

I'm more gratified when my partner sees me the way I see myself," he said thoughtfully. "If I'm accepted as a woman and my partner sees me as a woman, that's going to be a lot more self-affirming to me than if I try to have an erection and an orgasm playing the male role. When people are allowed to be themselves they're more liable to find that which is exciting and compelling and fulfilling."

"It varies from transsexual to transsexual," Alice Webb explained. "A lot of m-to-fs use the penis up to the time of the surgery. They won't tell people that, but they do."

Neither would offer a pat explanation for what's going on with pre-op transsexual, chicks-with-dicks prostitution. "There just isn't one answer," said Alice Webb. "The clients may be homophobic and this is as close as they can get to sex with a man. Maybe they are potentially transsexual or transgendered themselves. Sometimes they will be cross-dressers or merely people who want to date a pre-op transsexual! It's like anything sexual, there are too many variations to have one explain it all." Dr. Ihlenfeld agreed that it was impossible to give one explanation, and a mistake to.

As far as *being*, each discussed different angles of the social identity issue. Alice Webb wondered what was going on when her clients complained of being "read," noticed as being transsexual.

"They don't believe it when people say you're not passing because you're not doing it right, if you do this or that you won't have so many problems. If you listen to transsexuals who have never bothered to change their voice, they are living in a fantasy world as far as I'm concerned. If you have your back turned to someone and hear a male voice behind you and you turn and there's a woman standing there . . . that's confusing. A good therapist will confront that person."

I ask about political transgenderists who want acceptance for being the way they are.

Alice Webb sighed. "They insist they can cram it down people's throats and that people will accept it. They don't. We're not that evolved yet, socially. Gender roles are more equal but they're not blended and won't be for the next generation or two." She mentions the here and now. "If they perceive themselves as female with a gruff male voice and a beard and legs they don't cover . . . it's masculine, and thinking otherwise is a total fantasy."

"And yet . . ." Charles Ihlenfeld added, "I think people have the right to express themselves as they wish to, and other people have the right to respond the way they wish to. I can understand how someone who has felt oppressed by years of trying to conform to someone else's expectation would be angry . . . I think the extent to which we make social progress requires angry people who are willing to fight and make points as they insist on their rights."

And about that, Dr. Ihlenfeld said he was intrigued by what Kim had told me. "Maybe someone who is in transition hasn't had the opportunity *not* to feel trapped. One can experience greater fulfillment sexually if one is having sex the way one wants to, if one's deeper self is being affirmed by the sexual experience. Being a fuller participant of life is doing it with your whole self rather than the facade you've been taught to present."

It all presented questions of identity, sexual and otherwise. Who has the final word on what's real? At Halloween, Sue stopped over to show me her costume before she went to the famous New York Halloween Parade. She looked great. She wore a head to foot tan catsuit, including a long, curved tail Bert Lahr would have envied. She had matching plastic cat ears on her head, and cat whiskers painted on her face. She trotted into my apartment, meowing.

My cats had known and liked Sue for months. Across the room, Simone, my tiny Burmese cat, had been peacefully napping on the warm cable box. She opened her eyes and they nearly bugged out of her head. In two seconds every bit of fur on her body and tail was standing on end while she clutched her perch in terror. She was fluffed to the size of four cats, ready for a war, but the expression of disbelief in her face as she looked at Sue spoke Simone's thoughts. "Look at the size of that *&@#$$+& cat!!!"

Sue tried to calm Simone, thinking when the cat heard her voice it would be okay, but Simone stayed fight fluffed and clutched, the eyes riveted. I've never seen an animal look that shocked. Half an hour after Sue had left, Simone was still a trembling, fur exclamation point. DNA? Hormones? Never mind asking if Sue was a woman. As far as Simone was concerned, the biggest cat in the world had come into our apartment.

WORKING THE CLUB SCENE

I went to Edelweiss a second time a year after I first went there with Sue. Edelweiss is on 11th Avenue between 42 and 43rd streets, next to the bright glass and plastic of the Market Diner, one of the huge, reassuring places travelers, truckers, and people who need to eat in the middle of the night can do so. Spotlights from the roof throw teepee-shaped beams the width of two cars. Traveling west on the quieter darkness of 43rd east of 10th, in what would otherwise be a damned dark street, a shimmer of small cobalt blue lights leads the way.

There are cars parked with four or five guys standing outside and talking, watching the foot traffic as if this is some beach town in Jersey instead of New York City. Three of the cars are surrounded by groups of white guys, a crowd you could find at the local train station or Disney World, dressed in ordinary clothes: jeans white, polo or T-shirts, short hair, aged late twenties to sixties. They congregated to talk. In this vicinity their only possible destinations are the Market Diner or the club. They have a festive air, chatting, smoking, and enjoying themselves while they smile and wave to people passing by.

It was the blue lights. Their origin swam into focus. Bad light on 43rd Street prevented the immediate realization that they are the result of reflections from the twitching, swaying rump and cutaway back on a dress up ahead. A black woman with long long legs, high heels, and those blue sequins winding up the front and around the neck in a halter top, slithers that dress with sexy purpose along 43rd Street, headed west. She waves her straight hair like a flag over her twinkling lights and smiles a honeyed smile. The men call to her and look happy and excited, as if they've just run into a favorite friend going to the same big party they're going to.

I had not been quite sure if this was the right street, but following the blue sequins leaves no doubt. The figure in the glittery dress glides around the front of the diner to the club next door, and I see the sign: "Edelweiss. A Club For The '90s."

A couple of big bouncers take money at the door. A light-skinned black woman with gold braids looped up from her shoulders says good evening. The layout is as I remembered it, with the narrow front room, most of which is a mirrored bar. Two transsexual women serve drinks, one in aqua with a blond wig, slender, beachy, the other a substantial woman with a wrestler's body, a red tank top exhibiting muscular arms, and little black satin shorts showing muscular legs. Her hair is in fat black coils on her head. She looks like the cartoon of the big wife with the teeny husband whose presence is dwarfed by hers. I remember a dominatrix speaking of the popularity of wrestling sessions, about men who like having their heads squeezed between powerful thighs.

House music hits like a wave. Stairs head up from the first room to another mirrored room with tables and chairs to one side like a soda fountain, another bar lining the back wall, bare bosoms and bare backs reflected in the mirrors. To the right are stairs that go down, with squiggly painted designs splashing bright colors on the walls. Sensory overload make the first minutes returning downstairs (the place seems designed to propel the new arrivals to go up and down) seem surreal. There are men in leather and dance clothes and drag queens and transsexuals in fabulous outfits. Kabuki theater dodging and dancing with Hollywood and the Miss America pageant all at once.

Besides the thrill of the costume party, familiarity is an unexpected sensation. Why? I look around and get it.

Every familiar type of a female is represented. It's like watching porn and realizing much of it is crafted to match familiar settings and fantasies. A doe-eyed slender blond drifts by, wafting intimations of Clairol and you'll-look-better-in-a-sweater-washed-in-Woolite ads. A red French twist tops the high cheekboned, heavy eyeliner face of a stunner in a satin evening gown. "In Hollywood," filmmaker John Waters has said, "everyone is either in male or female drag."

Downstairs is the center, with a mysterious hallway for quiet conversation running right and left. In front is the big dance floor, with the disco spinning ball, and mirrors to reflect figures dancing with their reflections. In the center of the floor is an enormous black queen, in white satin harem pants, row upon pirate row of gold chains, big breasts pushed up in a midriff baring top, and cheeks and lips so lush they could be stuffed. Her hair is piled and mixed with strips of satin, black and gold cloth.

Standing in the floor, I can practically feel the sexual rush, the energy zapping around the room, current looking for current. Transsexuals in glamorous clothes languidly walk up to the men. Some connect and some drift off to eddy back onto the dance floor, show their bodies, and start the cycle again.

"It's headspace," Sue had said, time and again. The place where sexual fantasy originated. Because of Sue and her friends, I have a much better understanding of that space.

I know Sue is right, too, that under the fantasy there's plenty of harsh reality, that there will always be those who manipulate the fantasy for bad reasons. But for a moment, seeing this scene as the manifestation of people's needs strikes me as important.

"Open your heart, otherwise you'll never come to understand anything," Ava Taurel had said. Here I am in a room with beautifully dressed glamorous women who have penises. And men who are here because they are attracted to those women. Their fantasy, of mythological proportion, has it's own reality.

When I look up there are half a dozen men looking at me, and when I smile, they smile. The one closest to me, a small fellow with a sweet face, says hi and we shake hands. He asks me if this is the first time I've come to Edelweiss, and I tell him it's the second, that I was so interested the first time that I came to learn more about it. He nods.

"I'm from Queens. I've been here a few times, I'm into avante garde and counterculture things. Isn't this a great, wild sight?" We survey the pageant. We talk casually for a few minutes about the dancing, music, and other clubs he likes, some sexual, some not. Someone steps between us to reach the bar, and I'm face to face with another man, this one a bit older. He says something complimentary, and then another man comes on my left hand and starts talking as well. Both are very intent. I'm off balance, and realize I need to collect myself.

I didn't expect men to approach me. I came here to observe everyone else. I knew from the previous visit that if you came here as a woman (this was a differentiation that would be forever stamped in my mind), you dressed to kill. The pregame promenades at the Academy Awards didn't top the outfits here. I wore a pair of slim-cut black pants and a fern-colored floral vest. My hair had grown out to a short bob. The look was nice and understated, which was my plan, to blend into the woodwork and watch the fashion show. What was going on with these guys?

I finally get a hint when one asks, "You're genetic, right?"

I nodded. He leaned forward and whispered, "But are you a wild girl?" I looked inquiringly at him and he said, "You want to be the guy?"

I'm in over my head, and I don't want to show it. I tell him I'm going to get a drink.

The way out is upstairs. Cross the dance floor, up to the first level out the blue hallway. Everyone looks at me and I look at everyone. "Hi, there," says a tall, balding man with a handsome, thin face, smiling at the foot of the stairs. "Hi," I smile, continuing along the receiving line, hi, good evening, hello, how are you. Everyone looks at everyone. It's the looking capital of the world.

The stairway is for the moment empty, and it only takes a few steps before I'm fine, out of the social flurry. I'm at the top when someone who has come swiftly behind me speaks in my ear. "Wait. Are you here alone?"

I turn and there is a dark-haired woman with big almond-shaped eyes and a filmy gown fitted to the bodice and swinging free in tea-length skirts. She leans forward and smiles, with an expression that's questioning and friendly.

When I nod, her voice drops and I have to lean forward to hear her. "I thought so. Come, will you talk with me?" She leads me to the bar in the back of the second room and we settle on the stools. We introduce ourselves. "LouElla," she says, the syllables sung mellifluously in a voice with some sort of Mediterranean accent.

She barrages me with questions. "Have you been here before? How did you hear about this place? What are you doing here?"

I tell her that my friend Sue has taken me here once before, that she is a transsexual who does fantasy sessions, and she'd taken me to this club so I would see a place where more fantasy sex was available. I say quite honestly that I was back because there were still many thing that I wanted to understand and I'd returned because of my curiosity. "Do you mind if I ask you all about this?"

"I don't mind," she answers. "I like to talk. You can ask me whatever you want."

Her face—small chin, pretty cheeks and dimples—is framed by a dark bob. She has lovely big eyes, and every few minutes smiles a soft smile then quickly glances down. She has a rhythm: pretty eyes and face up, pretty eyes and face down. Her voice is perfect, dropping to a Jackie Kennedy whisper, rising with slight accent like a note of jasmine. Her rhythm means that to hear her, you have to lean close because the voice breathes off, and then she looks up and smiles and starts it all over again.

We start talking about the scene here. I ask if she makes a living from having sex with the men who come to the club. "I know that they want to have sex with a beautiful woman who has a penis. Do most of the women here still have a penis?" She nods. "And the fantasy . . . is that what they want? Is that most of what you do with the men here?"

"Mostly," she whispers in her little Jackie Kennedy whisper. "But you see, the hormones make your cock shrink, so I do not like to penetrate my male clients, even though many of them want me to. I do not enjoy doing that. Even if I had a bigger penis I wouldn't enjoy doing it."

"What do you do?"

She explains she gives them oral sex and enjoys being penetrated because she has "many nerves" anally.

"People have written that this is a way for men to hide their fear of being homosexual. They say that this way they get to have anal sex with a man but the man is a beautiful woman so that masks it and makes it okay for them. Do you think homophobia is part of it?"

"Homophobia?" she asks, puzzled. "No. They desire a beautiful woman. But she can be both. Both man and woman." I ask about her response. Is it as if she never had the operation and can have male homosexual sex this way? She shakes her head.

"It is not like that at all," her voice is soft and the accent musical. "You see, it is not what they hide, or I hide from myself. We know what we want. I would not be afraid to admit it if I wanted sex with a man as a man. Just to be a homosexual instead of a woman with a penis? No. No. When I was a man, I wanted what I have now."

"What?"

"To be beautiful. To be a beautiful woman." She smiles and hugs herself. "I love beauty. I love sensuousness."

"Well, you are beautiful. But why didn't you have the operation if that was what you wanted?"

"They want me to be both, the men. And I *am* both. I am a beautiful woman and man, but more woman. It's what I am. Why would I have to choose?"

"So . . ." I say slowly. "It doesn't have to be denial. It can be your choice to be like . . . a hermaphrodite." She smiles, nodding. She pulls down the front of her gown and shows me her breasts. "I didn't have implants, hormones gave me nice breasts." Many women who work here do have implants, she explains, but her breasts are real. "And my hips and buttocks are soft, so soft. I love my softness."

"Why did you stop me when I came in?" I ask.

"I'm bisexual and I like women very much. I think I like women more than men." She thoughtfully rearranges her skirts. "What I love is beauty and femininity," she says, raising her face and shaking out her bob. She never utters a sentence without accompanying gestures. "I want to be a beautiful woman and see myself in another beautiful woman, to enjoy her softness." She plays her palm up my arm, "and to have her enjoy mine." She sits back and hugs her arms on her shoulders, stretching her long fingers up to her neck, fanning them out to caress her jaw and ears, as if to suggest how wonderful her skin feels.

"Do you often have relationships with women?"

"I love to. But I want to have her touch me as a woman, never for me to penetrate her. But I want her to penetrate me, with a dildo."

"Let me see if I understand this. You were a man who became a woman. But you don't want to use your male organ on a woman. But you want the woman to use a substitute for a male organ on you."

She pulls her hair against her cheek. "Yes. I want to act as a woman with a woman acting as a man. But I want both of us to be beautiful and feminine."

I ask if she always thought she was transgendered. She explains that for many years when she was a man she thought she was gay, although what she longed for was female beauty. "I am not as young as I look. Guess my age."

She stares into my eyes, the kohl-ringed almond shapes radiating confidence. Whatever age, she knows she doesn't look it. I guess in her early thirties.

"Forty-five," she smiles, and casts her eyes down softly.

"You've made me understand a lot more than I did before, and I thank you," I say slowly. Her eyes look reproachful, but she nods graciously and we say warm goodbyes. Later, passing on the dance floor, she touches my hand with a quick greeting.

*   *   *

Back downstairs, two transsexuals nod to each other and come closer and look at me, then drift off, whispering together. A huskily built, extremely muscular man with a plaid shirt, doing a good imitation of a lumberjack, smiles flirtatiously across the room and starts to cross over when the same tall, slightly balding man who'd said hello earlier comes up. He starts talking to me in an animated fashion, and suddenly, with a perceptual drop in enthusiasm, says, "You're not a transsexual, are you?"

"No, I'm not. I'm Marianne. Hi."

It takes him an extra beat to give me the name he's decided to be, uh, Bill. Then he asks what I'm doing here. I tell him it's my second time, I found it so interesting the first time that I came back, love the clothes. You?

"I have this friend, you know the sort, the girl you knew since camp, best friends forever, you go out together when neither one of you is seeing someone else? Well, we're always playing practical jokes on one another. So she said, I'll meet you at this club at 43rd and 11th, and it turns out to be this place! Boy, wait till I fix her next time! I couldn't believe it!"

"That's a very interesting story." Two men next to us laugh. One of them is flirting with a black transsexual in a shimmering copper cocktail dress. She pivots on her spike heels and grabs Bill by the shirt front.

"Honey! It's you! Remember last time how you got so craaaazy! I will never forget gettin' on the dance floor, you picking me up and whirling me around and around. You were the wildest!"

"I've never been here before! This is my first time!"

"Oh, no, now sugar, don't be like that! Why you danced and danced and danced, I thought I was going to break an ankle trying to keep up with you. And remember later. . . ."

He starts yelling at her. "Oh, you're good! You're really good, aren't you? I tell you, I've never. . . ."

It seems like a fine moment to skid back across the dance floor to the bar. I'm watching the scene when a friendly voice in my ear queries, "Are you a reporter?" I turn and there is a medium-height man, athletic, with a short haircut, with an attractive face, very boyish. He's in his early thirties and looks mischievous.

Rather than answer that question, I shake his hand and give my name. He's Tom, from Boston, works as a stock market trader, and he frequents as many clubs like this as he can find. He sounds bright and funny, and after we compare a few notes and make each other laugh, I tell him that I first came with my friend Sue and yes, I am a writer. I speak about the people I've been interviewing and for how long, but that the commercial transsexual prostitute club scene is still something I'm trying to fully understand.

"You can ask me about it. I'm experienced," he smiles.

"Is this a big part of your sex life?"

"It's my favorite part of my sex life. My ultimate fantasy. I've tried to think if something in my background lead to this, but I come from a typical upper middle class family, professional father. When I was young I was totally fascinated with mermaids. I think I like the mythological aspects of the mix of sexes." We watch the dance floor action, which by now, after two A.M., has heated to a fever. Men are dancing with the girls, the girls are dancing with the girls. People are wacking each other on the butt and singing and swinging from the chains suspended from the ceiling. The tremendously tall one in the harem outfit is back and forth with two others in tight tight pants and little satin tops, with fashionable haircuts and lovely makeup.

I tell him I continue to be staggered by the outfits and beauty of transsexuals here. Tom points to one of the girls in the satin pants and says she has collagen shots in her ass to give it the firm roundness. The rest of her body is incredibly thin, tiny waist and ribcage, skinny arms, long neck. "Check the neck," he whispers. "A lot of times they do the hormonal change and electrolysis, but don't get surgery on the Adam's apple." Directly in front of us, a small Asian transsexual, with straight bangs and glossy long black hair, peels off a silver lamé gown and jumps onto the dance floor in white satin thong and bra.

"Did you always gravitate to this?" I asked.

He shook his head. "No, I'm bisexual, but I never really felt I was happy either with girlfriends or in gay relationships. I've come to this more and more."

"Some psychologists have written that this is one way for a man to allow himself to have anal sex with a man, because the person with a penis is a beautiful woman. Is that how it is for you?"

"Oh, no. Theories, love theories. Well, your turn. You tell me what you've discovered in your interviews before I answer that."

"I think people here who want sex with a pre-op transsexual, want exactly that. I mean, that's what they like. Although there seems to be variations on that."

"Very good. And what are some of the variations in people you've interviewed?"

"I thought the big draw would be men who wanted the woman with a penis to have anal sex with them."

"Yeesssss, but isn't it interesting how many ways the transsexuals orient themselves to it? Some in this room won't use their penis because it ruins their own illusion that they're a woman. I've talked to some who claim the penis is their clitoris. Did your interviewees tell you that?"

"One person I interviewed preferred to use a dildo because it was one step away from using her penis, and so was easier on her identity. Someone I spoke with tonight said she didn't like to use her penis to penetrate but she enjoyed being penetrated."

"I think they try not to use the penis so they can reenforce the fantasy they're a woman. By the way, was the second person you just mentioned LouElla? I saw you talking. You know, I think she's a little slutty." He made a disapproving face.

"Slutty? Isn't that a quaint thing for a guy who just admitted he enjoys chicks-with-dicks to admit?"

"Last time I was here when the club was closing she got on her hands and knees and started raising her rump in the air, as if she was begging someone to come and give her anal sex."

"Well, so she's into that. Aren't you being pejorative or do you just prefer subtlety here at Edelweiss?" The sexologist John Money wrote about how the cleft between saintly love and sinful lust is omnipresent in the erotic heritage of our culture, and gets programmed into everyone to some degree. In the midst of saying it, I realize I'm having a feminist fight to defend a male-to-female transsexual's right not to be thought of as a slut. Adaptable Marianne. I remember how a boyfriend I saw in my twenties told me he couldn't help feeling that what he'd been raised to believe was true: after a girl slept with him, he didn't respect her anymore. "God, I'm still having the same arguments, just in different settings," I think.

Tom smiles sweetly, and admits he enjoys baiting people. "Everyone here likes things just a bit differently and individual."

When asked what the attraction is for him, he answers, "It's perfectly in the middle of sex. It's got everything you would do as a man, as a woman, and what you would do with both or either." He explains he wants the mix of roles in one person. "I have to admit, when I came over to talk to you I was wondering if you'd be the woman who I could break my final virginity with."

"Which is?"

"I've never been penetrated in the ass with a dildo by a genetic woman. It would be so exciting."

"I've heard this conversation four times tonight. There can't be that many virgins. Or is being a virgin part of the fantasy?"

Did Madonna get *all* her stuff from clubs?

He playfully sulked, looking out at the floor. "Don't analyze too much."

He says he is surprised by my description of Sue, her intelligence, her awareness of personalities and sexual personas and how to use them. He says his experience with many transsexual bar girls is that they are trapped in one fantasy: that they're a beautiful woman, they never were a man. "Sue sounds really interesting. I'd like to meet her," he says.

"What about cross-dressing?" I ask.

"Many men here enjoy it. A lot probably have women's underwear on. Some want the transsexuals to be the goddesses. It varies. I like dressing. But I had a surprising thing happen. One of my male lovers, before I realized this is it sexually for me, dressed with me. I was excited about me being cross-dressed, but when I looked at him, I was completely repulsed. I guess it's true, I was my own fetish object. And a pre-op transsexual as a beautiful woman thrills me. But a man dressed . . . no. Is that some complex male/female role stuff? Sure. but . . . . . . but . . . !"

"But don't forget, there are variations on the variations?"

"Yes. Because plenty of guys get off on guys dressed as girls. You just can't figure it. What I do is try out all my fantasies, and if they don't work after a couple of tries, I move on to the next one."

It's late and I'm tired, but when I leave at three A.M., the club is still hopping.

WORKING NO MATTER WHAT THE GENDER DEAL IS

Kim completed her Ph.D., finished another novel, and is waiting to hear from the colleges she applied to for a teaching position. She already has some job offers. She's got an office job she hates right now but it won't be long before she's teaching again.

Sue moved out of her apartment in Chelsea that winter. A former business friendship had turned into a bitter feud. She was sick of hassles she got into, usually at wee hours in the morning. It was part of her nature to be impulsive, and rather than back down from a fight, Sue would go out and stick her small pearl-handled pistol in her former associate's face. The day I saw her apartment empty was a sad one. But it was better than having someone get killed.

She moved in with a former client and friend, but they clashed, and she visited me for breakfast and said she'd decided it wasn't going to work. "I'm moving out. My current roommate and I fought. He believes a woman shouldn't be the captain of the *Starship Enterprise*."

"You're leaving because of *Star Trek?*"

"It's the principle. He won't even watch the show. They have a female engineer, too, which is even more unacceptable to him."

I'd met him, a sweet heavyset computer expert who Sue had years ago befriended. "He's like a lot of submissive clients, he has his mother and his sexual fantasy mixed up. It's very common. The whole time I've known him he's said he wants to get a wife and children and settle down. He insists I cook out of his mother's pans and he only eats the food she used to make. He can't deal with a woman spaceship captain because it's outside the role he saw his mother in. He can't stand people who don't speak English but he loves the Spanish channel because the men are macho and the women are submissive. He says, 'The women are women, the way they should be.' He got offended when I suggested he get a Third-World bride."

"How did you become friends?"

"Through the clubs. It's my lost puppy instinct. Everyone kept screwing him over. The girls would rip him off. I felt bad and tried to bring him into my social circle, I always have a circle. Anyway, we'll stay friends, but I can't stay there."

"What will you do?"

"Don't worry, I'll stay in touch. I'm getting out of the sex business. It's not good for me anymore. I want to go back to producing. I've been talking to friends of mine about setting up a company to do Web page designs and corporate presentations for the Internet. The software is a bitch, but I think that's the direction I'm headed in."

"Where will you live?" Sue smiled and said I'd see for myself.

We talked on the phone. I knew she was working outside in the winter, as a mechanic. When she showed up in person in the spring, she was in great physical condition. She lead me to 10th Avenue, and there it was.

She'd restored a vintage mobile home, with sleek torpedo-like lines. It seemed to take up half the block. It was gorgeous, buffed chrome, new paint, and the motor hummed contentedly.

We went inside. It was bigger than several New York apartments I'd lived in. She had a kitchen, curtains around comfortable cushions in front, a shower. The back had counters and her computer, modem, fax, and cell phone. There were cabinets labeled: Long line bras. Girdles. Garter Belts. All fantasies could be accommodated on the road.

"The suicide rate for non-surgical transsexuals is the highest on this planet for any discreet minority group," Kim told me. "Sue is one of those people who if she wasn't terribly bright couldn't keep going. She's had a lot of problems in her life and her world always collapses around her. Somehow she always struggles back. She has so much knowledge, so much technical talent, so much creativity, that if you said to her, 'I'll give you five minutes to start an entire new industry out of nothing or I'll cut your head off, she'd do it!' "

And indeed, she did do it. She had the design and production skills from her years in advertising and film. It took months, but Sue mastered the complex computer software and opened her business with a partner. They're equipped to do corporate Web pages and presentations, but the first clients she pursued and sold ads to were people in the sex industry who wanted to enlarge their client base. Why not stick with a business where you knew the players, she reasoned? It might be a new line of work, but the territory was familiar. That helps when you're doing sales.

7

Sex and Escorts: The End

It took me five years to come to the end of my book on working sex. Five years later, I finally got it. I liked doing this work because I *was* this work. I needed more access to the hidden part of me, to all those different things a woman also is, aggressive and strong and every bit as sexual as a man. I remembered a group of young girls stopping me in a restaurant when the *New York* article first came out. "You made them seem like us," one whispered. "Can you go find out more?" I decided to follow up on escort services, take a new look and see if it felt different after all the changes I'd undergone in those years. The people in the book had taken me a long way. Now the journey would end where it started, with escorts.

When I opened the phone book to choose, I couldn't believe it. There were four times the number of services. It seemed we'd come a long way. Some of the ads said they offered male escorts.

This time, I was curious to find out the difference between paid-for sex and people's everyday sexual relationships. Did people want to buy something sexually they couldn't find in their own lives?

I'd read books, articles, and done many interviews with doctors and therapists, people who treated sexually dysfunctional couples. What I found most interesting about their work other than that it tied together many disparate questions raised by the lives of the people in my book was how it clarified the effect of rigid sex roles in our society.

Sex roles and mythologies ultimately destroyed sex. "The rate of sex problems in our culture is high," said Dr. Barry McCarthy, a Washington D.C.-based therapist who, along with his wife Emily, is the author of a number of popular sex books. "They're probably higher now than they were in Masters and Johnson's 1970s days. People are more knowledgeable about sex than they've ever been, except for how to maintain satisfying sexual relationships."

There were precious few models in our culture, he added. "If you look at movies and TV programs, sex is all premarital or extramarital." In soap operas, he added, marriage is the kiss of death. A married character either has to have an affair or is written out. "For many people, how you keep sex vital in an ongoing relationship is a real mystery."

The sex therapists pointed out to me that most people operated with an almost mystical faith that sex was supposed to work on its own, and if you had to think about it or communicate or, God forbid, work on it by learning and trying things, there was something wrong with you, or the relationship.

Even how we think of sex can spoil it by cutting us off from our experience to focus on performance. Dr. Shirley Zussman is a former president of the American Association of Sex Educators, Counselors, and Therapists, and for decades she and her urologist husband, Dr. Leon Zussman were called the "Masters and Johnson of the East." In the 1970s, Shere Hite pointed out that they were the first to integrate the fact that intercourse was not the way most women had orgasms, and that sex was a broad panorama of expression.

Had the Zussmans seen a dramatic change over the years?

"Our field has grown in diagnostic testing for sexual problems, but interactions between couples have not changed too much," she told me.

Barry McCarthy talked to me about how conditioning works against couples. The things that make sex exciting at the beginning contain the seeds of dysfunctional sex, because factors like romanticism, newness, experimentation, and excitement change over time. "You'd be better off coming for sex therapy six months rather than six years into the problem, but most come three to ten years after it starts."

Therapists try to get couples out of their lovemaking routines. They prescribe exercises to get them back to sensate focus and touching, experimenting with what feels good. "The more comfortable you are with affection, sensuality, erotic non-intercourse sex, the more alternatives you have," he explained.

Unfortunately, most males, and women who take their lead from them, are socialized to consider that sex automatically signals erection, intercourse, and ejaculation.

"A double standard gets males in big trouble, especially after forty," Dr. McCarthy added. At that point, the man doesn't get an erection easily and autonomously as in his youth. "Sex works better then when it's interactive, but most men resist getting help from their partners. That double standard says to males 'It's my job to turn her on and me on.' " Women do better in sex therapy, he notes, because permission giving and information giving is an easier sell to them. They're used to the idea that they'll need something from their partner to get into sex.

"If men follow these standards of believing sex is their responsibility, all this performance anxiety . . . " I started.

"The sex, even if it stays functional, will be much less erotic and much less arousing," he concluded.

If escorts exist because people want something sexually that they were willing to pay for, well, what sort of things do they want?

WORKING ESCORTS

My publishers advanced some money so that I could pay people in the escort business for their time, which I was sure would be necessary. Before I got the check, I tried to do it the old way. I knew there was a thriving escort business of men for men, but did women order men for sex?

I flipped open the Yellow Pages. There *really* were four times more ads than five years ago. And a good half dozen of them said "Male and Female Escort." Well.

I looked at another ad, one of the full-page illustrated ones. The Crown Club, my old friend Susan from the magazine piece. I wondered if she was still there. When I dialed and asked, saying I'd interviewed with her previously, a woman's voice told me to call back later.

I started getting in the swing of calling. I'd dial, and someone answered, usually without giving the service name.

"Are you hiring?" I asked.

"What is your name and have you done this before?"

"I certainly have. My name is Juliet," I said.

"Well, Juliet, tell me about yourself." This one sounded in her mid-to-late thirties, smooth and sharp. "Tell me about yourself" meant vital statistics and to see how practiced you were on the phone. The more

no-nonsense and self-possessed you were, the quicker you'd be accepted. In the previous two calls the person had to drag me through the
series of questions: breasts, body, are you attractive, are you experienced. . . .

"Thirty-four B-23-34, tall, slender, brown hair, blond streaks, good
face, will do kink but want to be paid extra for it. I'd like to be working
by the weekend. Is it possible to get an interview later?" She told me to
call after eight that evening.

I called more places and had much the same conversation. To keep
myself interested, I'd move my measurements up or down an inch,
came up with more hair color descriptions than L'Oreal, and sometimes wouldn't do kink at all, no matter what. I got four interviews for
the next day.

*   *   *

I was fixed up and ready to roll that evening, in a short dress and
stockings and high pumps, hair styled and sprayed, eyeliner, lipstick. I
called to confirm my interview. The booker told me what midtown
corner to call from, so they could give me the address. "You'll need two
pieces of ID," she added. "See you in a little while, Juliet."

Identification! How could I forget! Juliet wasn't going *anywhere*. I
waited twenty minutes and then called, apologizing and saying that I'd
had another call. They'd think I was trying out other places and taken
the best money offer, understandable.

I kicked off the high heels. Not tonight.

*   *   *

My friend, a police sergeant who'd been a source on a number of
stories, had moved to a job in city government. I asked if there was any
way I could get fake ID.

"Not possible," he said, telling me that his office had been approached by the FBI to get fake ID for an investigation, and been
turned down. He asked what it was for and snorted, "Those services
won't remember your name from that story! You're not talking about
places with institutional memories. Just give them an ID with no address."

Maybe he was right, but many of the people I'd reported on were
still in the business. And it was a tightly knit business. Going in with
my name? No. Fortunately, the next phone call I got was from the
publisher, saying the expense check was ready.

*　*　*

Time was of the essence. I hurried along Fifth Avenue, coming up to the Flatiron Building, at 23rd Street, trying to decide what to do first.

I had money. Enough money to buy upscale sex, even in New York. I could pay for a number of escorts' time. Where to first?

My approach had changed based on my experience. I *did* the reporting where I went in and got looked over. I knew how the business worked for women. What I now wanted from the women in the business was a look at economics and particulars of their calls.

But men? Besides gay escorting, for which I had good contacts, did women call men for paid sex? I thought of Gay Talese's book, *Thy Neighbor's Wife*, in which he'd concluded that no, women just wouldn't enlist men for sex, as if we weren't capable of it. Talese had concluded his book with a rumination on American society, likening it to people on a tour boat who'd sailed by him while he was at a nudist beach: ". . . unabashed voyeurs looking at him; and Talese looked back," he'd written.

Look at *this*, Gay Talese.

I had money. And I was supposed to write more about escorts. I had a sudden, unshakable thought. I wanted to take the money and buy a man.

Startled, my mind raced on down the street as if a pursesnatcher had taken it. I'd never thought about this before. What would it be like?

What would I do if I called a place and half an hour later had a man standing in front of me? It was amazing to contemplate. He's mine for this hour. I can do whatever I want with him. Pat him like a horse, strip him, touch him, make him touch me. I was lost in my fantasy. It wasn't that it would be better than partner sex. It would be different. I wouldn't have to worry about his feelings or pleasing him. I got to think only about what I wanted.

Jesus! I'm a monster, was the very next thought.

No, I'm not. Why was it different for women? So many of the men I knew had told me stories of being with prostitutes, good stories. I had mental images like snapshots. Loneliness: one friend who'd told me of being comforted by a pregnant streetwalker during a moment of his life when he was devastated. Or just plain lust and high spirits: another had gone to Nevada, picked someone who matched his fantasy, and they'd both had a great time. She later visited him in New York. If I could understand them . . . then they have to understand my eroticism, too.

How could you be thinking this? the other side of my brain wailed. What's gotten *into* you? My friend Eddie told me I was bipolar. Bipolar? I wish there were only two aspects of a modern woman.

I was almost at the corner when a sudden bleak feeling washed over me. What if some man I liked could know my thoughts? I felt shame, and then, I had a sudden fierce conviction. I don't care. Let him know. Let him know how I feel and what I truly am, not what I'm supposed to be. I realized from this moment on I would never be with a man who couldn't do that. We're not the second sex. We're not opposites, men and women. We've got a lot in common. It felt as if I was coming to the end of a long journey.

WORKING SEX: PRESSTITUDES

The headlines on the *New York Post* and *Daily News* got my attention: "CALL GIRL RINGS BUSTED." The only escort service to ever be busted in New York City in the past decade was Sydney Biddle Barrow's Cachet. Why was this happening this week?

The *Post* made reference to WNBC/Ch.4 breaking the story first.

"Three call-girl services patronized by celebrities and high-powered businessmen were raided last night by the Manhattan District Attorney's office. . . ."

Intimations of glam clients: "several prominent financial and entertainment firms . . ." Creative financial reporting: "The three services raked in more than six million over six months—and perhaps $10 million a year by charging as much as $455 an hour."

When I tuned in on NBC's second report, they flashed that AMEX stub with the $455 written in the little box. Interesting. When I'd called the day before to reapply for work, I'd been told the rate was $300.

It was the Crown Club, and my old acquaintance Susan.

NBC News and the tabs reported that the $6 million escort fees were moved through a dummy limousine company and gallery, that prosecutors said the scam could be an avenue into a major racketeering case, potentially involving money laundering and tax fraud.

Sydney Biddle Barrows had a trenchant observation to make about all this.

"Did you notice that they are not going after them for being prostitution rings anymore? They've learned that the public doesn't want their tax dollars squandered on prostitutes. So now they call it money laundering," she declared.

But she showed me how it didn't stand up. "Who is laundering money? You can only launder *cash*," she added. "If in point of fact credit cards are being used by clients, those credit card slips are being deposited in a bank under the name of a company, and at tax time, that money has to be accounted for! If they're worried that the clients are writing off the money for a tax deduction, is that not a matter for the IRS? Why is the New York City police department worrying about the Federal Government's money! This is an effort on the part of the D.A. and police to whitewash what they're doing. 'Money laundering' makes you think of drugs, a major criminal element. Adults having consensual sex? So fucking what?" Sydney demanded.

We started talking about the money, and she did the math: "Six million dollars in six months? If you pull out your calculator and divide it up, that means every single hour of every single day in the last six months they had to have fourteen girls out making $450 an hour. That is not happening!"

Mike McAlary's reporting for the *Daily News* was a pathology printout. "Lonely Man Loved the Call Girl," wrote McAlary.

"The story starts with a lonely rich man . . ."

and went downhill from there. Sexism? Naah. The "love affair behind a million-dollar racketeering case" began, according to McAlary, when this sweet, kind, lonely man fell in love with a "curvaceous 28-year-old blond" he met at the Crown Club. A relationship develops. She tells him "call girl secrets," like putting a sleeping pill in the client's drink to bill a second and third hour.

This is goofy, a bad movie plot. Imagine trying to pull that off. I'm not even going to walk you through it. Just think of the effect on repeat business.

So they go to Vegas "She went for love. *Or so he thought*" and get married, even though he's already married. He wakes up "aghast" realizing he's a bigamist.

Nerissa Braimbridge, who runs International Escorts, mused. In her cultured Jamaican voice, she noted that "This intelligent fellow forgot he is married? How unusual."

Anyway, the poor lonely guy goes back to Manhattan with her and immediately "went to see a lawyer, lots of them. The marriage is illegal, or so he hopes." She goes back to work as an escort. What's she supposed to do? She even files taxes, and leaves him, filing for divorce, to which he responds by turning her call girl papers over to the Manhattan D.A.'s office to soothe his lonely, broken heart.

You get the idea. The next day McAlary told us: "Suspected Madam's Hard As Nails." She "muttered a curse or two" upon being arrested.

"Well of course she did!" exclaimed Sydney as we reviewed the copy.

And "as newspapers were hitting the newsstands, she buried her face in her hands." What a hard woman.

> "She routinely worked 10-hour shifts, leaving as the last of the suspected call girls dropped off their credit card numbers for processing."

That means she was good at her work, in the best possible way. I talked to many women in this business, and the last thing they want is to be out on a call and not have the agency check to see they're back. The good ones, the responsible ones check. What they told me five years ago about watching out for the people who worked for her was true. Susan couldn't control everything, but the things she could check up on, she did.

The *Daily News* had more about "the tough matron": "She sounded polite, almost motherly."

When John Miller, the reporter at WNBC, returned my call, I apologized for having left a phrase like "discrepancies in your reporting" on his phone mail.

"That's okay," he sighed. "It was the nicest thing anyone said to me all day."

WORKING ESCORTS/WOMEN

In the subway uptown, I was trying to decide who to be. Marianne or Juliet? I guessed I'd just go with the moment.

It still struck me, when I was given the address, that I always ended up in these nice neighborhoods, Madison or Fifth Avenue. I went to the door between the antique store and the French restaurant, up a flight of stairs, and found myself in a room with computer terminals, four phones with multiple lines, and this time a friendly young black woman who carefully looked me over, smiled, and handed me a clipboard to fill out.

I knew who I was going to be. "Listen, I want to ask you a question, and if it's the wrong one, just tell me to leave, alright?" I said. She looked torn between a laugh and keeping an eye out for a gun. "Ooooohkay," she said nicely enough, eyebrows raised.

"I'm a writer. I'm finishing a book about people who make a living through sex. I'd like to interview you or people who work here. I'll pay $100 for the interview time. It's anonymous. I'll be discreet about the place or anything that might give you a legal problem. What I'm looking for are details about the business. I'm not judgmental about it. I think it should be legalized."

She looked at me carefully and shook her head, glancing worriedly out the door. "The people who own this place wouldn't go for that," she said. "I'd lose my job if I even suggested it." She thought for a minute and spoke quickly. "Maybe I can help you." She slid an index card across the table. "Write down your name and phone number. I'll call you later. Do you have any. . . ."

"ID? Yes, here, I'm on the level." I handed her the original *New York* magazine. That thing comes in handy. She nodded, satisfied. "I'm Leah. But please, put down something on the clipboard. There's a video camera overhead."

The form had the usual. I made up a name and phone number. I liked the last line: IS THERE ANYTHING YOU ABSOLUTELY WILL NOT DO? "No golden showers," I wrote. I slipped her twenty dollars hidden under my form and left.

WORKING ESCORTS/MEN

The first phone call was to an escort/limousine service.

A young woman's voice answered. "Good afternoon." When I asked if this was X company, no response. "Who's calling?" she asked.

"I wanted to know if it would be possible to get a man as well as a woman," I said.

Her tone of voice was human, and urgent. "Oh, no, we don't handle men. But word to the wise. Men normally go see men. That's to yourself, a word to the wise, okay, honey? Good luck." She hung up.

"I notice the ad says you have men. Do you have them regularly and at what rate? " I asked the young-sounding booker at an escort service called Pretty Woman. The obvious question I left out: Why is it just called Pretty Woman if you have men?

"If you want someone now they could get there in twenty minutes, $300 cash per hour," she said.

"Is there a way to select them?" I asked.

"Yeah, you tell me what you want and I send that to you," she responded. I said I wanted someone for the weekend. I'd thought they needed advance notice, but she said, no, she had over forty guys and all I had to do was describe what I wanted and they'd send him right over. Call back when I was ready.

I got one very tough, suspicious sounding woman at another escort service who growled into the phone, "Where you located? Is it for you?" She sounded as if she didn't believe me. At the next call, the young woman who answered the phone heard my questions, sounded confused, and put me on hold. Finally her boss, an older man, got on the phone. He sounded gentle and handled the conversation well. It was clear he thought there was something fishy about me, but he was impeccably polite. He explained their gentlemen were the best in the city, *GQ* models and so forth. When I knew what I wanted I should call and they could accommodate me.

I sat holding the phone. Okay, a woman *could* get a man sent over. This was, after all, New York. But my immediate impression was that it wasn't business as usual.

*   *   *

I called a gay male friend who sometimes hires beautiful young men for sex, and knew how that part of the business ran. I described the trouble I was having, and he snorted, telling me that the services advertising "Male and Female" were all connected by the same beepers. "If you're going to investigate this, let me give you the best. Call this number," he said.

The male voice that said hello was like raw silk.

"I got your name from a friend. Do you supply men for women?" I asked. There was a millisecond of a surprised pause.

"Used to. Depends on the guy. What is your name and how did you get my number? The more legitimate you make yourself the quicker and happier I'll be." We went through a dance (Juliet), and then he said his name was Jay. He asked me why I was calling. I said I wanted a nice experience with someone who was fun and good-looking. I asked if he had books of photos for me to look at and he said, no, he supplied people as they came through town.

"Do many women call?"

"No. Years ago I'd get calls from couples looking for threesomes. But since AIDS that's changed. And there's no avenue for tapping the straight women market that I know about. I don't know any women like you who would call up like you're ordering a cheese pizza."

He asked what I would like, and I found myself thrown by the questions. He was asking about penis size, build, and hair coloring. I knew if I hesitated I'd sound as if this whole thing was fake. Okay. . . . in twenty seconds. Who do you want to sleep with in half an hour?

"Give me a Jeremy Irons who's discovered the gym. An ectomorph who works out, not a beefcake. I'd like smart and a sense of humor, if you could manage it. Do NOT send me someone brain dead and hung, if that's the choice." Very good. First time out and already I'm a Roman Emperor.

"Let me see what I've got. I'll call you back."

*   *   *

On the other end of the phone, I learned later, Jay's mind was shouting, "This is it! I knew there were women like this out there somewhere!"

"I have two guys who got hard just hearing about this," he told me when he called back. He described one as being young, blond, beautiful body, from the south, with a sweet, winning, open personality. Very well endowed. The other was more sophisticated, older, dark haired. "Do you have Madonna's book *Sex*? There's a picture of him in it. He's the only one with full frontal nudity."

"That sounds interesting. I wish I could see that."

He asked me where I lived and to our surprise, we discovered we were closer than a ten-minute cab ride. He said he'd be intrigued to meet me and if I wanted, I could come take a look at who was there.

*   *   *

"Listen, Jay, there's something you should know. I'm a writer . . ."

I'd met the young blond boy when I arrived. He was perfectly sculpted, very sweet. I felt maternal toward him, not sexual. Later I had to explain to someone that the term "boy" was ubiquitous terminology to describe "young man in sex trade." Likewise "girl." They weren't real big on pc language.

My confession was a disappointment. "I knew it was too good to be true," Jay said. "When something feels screwy, it usually is. Okay, what's your story?" When he heard it, he was incredibly nice. "I *read* that piece! I can't believe it's you. Well, what do you want to know?"

"Do you know of a service where women call for men?" I asked. He shook his head. "If they do," he said thoughtfully, "it's not like the rest of the escort business. How did you feel about ordering a male?"

"Scared," I said. "I love it as a fantasy, but the reality is too intimidating. Unless I had a gun on him, I wouldn't feel safe, and then I wouldn't feel relaxed or sexy."

Jay told me that he did not believe women used escort services to request men. He thought the ones that advertised male and female escorts were really aiming for a businessman who wanted to explore his bisexual side but was too closeted or intimidated to pick up a gay publication. Sydney Barrows concurred, saying she never got a legitimate request from a woman for a man. She thought Jay's scenario was accurate. "If you're a bisexual man, you can have sex with women any time, because it's societally sanctioned. You have a wife, a girlfriend. If you're going to New York City to buy sex, to do something naughty, you're going to get it from a guy."

At that moment Jay's phone rang. "No, no. False alarm. No, Rocky. Yeah, she's good-looking, but it's not what we thought. She's a writer. She was trying to find out if women call men for escort sex. Yes, you can say hello . . ." Rocky was friendly, saying that his appearance in Madonna's book had resulted in more modeling jobs, a forthcoming book project, and that yes, he did know of women who paid men for sex. He said he'd be willing to talk about it in the future, but right now he was busy.

"Why did you say his dick would get hard just thinking about it before?" I asked after Rocky and I bid farewell.

"Are you kidding? A woman wants to pay me to fuck her? It's the ultimate male fantasy, even for gay and bi guys. The seal of desirability. Even better, you sounded really hot on the phone."

"If women do pay men," he resumed, "I think it's probably part of something ongoing. The pool boy. Someone at a club. More like a relationship or at least familiar territory. I'll make a few calls."

Jay was an intriguing fellow. He was an unusual mix of characteristics, all of which played across his personality in a constant and conspicuous way. He was smart, sensitive, jaded, with a conscience, cynical, *and* romantic while being suspicious of all of the above, kind, angry . . . he wore his nerves on his skin.

He'd been doing this for a long time, but also had a day job in the arts, his real love, which he wouldn't talk about.

His phone rang constantly. "Hello? Sebastian will be back in January. Why don't you check back then. . . ."

He said that his service didn't allow drugs, which had been the downfall of his chief rival and enemy in California. But he growled, "I'm not St. Anthony." He winced telling me about his work, alternating between explaining how a successful service worked, and acknowledging how society would judge him.

"When I read *The Mayflower Madame* I thought, 'nobody will believe she contributed to the lives of these women.' But she taught them how to dress and act. They made a good living. You wouldn't believe what I have to go through, even personal hygiene with these boys," he said.

He told me of young men who came to New York and were living in cars before they worked for him. We spoke of broken families and economics and class backgrounds. "You and I were raised to have a dream, and the American idea is to obtain the dream," he said. "I ask them what they're going to do and it's 'huh?' Many blow the money. They don't have anything in a few years. Car, Rolex, clothes, whatever they made, gone." Jay insisted that there was a right way and a wrong way to run an escort service. Drugs were the wrong way, but some places tried to hold on to boys that way.

We talked about fielding the calls. "Do they *all* want these Greek gods?" I asked. Jay didn't even hesitate. "Absolutely. You should see the handsome guys who have a good body but not a great body who I have to turn away all the time. My clients know exactly what they want: beef, big cock, beauty."

"How do you feel about that? Every day you deal with these perfect specimens, and then there's someone like you. . . ."

A flaming blow torch flew across the room. "Thank you very much, fucking bitch!"

"I didn't mean it like that!" I floundered, looking at his face, then got traction. "I mean, it would be like me comparing myself to some twenty-year-old and saying, 'That person personifies sex. People my age do not.' Frankly, if I had a choice between that sweet blond kid and a forty-five-year-old like you with your face and dark eyes and I like your body, by the way, you're solid but very nice, it would be you I'd go for."

He was looking less as if he wanted me dead, and he could tell I meant it. "I have this same conversation with a friend of mine who is gay who only wants sex with guys like your blond," I nervously marched on. "I'm sorry, I think it's sad when someone can't find sexy or fall in love with the equivalent of themselves. And I'm not just talking about gay men, it's the same with hetero men who only want beautiful women under thirty. Don't you think anything else can be sexy?"

"I know what you're saying," he said. "But it's what my clients want. I only deliver their dreams."

Jay and I talked for hours. He lived an interesting life that crisscrossed the mainstream. He felt he provided an important service and ran a responsible business. On the way out, he showed me his hall of fame, a collection of books ranging from Colette's *Cheri* to modern bestsellers, all about prostitution. He pointed to a framed poster of *American Gigolo* with Richard Gere and said how incredibly brave Gere had been to do full frontal nudity when he only had a normal size penis. That had never occurred to me.

"Wait a minute, yes, it's here. . . ." He reached into the shelf and pulled out the *New York* magazine with my escort story. "I knew I had you." I looked at my spot on his shelf. I was honored.

"Let me see if I can discover the answer to your question about women paying men," Jay said. "I'll be in touch."

WORKING ESCORTS/WOMEN

Leah and I met as arranged at a coffeeshop near her escort service on the upper East side. We talked for almost two hours. She confirmed many things I'd heard before, that the johns left their names and credit cards in the computers with the services. Most of the business was done via credit cards with a cover company name such as a car service, so Zippy Escorts would be Zippy Limos on the bill. They didn't get many fee disputes, Leah confirmed, because the last thing the client wanted was to have the service fight them over payment.

That customers were mainstream was impressed on me again and again. She told me the majority of their clients were traveling businessmen calling from hotels.

Leah had been at her job as a booker—running phones and dispatching escorts—for over a year. In that time, there had only been a couple of bad incidents, such as clients fighting a girl about paying. The Christmas season was always the worst, being an emotional time of year. "One call went fine, normal, then when the girl was leaving he went crazy, put his hand over her mouth, started smacking her around, dragged her outside, and threw her clothes after her. It was horrid." She thought the girl would quit, but she decided to come back.

"These women are something else," Leah said. "The mental strength they have, even to do this job . . . I pat them on the back, I really do!" She looked emphatic.

I asked what was the worst thing they had to contend with, and she unhesitatingly answered "humiliation. You do this. You do that. I'm paying you. They talk down to them and insult them. They treat blonds the worst, and blonds get the most calls."

"Is it that they resent what they desire?" I asked. She nodded. I told her about how I felt about ordering a man. Leah said this was what she had to emphasize to women who came to work for them. "I interview new people every day, and I ask why they think they could be escorts, and they say, 'I've dated a lot.' I have to say, this is not a date. These guys think they hired a maid who will do whatever they want them to do."

Leah told me one thing that stunned me, but it fit perfectly with what the therapists had said about men's conditioning and performance. I'd asked if they were strict about the hour, believing that the services called to signify the end of the session because all men would naturally want to run overtime.

"The girl is usually there for ten, fifteen minutes, twenty tops. For $300," she said.

"You're kidding! Doesn't he want, like, a backrub afterward?" She shook her head. "That's it. And that's it most of the time."

I found this stunning. My idea had been that men would use an escort service to have the sex they fantasized about. Twenty minutes? Why didn't the guys just masturbate if they were going to have the same unimaginative sex they could have at home? Later, I asked Sydney about this, and she instantly confirmed it.

"Boring and quick. Absolutely. I'm not saying I didn't get calls from people who wanted fantasies. We referred those to specialty services. It was rare for the client to want anything but straight or oral sex," she told me.

"Doesn't he want to build up? For that money? A bath maybe?"

"No, not usually," Sydney said. "They want you to go away so they can go to sleep. That's another reason they pay for it—because you *will* go away. That's part of the deal. Why do you think people like Charlie Sheen and Billy Idol pay for it? So she'll go away. Someone the other night was expressing great shock and surprise that celebrities, people who could have anyone, pay for call girls. I said, when was the last time you read in the *National Enquirer* that a famous person had stepped out on his wife with a hooker? Hookers don't talk. You know who talks?

Fans talk, girlfriends talk. Working girls don't talk. You are safe having
sex or an affair with a working girl because their business depends on
being discreet."

I said I was still surprised men would pay for whatever they wanted
and then only asked for the same limited sex they could have for free.

"More limited, I bet. When these guys are with working women,
they're never thinking 'How can I make it good for her?' They want to
be totally selfish. Men love quickies! Not to say they can't be sensuous
with their partner, but here they want to get it up, fuck, be done. They
can't do that with their regular partner. She'll be upset. But you can
with a working girl."

Back in the coffeeshop, Leah and I talked about what skills were
important to work as an escort. An ability to compartmentalize, she
believed. She thought it soon became a job, and it could be a very hard
one.

"What is the percentage of women who can handle it, and who
can't?" I asked.

"A lot of times there are women who act like they're handling it, and
then I discover that everything else in their life is falling apart."

"What makes that happen?"

"You're living two lives. Some of them are married, some have boyfriends, lots have children. Most of the time it's secret, and that's the
scary thing, because they're afraid their partner is going to find out. I've
dealt with two girls lately where their boyfriends found out and beat
them up. It's difficult leading two different lives," she emphasized.

Leah agreed with Jay that she'd seen only a small percentage of
escorts who managed to save the money they were making, or plan for
the future.

"It's like an addiction, that money. Once you realize you can make
thousands of dollars a week, are you going to quit for a secretarial job?"

But choice wasn't the case for most escorts. This was their only
profitable job option. Leah told me seventy-five percent of the women
who worked at these services were single mothers. I thought I didn't
hear correctly. I asked, "Not actresses, models?" She shook her head. "I
think we have, like, one actress. Most are single mothers." She looked
angry. "It's pitiful. Most are single and a parent and either lost or can't
find a job, because it's hard to get a good one these days"

I asked about the job backgrounds of the women she had working
for her, and she tapped her finger, thinking. "Home health aids. Bank
clerks, secretarial . . . Some don't have enough schooling. For them
it's minimum wage. You cannot support a child, pay rent, pay Con Ed,

with minimum wage. You just cannot do it these days. They can't work two or three jobs because there's no one to take care of their children."

"Can you type?" I asked.

"My speed is down, I haven't in a while."

"Do you think many of the women have those skills? But even so, temp jobs don't pay that well." I thought, I came from a well-off background, went to college. I am white and attractive. Temping? I temped for five years when I became a freelance writer. When I worked fifty-two weeks a year I broke even. Other years the work fluctuated, sometimes was not to be found. How did I support myself and have the time to become a writer? I borrowed money from everybody I knew. I'd *still* be temping if I hadn't. This woman is black, personable, a hard worker, has a kid. Who do you think is going to get called first for the lousy temp job? What options does this woman have?

Leah interrupted my thoughts. "Some may type, but you're right, those jobs do not pay well, and some have two, three kids and the men are not there. This one woman was married, her husband wasn't working. When he decided to get a part-time job he made her quit, claimed he couldn't handle it. But he handled it before. He sat home while he knew what she was doing. I have no respect for men like that."

I asked Leah if she could arrange for me to pay to interview some of their escorts, but she shook her head, telling me it was a small world. The agencies communicated, and it might get out she was speaking to me.

"We'd get fired. Some go from service to service, and a girl can be blacklisted. On top of not getting a regular job, being blacklisted from this . . . you're in trouble."

"I have a child to take care of and she's at the age where she wants to come to Mommy's job," she said softly.

When I'd come in to fill out the application, Leah had been on the phone, talking affectionately to a child. "I don't like living the lie." She has a boyfriend who knows about her job, but he is the only one of all her friends and family. He knows she does only phone work but occasionally gets jealous wondering if she'll switch to escorting. She says she loves her child too much to take the risk. She's afraid. "We have security. We run our place right, calling the girls before and after . . . but you can't control everything. The money, though . . . ."

"How much do they make?"

"The popular ones, three or four calls a night. Sometimes they'll be out for four or five hours. They rack up. They can make a couple thousand a week. We have two girls who look like models, absolutely gorgeous, and always out."

"What do you think it's like for them? Do you get a sense?"

"I get a sense that it's difficult. Some break down. I see the change in their moods and attitudes. It's rough on them. Some came to New York from other states just to do this. They left their parents, friends, and they miss their family. 'I can't let my parents know what's going on, but I need to be on my own.' That pride thing, I can't ask them for money at my age. I can see what it does to them. But they do make a choice and it is a lot of money."

"Does it make you upset or angry?" I asked.

"It upsets me that women have to do this as the best job available. That there's not child support or adequate health care. So many men aren't supporting their children. The state is saying we'll make them pay but nothing happens."

She rolled her eyes, pragmatic. "You can't get child support from someone who is not working. Are you supposed to sue them? What is a mother supposed to do? Go on welfare? You cannot support a family on that. Women are forced into doing things they shouldn't have to do."

"This is not the example I want for my child. At all. So of course she doesn't know what I'm doing. I don't like to hide anything from her. We're like sisters, me and my child. But at the moment, I have to put food on the table. I don't want to be on welfare. I have rent to pay. You do what you have to do in order to get by."

She hesitated, saying she didn't want to sound judgmental, but morally, she did have reservations. "Maybe if it was legal and it was an acceptable thing in the world, I wouldn't have such a problem with it. Now I have to sneak around and say I do one thing when I do something else."

Prior to this job, Leah had worked as the manager of a 900 phone line for four years, eventually managing sixty women. Some fine perverse changes were put into effect at her company, a result of changes in the laws. The woman on the phone was not allowed to start a sexual conversation, but . . . surprise, the man was! Talking about coitus and oral sex was okay. Anal, no. And noises—grunts, moans, breathing—absolutely not. It's great to give the government the power to decree what shall be performed as a fantasy over the phone. The United States Government. Coming soon to a bedroom near you. Maybe yours.

Because of the new rules and increased competition, Leah's bosses decided she was making too much money working the slower daylight hours and wanted her switched to night. She couldn't, because of her daughter. "Back then, I was doing real good," she says in a happy voice. "I was making good money. I had my child in Catholic school. It was great."

"Did your child have to switch schools?" Well, guess the answer to that one.

Leah went through the want ads. "It all was temp. No benefits either." She makes seven dollars an hour at the service. She wanted an office job, with career possibilities and health insurance. And later, thinking about her situation, I thought, what's this woman going to do when an opportunity occurs and they ask for job references?

"What are the biggest misconceptions about escorts?" I asked when we were leaving.

"The quality of the men, because people think they're sleazy. Our clients are normal people, children, the dog, the wife. It's upscale. Also the quality of the women. They think the women do it because they're sex addicts. No. They do it because for ninety percent of them, this is their best economic choice for work."

WORKING ESCORTS/MEN

"I wonder if I'm losing my ability to relate sexually on a personal level," Jon told me, sitting on my couch on a Sunday morning. "You lose sight of what makes you happy because you get so used to accommodating other people's needs."

There was a pause, and he said thoughtfully. "It's going to be years before I understand the effect this all had on me."

We had to walk around the block to get more tapes on this cold December morning, blinking like bats in the daylight.

"Your job must be difficult," I said, once we were back inside. "I'm just following people in the escort business around and I've been up until three and four A.M. each night. When I'm writing I do that, but the thing that exhausts me with your work is how demanding it is on so many levels."

He nodded. "It's *always* like that when we're working. You can't imagine." Jon leaned forward, mixing thoughtfulness and mischievousness. "Why do people hire me? It's a safer alternative, with well-established boundaries. They know why I'm there when I dance. The customer gets to see everything before they take me home."

We looked at each other and laughed, appreciating the irony of seeing a gorgeous naked man and taking him home to interview him. Of all the sick, twisted. . . .

He couldn't resist teasing me. That night when he called to leave a message arranging our concluding phone interview he added, "I know a handsome, well-built escort you could have a lot of fun with . . ."

We'd first met a year ago, after I'd seen him dance at the Gaiety. He had a sculpted body, a classically handsome face, and a sense of throwaway glamour and humor that humanized him and made him even more appealing. In the first interview, he told me he'd grown up in a strictly religious home with a father who was an ordained Baptist minister. With the exception of a younger sister, his family detested what he did for a living, and all they knew was that he was an exotic dancer, not the escort part.

"They both resent and envy me. I have a six-figure income, and travel a lot to places they only dream about. But they're the first to ask when they want a loan, so it's hypocritical. I wish I could be open with my family about what I do without fear of being judged," he said. "They consider what I do a crime against God." He was quiet for a moment and then he told me a story of riding in a car with his father.

It was the voice in which he told the story that made it terrible, the father's hard, sad, and cold, "Jon, isn't it important to you to know that your father is proud of what you do?"

"I said, 'Yes, Dad, it is important to me.'" His voice shook with emotion. "But I'm disappointed you can't be proud of my success or that you can't respect the fact that I'm doing what I feel is right for me in my life. You taught me the difference between right and wrong. I'm an adult now, and I have to justify the decisions I make. I square them with what you taught me. But if I tried to live my life to please someone else, I would be very unhappy."

"What did he say?" I asked.

Jon sat tensely in his chair, a contradiction between his perfect body and the vulnerability in his bitter and hurt tone. "It wasn't registering because there was that Berlin Wall that separates us and I can never get over," he answered. "I'm always stonewalled trying to say what I'm feeling and what it is I believe. No matter how hard I try, they can't comprehend and can't respond to me."

I wondered aloud how he'd made the leap, considering his background. He said he'd majored in philosophy.

"I did a lot of thinking. I didn't just casually abandon my Christianity. I did extensive reading. I conducted a reasoned analysis of my belief system and I reassessed my thinking based on that."

I was intrigued by the combination of his conspicuous beauty and his eloquent struggle with conviction and its cost.

"I'm basically an agnostic. I believe it's the most intellectually honest position to have," he said. "It makes my life tougher though, because I'm without those moral absolutes that help make decisions in life. I apply the golden rule and that's about it. But what I do is . . ." his voice shook, hardening, "definitely wrong in their opinions. It's not open for discussion. There are a lot of people that feel that way! I'm not ashamed of what I do. I stand by the decision I made and if what I have done closes doors for me, so be it. It's a door that should be closed."

A year after our first conversation, Jon sat in my apartment and told me about the incredible variety of things that his clients, all men, wanted to do. Jon was bisexual and until recently, had lived with his girlfriend Cathy. She knew what he did, but had found it increasingly difficult to share him. He was upset and angry by the breakup. At one point we were tracing his work story, and I asked about doing escort work for women. He'd found no work at the agencies he'd checked.

Women had offered him money for sex when he first began dancing. I started asking questions, but he shook his head and said he'd never acted on the women's offers. "Why?" I asked.

"I was in love with Cathy. I couldn't," he said, surprised by the question.

When men hired Jon, he told me the sessions were often elaborate, not at all like the meat-and potatoes sex the female escort service people had described.

"I get fetishes of all sorts. Domination and submission, bondage. I have one guy who has a road kill fetish. . . ."

"What's that?" I asked dubiously.

"We drive around, and he masturbates while asking me to talk about animals I've run over. I make everything up, but he loves it. Then he talks about animals he's run over. We finish by putting pumpkins in the road and I hit them while he stands outside, watching, and then he climaxes."

I know this sounds seriously strange, but this is a deep part of what psychologist John Money identified as this man's lovemap, how he's wired, likely how trauma was eroticized when he was young, and it is sex for him now. What Jon does gives this man an outlet, and that's important work. Without Jon, he might hit your poodle instead of the pumpkins. It's not harming anyone.

Another recurring session is body worship. Jon is an Adonis, and many clients just want to oil him and feel parts of his body, biceps, arms, chest. I spoke to a man who loves these sessions, and I asked him why. He said when he was young, he was beautiful. On nights when he didn't pick anyone up, he would face the mirror, look at his own perfection, be his own sex object and masturbate. Hiring young men for body worship provided a mirror, a sort of Narcissus looking in his pool, an autoeroticism transformation.

"Are your sessions always different, or do certain activities constitute the majority of what people want to do?" It was all different, he said, there's no common thread. Interesting. Jay had said the same thing.

The third time we spoke, Jon had an edge in his voice that I hadn't heard before. We spoke on the phone the morning he was leaving to go home, and I asked him about it, saying I couldn't help being concerned.

"Sometimes I think I'm too nice to do this work," he said. "I'm not a cynical person. I'd rather trust people, and sometimes this work is tough for me. I can't seem to get desensitized to it." He'd been stunned by a heart problem in the past months. There had been occasions of arrythmia, his heart racing at 200 beats per minute, that had resulted in him seeing a cardiologist. He was scheduled to go for more tests the following week.

ORGANIZED WORKING

"I always know when it's sweeps week without even looking at the television. The shows all call me," Diane Wolf of PONY (Prostitutes of New York), told me. Her grandchildren clamored while she made dinner, giving me names of other national and international prostitutes rights groups, many of which are now much better organized due to the Internet. Representatives of the International Commission for Prostitutes Rights went to the women's conference in Bejing, China this year.

"This is a serious topic," she says. "The producers call up and say please get us three blond underage prostitutes. . . ."

"Sounds as if they were ordering call girls," I commented.

"I never thought of it that way before, but you're right! People think those daytime shows are news, but they're not, they're entertainment. But *Nightline* or *Charlie Rose*, CNN, we're right there. Don't even send a car, we'll be there for a good, honest news show any day."

"I actually was not a good prostitute. It was not for me, because it's really about being a psychologist. It was mentally exhausting. My personal theory is that men are not supposed to show their feelings, and they aren't supposed to go to a psychiatrist, so they go to prostitutes, which is something equated with being masculine."

"My real job was to be a therapist. Most of my calls were about 'My marriage is failing, my God, what do I do? I have to have a woman's opinion.' I was young. This was in the late 1970s. I was confused, because these men were old enough to be my father. My parents had an okay marriage, so the idea people could be unhappy in marriage was a revelation to me."

Once more, I asked if the men were interested in trying new things sexually.

"The only time they wanted to see new, fancy, was their version of new fancy, which was something other than missionary position, bounce up and down. There were things they wanted to know, but it was as if they'd heard of oral sex, but didn't know how to do it. Or they wanted to know what would turn a woman on. They knew their wives weren't frigid, and they knew the lack of sexual satisfaction had to do with ignorance."

We talked about her years with PONY. She said prostitution would never be legalized in her lifetime. Surprised, I asked, why all these years of trying to work for it, then?

"Just because it's not the popular thing to do doesn't mean you shouldn't stand up for it," she responded calmly. "People in my family were civil rights lawyers in the deep South in the 1920s and 1930s, not exactly a popular concept then. Sometimes you work for things you yourself will never see just because it's the right thing to do."

WORKING ESCORTS: MEN

I'd been up until four A.M. for a week, out of bed working again by eight every morning. So at midnight this night I fell face down in bed to recharge. . . .

The phone rang. I picked it up.

"Hello, is this Marianne Macy?" asked a deep, soft voice with a slight Southern accent. "My name is Chuck. I'm calling you from Los Angeles. A mutual friend named Jay thought you might want to speak to me . . . ."

We got to the point quickly after we'd established we both knew Jay for professional reasons.

"So, do you have women clients?"

"Yes, aaah do." What a voice. He sounded as if he should be on a horse.

"Is your business predominantly men with only the occasional woman?"

"No. Women." Three syllables sounding sexually alive.

"You're kidding!" I exclaimed, and he laughed. "No, ma'am." He explained he knew Jay because they had mutual friends.

He started as an exotic dancer in Atlanta, working the male dance review Chippendales. From the start, women approached him in many different ways.

"They're not like a man," he said. "Men are . . . well, men are just pigs. Women are very slinky about everything. . . ." His soft Georgian voice made this information more entertaining. "They say, 'May I take you to dinner' and this and that. 'I'll pay you this and that.' When you go out, if you show a lot of interest in her and be nice . . . you know . . . they . . . ." He stopped, the southern gentleman.

"Initiate things?"

"*Yeesss.* "

I asked if the dates would end up in bed the first night or if the ladies would want some courtship. He reckoned it was eighty percent that had sex the first night. It was up to him if he wanted to repeat the encounter from that point, because most of the women did. He had a few clients, just a few, where things had worked out nicely.

"I have one married lady in Atlanta that I've been seeing for five years now. I have a lady in L.A. who I've been seein' six months. She's married, too."

"Do they tell you why? Are they frustrated? Do they need the novelty?"

"You know what it's like . . . ." he paused thoughtfully. "Sometimes people get so much money, that they think they're so happy, when actually they're really so sad. Sometimes I feel bad cause I'm manipulatin' them in some way, in a fashion. Some become good friends of mine. It's different. You get an attraction to them, but most of the women I see *are* married."

"Are they all wealthy?" He instantly responded, yes, very much so. Did they tell him if they were unhappy with their married sex lives?

"Unhappy. They say," here his voice mimicked a lighter, slightly neurotic tenor, " 'I wish you were a blowup doll I could take home to my bedroom to show my husband what to do!' "

His voice and the way he spoke demonstrated his appeal. He

sounded like Gary Cooper with a Southern accent, terribly attractive and masculine, while being the polite strong silent male all at once. Something along the lines of, "Well, all right, ma'am, since you did drag me into this here bed. . . ."

"A lot of people are looking for somebody just to care, more than sex," he said.

Currently, he had three regular clients, plus the occasional client who sent for him from places like Paris. When I asked if his work paid well, he laughed softly. "Ah have a place in L.A. and a home in Atlanta and cars paid for in both," he answered.

He was a model who had done commercials. He was in his late twenties. He started exotic dancing when he was in college. He was dubious about the idea of male escorts working like female escorts, with hourly rates and clients calling for people to be sent over.

I told him about my conversations with Jay, that while hiring a male escort seemed like a great fantasy, it would be a scary thing for a woman to do. "Do they have to meet you through an intermediary? Or do they get to know you from hanging out and talking to you? How does it work?" I asked.

"Well, here in L.A.," he offered, "you get invited to all these parties if you're attractive and all. It's the only way you meet people here. People might tell you otherwise nine ways til Sunday, but they're lyin' to you. The most important thing is, you have to go to parties. I've been to so many, and I hate to be there. It's like you're a toy being paraded around."

Chuck continued, "You get shown to these wealthy people, and there are going to be one or two who find you attractive. So they'll ask one person and ask another person, and someone's going to know your number."

"So there is a network that screens you," I said, thinking, when you got to the highest level, society itself was the service. "It's not as if you could come off the street and do this."

"No, no, it doesn't work like that," he laughed. "And plus, someone with ten million dollars is not going to be with someone who has no class. It has to do with how you present yourself. You better have a thousand-dollar suit on."

Chuck said everyone took their parts in this play. "Their husbands will be there. You're at the party to help serve the alcohol. You're by the bar, saying hello to this lady who knows you, but her husband doesn't. And friends of the lady try to lure you sometimes. It's a little game."

"Is is about status?" I asked, to which he sighed deeply. "Oh, yes."

Were the wives taking some sort of revenge on the husbands for extramarital activities? "I don't know. Some people are just unhappy, unhappy sexually or with their marriage. They try to show you off a lot. They can't be happy by themselves, so they have to have control over someone."

"Are they controlling sexually?"

"Not with me." He laughed again at the idea. "They have it in them, but it's my manly role to be the dominant one, and they like that." He said he was six foot, two inches tall, 225 pounds, four percent body fat, with a forty-nine-inch chest. "I'm not a little boy. People describe me as a very big James Dean."

"Do you know anyone else who has women clients? How common is it?" I asked.

He said that it was fairly common in L.A. as in New York City. There were many married, divorced, or even single women with a lot of money. There were discreet circles through which these things happened.

The fantasy involved was essential to the client, he explained. They wanted to feel they were buying things that other people couldn't afford.

"The lady I see in Atlanta, the first time I was with her she gave me $2,000 for the night," he explained. "After that, they don't pay you for every time, they help you with things you need." For Chuck, those things had included $5,000 worth of fancy fixtures for his car, or the occasion when the lady had said, "Give me the mortgage book for your house, I'll take care of that."

"My car here, a brand-new BMW, is paid for," he said. "Just things like that. They ask what you need, and it's only a phone call away. Women are different than how men are with the escort business."

"Do you fall in love with them or do they fall in love with you?"

He laughed. "Ah, me! I don't spent too much time in Atlanta because there's a few women there who. . . ." he fumbled. "Well, sometimes they do fall in love, and that's hard."

Another problem was that some of his clients expected him to be Superman in bed. "They want it ten times a night. I may be potent, but I'm just human. I can only do so much. That's kind of hilarious, considering my age, twenty-nine. My clients are in their forties."

I asked if in addition to the affection and attention he'd mentioned, if the women also acted aggressively. He said yes, that he'd even get emergency calls that needed to be satisfied.

"Do they want to act out their fantasies? Is there a big range of what they want to do?"

"Yes, they do. They want to play this out, that out. They like to do a lot of different things." Escapades had included lovemaking in exotic or outdoor locations where part of the excitement involved the possibility of being discovered. His clients also enjoyed bondage and exotic fantasy role-playing. He'd learned to be ready for anything.

Chuck said his girlfriend was a model. She knew that he had older ladies who took care of him, but as long as it was business, she was not jealous.

He used the term "pigs" to describe men again. "They have no respect for you." Later Jay clarified that at one point, Chuck had worked briefly as an escort for men. Chuck told me that he much preferred women. They were kinder and the experience was more en-joyable. He was at the top of the business, and speculated that other levels where women paid men for sex might include their trainer in the gym, but he suspected it was not common.

"I would say there are only a small number of people established at this level, and it is different. We're educated, not doing drugs. . . . I look at it that these people have so much money and they want to help me through life." He added, "You try to be so sweet, but you have to watch your emotions, because they get very attached to you. And you might not want to admit it, but you can get attached to them too, sexually, financially, different ways."

I asked if he thought that any of his clients could or did separate things so that the relationship was just sex, them employing him to satisfy their lust and only that.

"I wouldn't say women do that. They want to, but when the shield comes down, they open up."

I asked about the escort services in New York that offered men. Chuck agreed with everyone else that it was men who called for the men offered. He laughed at the idea of women calling an escort service for a man for sex. "No, no!" he insisted. "A lot of times they're a widow, or divorced. I knew a lady who is sixty-two, a sweetheart, she never had a son, and wanted to treat someone like a son. She gave me everything! I had to stop it. Sometimes they might want just sex, some want a friendship, but it all derives from forming a relationship. It's not ever that one time and that's it with a woman."

"And they don't go from you to someone else. They don't have me and someone like me at the same time. Someone who is upper class, they might meet you through someone, but once they meet you, it's not a one-night thing. The sex is just wonderful."

Chuck found the separation between the working and nonworking parts of his work difficult to balance. He'd wonder why he was with someone *unless* he was getting paid. When he was with a girlfriend he'd have to remind himself to be his other self.

Chuck may have his BMW and house paid for by his women clients, but in ordinary society, women he wanted to date wouldn't go out with him. He told me quite seriously that if he walked into a bar and tried to find a date he'd have trouble. Women reacted to him suspiciously because of his looks. "You don't know how many times I hear, 'You're too good-looking, I won't go out with you.' A lot of women will accept less just to feel it's stable."

I asked Chuck about his future. He wants to continue doing commercials. He doubts he'll be in this game in ten years. "I'm naturally attractive, but it's more about how you take care of yourself. If I walk into a room and make women turn around when I've got my clothes on, I'm doing something right."

Finally, he adds, the guys you see on TV who talk about having women who pay them for sex are lying. "I could never discuss this on TV. I'd lose my clients. I keep a low profile. Those of us who reach this level don't speak about it in public."

WORKING ESCORTS/WOMEN

When we first sat down to talk, I spent three hours with Nerissa. She called back at midnight, and we talked for three hours more.

I nearly didn't go to see her, because our history had been so odd. Nerissa Braimbridge ran the lavish International Escorts, which was in the original magazine piece. She had a witty, cynical line of jive to accommodate a hypocritical world: "Our place is an upscale escort service. We send out beautiful intelligent women for our clients' sophisticated lifestyles. Of course, we don't fool ourselves that sometimes people become attracted and sexual things may happen, but they are adults. . . ."

I was entertained by Nerissa then. I thought she was smart and a great publicist. She put me under her spell. I came out believing she was brilliant, a visionary philosopher, as well as a hell of a businesswoman. Nerissa Braimbridge impressed me, and I wasn't expecting that at all.

When the original story ran in *New York* magazine, she put them on the defensive, terrorizing with phone calls in which she took issue with things in the article. She declared that International's purpose was not sex for sale, but more about professional entertainment. They printed her letters. I believed she was a publicity genius. She got her message out: International was the best escort service in New York. I thought she had brass balls.

Nerissa was a tall, beautiful black Jamaican woman with presence and elegance. She watched and watched me the few times we conversed. I'd asked her if we could talk about escorts when I was doing that part of my book, and she said yes. After a few attempts, I was convinced it would be an exercise in futility because of our disputes around the article.

Still, I called. Everything else had happened, Jay, the bust, Jon, going to services. . . . The urge to go back to where the story started was compelling, but I thought she would either put me off or give me an hour of what I'd heard before.

International Escorts has the best office space of any escort service in Manhattan, and that's no small claim. High up on Columbus Circle, walls of glass looked out over Central Park and Donald Trump's scaffolding covering the Gulf & Western Building. From International's windows you could see down the avenues of Manhattan.

Inside it was all grey tones, soft art, and miles of deep black leather couches, as well as a number of glassed in offices. In one, a willowy blond in black leather pants was being interviewed. Nerissa, who lived a block away on 57th Street, entered, casual in leggings, dark sweater, and boots. She waved away my thanks for her time, saying she didn't have to be anywhere until the opera at eight o'clock.

Her assistant, a Nordic-looking woman, went to get cappuccino, and Nerissa settled behind a big desk.

"We're proud of what we do. I'll tell you why. I studied anthropology and world history. People and cultures are very important to me." Different cultures, she pointed out, had a wide variety of sexual mores. Knowing this helped her see her business in a larger perspective, where not all the rules were defined in the same way.

The richness of her voice, with the Jamaican phrasing and musical tones, intelligence and clarity, immediately captured the ear.

"Also I don't have the hang-ups that most people have, religious dogma and all of that. I am free. I transcend all of that, even though I grew up in very religious homes, Protestant and Catholic. What I have studied makes me think, and I think a lot."

"I have a great amount of respect for womankind. I'm pro-woman, not anti-man. I love men. But I have to tell you I think women come first. I come from a society where women had to walk behind men all the time."

Nerissa has traveled around the world three times. Since 1978, she told me, she has collected art and photo images of women from all cultures. "Our power has been taken away from us. Every time we try to do something, men try to keep us in a certain place. For example, this business. It becomes soiled, and you start to wonder. Why do they do this? If they weren't the market, we wouldn't be here."

"We are hammered. We are whores, we are prostitutes. We are every horrible name you can think of. I started when I was modeling. How it really started was very innocent."

"One day I was sitting with a bunch of models and I said, 'Here we are. We're well-traveled. Most of us speak at least one other language. We know how to dress well. We know how to behave socially. Why don't we do something where we can utilize this?' When I started International Escorts in 1973, there were no such things as escort services anywhere."

Nerissa spoke of what it cost to live well in New York, the price of an apartment, clothing. She decided, she said, to start her escort service so that she and her friends could do the things they always loved to do.

The more she spoke, the more fantasy and reality wove in and out. According to Nerissa, the escort service became the way for beautiful women to live a glamorous life. The fantasy built on the fantasy, and pulled more people in. I had been watching early Louis Malle films with Jeanne Moreau, these stunning studies of bourgeois French life. The women wore Paris fashions, jewelry, and lived hothouse adventures of affairs. Malle was fascinated by the lives of these women in their claustrophobic, opulent universe, financed by males but in which the women designed their own course.

Nerissa's fantasized a world where women lived in the same way. But she would be the powerful financial one. She just needed to create a saleable image.

It was fascinating hearing her talk about getting started. From the very beginning, the media gave them a lot of coverage as being something new. "Tom Synder was the first to feature us. Ted Knight had been given a show by Mary Tyler Moore. He was pretending to be the manager of an escort service. The girls he had looked like bimbos, and I said, no, that's not the way. He and I were both guests on a show

Mike Douglas did about escort services on his CBS program." More clients came to International.

"When I started this I couldn't find a newspaper that would print the word 'escort.' The Yellow Pages took two years before they would allow the word 'escort.' For the first two years, it was listed under International Entertainment. On the third we were finally listed under 'Escort Service,' and we were the first and only one."

Nerissa talked the *International Herald Tribune* into taking her ads, saying they would be doing their readers a favor. "People are traveling here from around the world. It helps them so they know when they come to New York they can meet a friend, have companionship."

"When I went to the *Village Voice*, that's when I really lost it."

I liked this story because of the irony. In 1973, the *Voice* was one of the country's most influential voices of the counterculture. They refused to run her ad unless it used the euphemistic "International Promotions."

"I got angry and said I wanted to speak to the manager," Nerissa recalled, delicately putting down one of the little chocolate cookies she'd nibbled.

"They said I couldn't. I started crying and pushed into this half-open door. There was the publisher. He saw I was really agitated so he asked if I wanted a cup of tea."

"I said," Nerissa's voice rose, relating the moment, " 'Are you telling me that all the time I lived on my tiny little island that I heard about this big country America, they have such freedom of press? You are telling me that Americans are so stupid that if I place an ad that they don't want it's going to influence them to use my service? They're so dumb they can't make up their own minds? Are you telling me this society of people I've always thought of as so progressive needs you to dictate to them what they can and can't read? They need you to censor an ad so that they can't make up their own minds?' "

The publisher of the *Village Voice* told Nerissa that they would give her an answer in two weeks. The ad ran.

Nerissa Braimbridge ran her ads for her escort service in *New York* magazine for a number of years through the 1970s. One day she got a call from their advertising department, saying they could no longer accept her advertising. The very next week she opened the magazine to find a story that splashed its title across two pages: "Whores." It was about women who worked as call girls.

Sydney Biddle Barrows told me that she remembered *New York* had an escort service category for a while, but they dropped it. "Now they don't have ads for escort services, they have massage and role-play ads, which is exactly the same thing. I don't know who they think they're kidding."

At this moment, Nerissa's assistant came to ask us if we would shift to an inner office. A client was coming in to peruse their books of escorts. We picked up our things and moved, passing a tall, extremely handsome young businessman with heavy dark hair falling down over one eye. His clothing was expensive and he wore it well. I overheard pieces of the conversation. He was the fantasy client, here in the flesh.

In her office, she gave me copies of her advertising, and her written promotional material. With full-color illustrations, International Promotions described the lavish possibilities that were available, with escorts as "Corporate Hosts d'Affaires, multilingual and exceptional social companions . . . get-away companions, vacations, sporting events, leisure, the arts, and adventure."

There was the chance to "Give An Escort," "A unique gift idea for visiting business associates, clients, relatives and friends." "Beautiful People Unlimited—Models, spokespersons and other creative talents available to enhance and project your companies image graciously, adding glamour, sparkle and pizazz to any occasion: publicity, presentations, special events."

She provided a sheet of "Recent Examples," of her company's use, little vignettes:

> "A grateful businessman wanted to show his appreciation to his attorney and friend (a bachelor), who had recently won a case for his company, and was in town for a short visit. He arranged . . . to devise an 'Evening-on-Town' package which was to include a very beautiful and elegant escort who would accompany his friend to dinner in a top restaurant followed by some dancing at a popular nightclub, complete with a limousine that was always at their disposal. The attorney, who did not know anyone else socially in the city, was very pleased with his friend's thoughtfulness."
> "A female client (A European aristocrat) regularly retains distinguished-looking male escorts to squire her to her black tie affairs . . . ."

Nerissa also wrote of shopping expeditions for corporate wives, the thirty-five escorts at the shipping party whose job it was "to look terrific and mix and mingle with the guests, steering conversations toward

subjects their clients were interested in promoting," and the toy manufacturer who hired an escort to dress as the doll he was promoting.

I was confused reviewing this material, not knowing if any of it was
real. She handed these elaborate brochures out to clients. I became
impressed by her imagination, and realized that Nerissa *would* supply
all the above. It was her fantasy business. Whatever her clients dreamed
about, she would create.

* * *

Nerissa has four daughters, one a doctor who first received a degree
in engineering and then decided she wanted to use that technology in
medicine. She went to medical school and got a second degree. Another daughter has a masters in education and is married to a doctor. A
third daughter is studying electrical engineering, and the youngest
graduated as a mathematician. They live in New Jersey and Florida.

"My daughters are strong and independent women," Nerissa said.
"When you grow up in a society like I am from, you recognize that you
were held back as a woman. You come to a country like this and you see
that women have a certain amount of power."

"Once I started this, I was not going to back out. I believed in what I
was doing." She said that with off-season Broadway actresses and dancers, flight attendants with spare nights in town, and former beauty
queens, they soon had a group of extraordinary women. Their media
continued to cover them, with stories appearing in international business and popular culture magazines and newspapers. A big article about
International appeared in *Cosmopolitan* magazine. Nerissa, who'd long
admired Helen Gurley Brown's "message of enhancing and celebrating
womenhood," deeply appreciated this.

In her office, flipping through the pages of media coverage that
spanned nearly twenty-five years, Nerissa paused thoughtfully. "When
you need to survive, you do what you have to do," she said. In her case,
to survive had meant learning the language of the society that used
escort services, but insisted that the services be hidden. Nerissa had
created the best escort service in town, with fantasy parties on yachts
and fantasy catered affairs, for clients who wished to remain invisible.

* * *

"I have no end of respect for the girls who work for us. They have to
make their way, and it's tough," she said. She slid a sheaf of papers
across the desk to me. "This is an agreement that the girls have to sign.

You may want to keep this. This is just between you and me. Do not. . . ."

"Don't write about what's in this?" I asked, and she nodded.

"Yes. This is just between you and I," she emphasized. "Just so you get an idea of the agreement that these girls have to sign. And these," she gave me more papers, "Are the actual rules and regulations for the escorts." She went on to say that not everyone wanted to work for her because she required them to divulge their name, address, and social security number, which is unusual, as many people in the business want to avoid paying tax. International maintained employee's anonymity and never divulged who they were. Over the years, clients as well as escorts learned to trust her.

She talked all afternoon, about sex in other cultures, and philosophical considerations of prostitution. She thought legalization would make things worse, because bringing prostitution into the open would not change attitudes. "You can make it legal but not respectable," she said. She told me she had traveled to Japan to learn about the geisha, a role that was regarded as honorable, unlike the Western concept of the same.

"I stood on the steps of the Acropolis when I was in Greece," she told me. "And thought of how the Greeks believed their Gods were literal, and now, we call them myths. Is that how our religions will be seen one thousand years from now? Will none of this matter?"

*   *   *

Nerissa left a message on my machine a week later, saying she'd talked to her lawyer. She'd made a terrible mistake in showing me the contract from her escort service. I must promise never, never to reveal its contents. The lawyer said she was a fool to trust me with it.

The one thing I did know was that she was no fool. Giving me that contract was her way of influencing the story, of forcing society to acknowledge its connection to her work. It was no accident. Nerissa Braimbridge gave me that contract so that in the end, I would have the opportunity to give it back to her, signed.

Afterword

When I began the reporting that became this book I knew little about the people I would encounter and less about their lives and work. I thought of it in terms of "them" and "us," seeing little connection between "their" world and "ours." Now I know we inhabit the same social spaces, different parts perhaps, connected more deeply that I could have imagined.

We'll always have sexual behavior (seemingly) outside the confines of polite society. It's not going away, nor should it. There are problems that are not easy to resolve because they are most often the consequences of the very sanctions society imposes on unorthodox behavior. We want to buy sex we can't find at home. But if you work to provide that service for us and get paid in the bargain you will earn our disapproval. We may have to punish you, but don't stop delivering the goods.

It's a very intimate relationship.

We have a sex industry because we need and want one. Understanding the people in this huge industry is not helped by either idealizing or condemning them. The idea here is to learn from them, to use the opportunity to bisect with their lives, to see better how society measures the conventions it imposes with prescribed behavior and regulations. It is not only our secret wishes and disavowed parts that take form here, but questions we wrestle with in our private and public lives: definitions of what's moral and healthy, good and bad, and notions of sex roles and sexual identity.

Sexual activity considered abnormal or deviant (not to mention immoral or dangerous) is hard for much of society to tolerate. This seems because it is a mirror we're fearful of stepping through: the reflection can unsettle. What I hoped to do in writing this book was to allow the people in it to be seen as individuals who warrant our respect, even our admiration. The way I was conditioned to see the world before this resulted in seeing things in a disavowed, shadowy way. This provided an education. I also wanted to do something like that child who mentioned that the Emperor was actually naked: once you acknowledge what your eyes report, the collective deception begins to lessen its hold. *We* provide the work for the people in this book. They act out our hidden desires. The more we acknowledge this exchange and learn about them, the better we could understand aspects of our selves and our own sexuality. As I said, it's an intimate relationship, possibly best expressed in the wedding between an aerialist and a dwarf in Todd Browning's 1932 film *Freaks*. "One of us, one of us!" chant the freaks as the assembled characters raise their glasses in a toast.

Suggested Reading

It's impossible to put together a complete list of sex-related books and papers consulted for *Working Sex*. Here's a start . . .

And The Band Played On: Politics, People, and the AIDS Epidemic, Randy Shilts, Penguin, 1988

Bowers v. Hardwick: The Enigmatic Fifth Vote and the Reasonableness of Moral Certitude, Allan Ides, Washington and Lee Law Review, 1991

Boys Will Be Boys: Breaking the Link Between Masculinity and Violence, Myriam Miedzian, Anchor/Doubleday, 1991

Coming of Age in Samoa, Margaret Mead, American Museum of Natural History Press, 1928

Cross-Dressing, Sex, and Gender, Vern L. Bullough and Bonnie Bullough, University of Pennsylvania Press, 1993

Defending Pornography: Free Speech, Sex, and the Fight for Women's Rights, Nadine Strossen, Scribner, 1995

Disorders of Sexual Desire and Other New Concepts and Techniques in Sex Therapy by Helen Singer Kaplan, M.D., Ph.D., Brunner/Mazel, New York, 1979

Erotism: Death and Sensuality, Georges Bataille, City Lights Books, 1975

Female Perversions, Louise J. Kaplan, Anchor Books, 1991

Feminine Psychology, Karen Horney, M.D., W.W. Norton, 1967

Feminine Sexuality, Jacques Lacan, edited by Juliet Mitchell and Jacqueline Rose, W.W. Norton, 1982

Fragments for a History of the Human Body, Parts I, II, III, edited by Michel Feher, with Romona Naddaff and Nadio Tazi, Zone Books, New York, 1989

Freaks: Myths and Images of the Secret Self, Leslie Fiedler, Simon & Schuster, 1978

Free Speech for Me—But Not for Thee: How the American Left and Right Relent-

lessly Censor Each Other, Nat Hentoff, Aaron Asher Books, Harper Collins, 1993

From Reverence To Rape: The Treatment of Women in the Movies, Molly Haskell, University of Chicago Press, 1987

Gender Politics: From Consciousness to Mass Politics, Ethel Klein, Harvard University Press, 1984

Getting Together: A Guide To Sexual Enrichment For Couples, Drs. Leon and Shirley Zussman with Jeremy Brecher, William Morrow, 1979

How To Attain and Practice the Ideal Sex Life by Dr. J. Rutgers, Intended For Circulation Among Mature Persons Only, Cadillac Publishing Company, New York, 1940

Letters To Judy: What Your Kids Wish They Could Tell You, Judy Blume, G.P. Putnam & Sons, 1988

Liberty & Sexuality: The Right To Privacy and the Making of Roe. v. Wade, David J. Garrow, Macmillan, 1994

Life After Hardwick, Nan D. Hunter, Harvard Civil Liberties Law Review, 1992

Lovemaps: Clinical Concepts of Sexual/Erotic Health and Pathology, Paraphilia, and Gender Transposition in Childhood, Adolescence, and Maturity, Prometheus Books, 1986

Lust, Lack of Desire, and Paraphilias: Some Thoughts and Possible Connections, Charles Moser, Ph.D., M.D., Journal of Sex & Marital Therapy, Vol.18, No. Spring 1992, Brunner/Mazel, Inc.

Making Sex: Body and Gender from the Greeks to Freud, Thomas Laqueur, Harvard University Press, 1992

Man and Women, Boy and Girl: Differentiation and Dimorphism of Gender Identity From Conception to Maturity, John Money and Anke A. Ehnhardt, Johns Hopkins University Press

Masochism: Coldness and Cruelty, Gilles Deleuze, and *Venus In Furs*, Leopold von Sacher-Masoch, both by Zone Books, New York, 1989

Observing The Erotic Imagination, Robert J. Stoller, Yale University Press, 1985

Pain and Passion: A Psychoanalyst Explores the World of S&M, Robert L. Stoller, Plenum Press, 1991

Perversions and Near Perversions in Clinical Practice: New Psychoanalytic Perspectives, edited by Gerald I. Fogel, M.D., Wayne Meyers, M.D., Yale University Press, 1991

Refusing to Be a Man: Essays on Sex and Justice, John Stoltenberg, Breitenbush Books, Inc.

Ritualized Homosexuality in Melanasia, Gilbert H. Herdt, University of California Press, 1984

Sadomasochism: Etiology and Treatment, Susanne P. Schad-Somers, Ph.D., Human Sciences Press, 1982

Sadomasochism: Studies in Domination and Submission, edited by Thomas S. Weinberg, Prometheus Books, 1995

Sex By Prescription, Thomas Szasz, Anchor/Doubleday, 1980

Sex For One: The Joy of Selfloving, Betty Dodson, Crown, 1996

Sex Law: A Legal Sourcebook on Critical Sexual Issues for the Non-Lawyer, Scott E. Friedman, McFarland & Co., 1990

Sex, Sin & Blasphemy—A Guide To Americas Censorship Wars, Marjorie Heins, The New Press, 1993

Sexist Justice, Karen DeCrow, Random House, 1974

Sexual Awareness: Enhancing Sexual Pleasure, Barry and Emily McCarthy, Carroll & Graf, 1993

Sexual Excitement, Robert J. Stoller, Pantheon, 1976

Sexual Violence: Our War Against Rape by Linda A. Fairstein, Berkley, New York, 1993

Symposium: The Sex Panic: Women, Censorship, and "Pornography," New York Law School Review, 1994

Taking a Sex History: Interviewing and Recording, Wardell B. Pomeroy, Carol Flax, Connie Christein Wheeler, Free Press, 1982

The Act of Marriage, The Beauty of Sexual Love, by Tim and Beverly LeHaye, Zondervan Press, 1976

The Best of Skin II, edited by Tim Woodward, a Richard Kasak Book, 1993

The Celluloid Closet: Homosexuality in the Movies, Vito Russo, Harper & Row, 1981

The Female Eunuch, Germaine Greer, McGraw Hill, 1971

The History of Sexuality, Vols. I, II, III, Michel Foucault, Vintage Books, 1990

The Horny Teenagers' Guide to Sex . . . and Drugs, AIDS, Parents, the First Time, Broken Hearts, and More, P. Bragg, a P. Bragg Book, 1988

The Love Teachings of Kama Sutra, Crescent Books, 1980

The New Male Sexuality: The Truth about Men, Sex, and Pleasure, Bernie Zilbergeld, Ph.D., Bantam Books, 1992

The Second Sex, Simone DeBeauvoir, Alfred A. Knopf, 1952

The Sexually Abused Male, Volumes I & II, edited by Mic Hunter, Lexington Books, DC Health and Company, Lexington, Massachusetts/Toronto, 1990

Transsexualism and Sex Reassignment, edited by William A. Walters, Michael Ross, Oxford University Press, 1986

Vandalized Lovemaps, John Money, Prometheus Books, Buffalo, NY, 1989

Women Against Censorship, edited by Varda Burstyin, Douglas McIntyre, New York Law Journal, 1985

Index

AASECT, *see* American Association of Sex Education, Counselors, and Therapists
Abrams, Floyd, 76
Abstinence, good health and, 20–21
Ackerman Institute, 156
Acrotomophilia, 188
Adam & Eve, 80–89
Adults Only, 36
Adult Video News, 87
Adult videos, *see* Videos
Alan (transsexual), 203, 207
American Association of Sex Education, Counselors, and Therapists (AASECT), 65, 68, 81, 214
American Psychological Association, 71–76
Anderson, Kurt, 170
Antipornography activists, xv, 40–41, 46, 49, 50, 57–59, 60, 65, 66, 69, 71, 72, 73, 76, 78, 79
Ask Me Anything: A Sex Therapist Answers the Most Important Questions for the '90's (Klein), 185

Backlash (Faludi), 60
Ball Games, 53–54
Barbach, Lonnie, 65
Barber, Candy, 54
Barnard conference, on women's sexuality in society, 58–59
Barnes v. Indiana, 95–96, 118–20
Barrows, Sydney Biddle, 8, 9, 246–47, 252, 271–72

Bayer, William, 8
Becker, Judith, 32
Becoming a Sexual Person (Francoeur), 21
Becoming Orgasmic, 81, 86–87
Benjamin, Harry, 209–12, 224, 227
Benjamin, Harry, Scale, 210–11, 224
Benjamin, Harry, Society, 212, 227
  Standards of Care of, 212
Bentkowski, Tom, 22–23
Bernard, Jami, 65
Better Sex Video Series, The, 82–86, 88
Behind The Green Door, 43
Bill (transsexual), 235–36
Bird, Lance, 151
Bisexuals, 211
  transsexuals as, 234–35, 236–38
Black Book, The, 98
Black, Timothy, 80
Blanton, Lavada, 58
Blue Magic, 56
Blume, Judy, 77
Bodysex Workshops, of Dodson, 13, 14, 15, 18, 19, 20
  for men and couples, 27–29
  for women, 13, 14, 15, 18, 19, 20, 22–27
Bondage, *see* Domination and submission (D & S)
Bookers, for escort services, 3–4, 7, 244, 254–59
Bowers v. Hardwick, 119
Boy Scout Handbook, masturbation and, 21
Braimbridge, Nerissa, 247, 268–74

Brent, Bill, 98
"Bright Lights, Big Titties," 32–33
Brody, Jane, 20
Brown, Rita Mae, 57
Brown, Helen Gurley, 273
Browning, Todd, 276
Buchanan, Pat, 77
Bullough, Vern and Connie, 212–13
Butler, Jerry, 64
Byrd, Robin, 97, 100, 101–4, 140–41

Cachet, 246
CALACT (Californians Against
    Censorship Together), 44
Calderone, Mary S., 31
Califia, Pat, 155
Call girls, *see* Escorts/escort services
Carrie (slave of Ava Taurel), 167, 177–
    80, 198–99
Child pornography, 36
Chippendales, 98, 109, 114–15, 116–17,
    264
Christian, Damon, 51
Christine's Secret, 64
Chuck (male escort), 263–68
Club 90, 32, 62–63
Cole, Sandra, 68–69
Cole, Ted, 68
Condoms, Harvey and, 80–81, 87–88,
    90
Conference on Women's Sexuality, of
    National Organization of Women,
    19
Contract, in domination and submission,
    143–44, 146, 150, 155
Cornflakes, as antimasturbation food, 21
Cosmopolitan, escort service article in,
    273
Couples
    domination and submission and, 174,
    184–85
    masturbation taught to, 28, 29
Courts
    on pornographic films, 43, 49, 57, 88,
    89
    on stripping, 95–96, 117–20
Cousteau, Desirée, 50, 51
Crary, Jonathan, 168
"Creating Adult Erotica That Presents
    Positive Sexual Role Modeling,"
    71–76
Crichton, Michael, 92

Cross Dressing, Sex, and Gender
    (Bullough and Bullough), 212–13
Cross-dressing, *see* Transvestism
Crown Club, 4, 243, 246, 247
Crystal, *see* King, Dianah

Deane, Mark, 117, 118, 122, 127
De Beauvoir, Simone, 92
Deep Throat, 35, 43
DeGrazia, Ed, 43
Deleuze, Gilles, 144, 145, 151, 164
De Sade, Marquis, 144, 145
Devon (male stripper), 115–16
Diary of a Conference on Sexuality, 59
DKT, 87–88
Dodson, Betty, xiv, 13–29, 70, 90
    art of, 16, 17, 18–19
    Bodysex Workshops of, 13, 14, 15,
    18, 19, 20, 22–29
    "Liberating Masturbation" (article) by,
    17–18
    Liberating Masturbation (book) by, 19,
    58
    mission of, 17–18, 20, 23, 25, 26, 27
    popularity of, 19
    pornographic films and, 56, 58
    reactions to, 13–15, 17, 18, 19–20, 25
    Sex for One, The Joy of Selfloving by,
    15, 18, 19
    videotapes produced by, 19–20
    workshops for men and couples run
    by, 27–29
    workshops for women run by, 13, 14,
    15, 18, 19, 20, 22–27
Domestic violence, 156–57
Domination and submission (D & S),
    143–99
    consensual versus nonconsensual, 155–
    56, 182–86
    contract in, 143–44, 146, 150, 155
    couples and, 174, 184–85
    critique of, 72–73, 74, 153–57, 182–
    86, 197
    definition of, 172
    dominatrix and, 143–44, 146, 147,
    148–53, 157–68, 182–86, *see also*
    Taurel, Ava, *below*
    earnings, 153, 162
    fetishes and, 145–46, 153, 161–62
    gay, 155
    phone sessions, 159
    political philosophers on, 143–46
    Ava Taurel and, 71, 72, 73, 146, 148,

Domination and submission (D & S)
(cont.)
152, 161, 166–67, 171–83, 186–91,
194, 195–96, 197–99
therapists/sexologists on, 145–46, 147,
153–57, 158–60, 174, 182–86, 187,
197
Veronica Vera on, 36–38
dominatrix, 143–44, 146, 147, 148–53,
157–68, 182–86
see also Taurel Ava
Donnerstein, Edward, 32
Double-O-Sappho (Kim), 222
Dowd, Maureen, 91, 92, 93, 94
Dworkin, Andrea, xv, 41, 56, 60, 73

Edelweiss, 219, 221, 229–38
Eisenberg, Lee, 23
Ellis, Albert, 210
Ephron, Nora, 78
Erotic films, *see* Pornographic films
Erotic products, Adam & Eve selling,
80–89
"Escort: What I Learned Job-Hunting
In the World of Sex For Sale"
(Macy), xi–xii, 3–11
Escorts/escort services, 3–11, 241, 243–
74
bookers for, 3–4, 7, 244, 254–59
busted for prostitution (Cachet), 8,
246
earnings of, 246, 250, 255, 256–58,
265, 266
madam and, 4
media accepting ads from, 270–72
men requesting men, 259–62, 267
men requesting women, 254–59, 268–
74
nature of women working as, 257–59
nature of work of, 6, 7, 11
New York magazine article on, xi–xii,
3–11
raided for money laundering, 246–48
requirements for, 3, 4, 5, 6, 243–44,
255, 256
therapists/sexologists on, 8
women requesting men, 245–46, 249–
54, 261, 263–68
Evergreen Review, Dodson in, 17
Eve's Garden, 58
Exotic Dancers Directory, The, 97–98
Exotic dancing, *see* Strippers
Explicit films, *see* Pornographic films

FACT, *see* Feminist Anti-Censorship
Task Force
Faludi, Susan, 60
Fantasies Unlimited, 109, 112
Fascination, 54–55
Female Eunuch, The (Greer), 15
Female Perversions (Kaplan), 59, 158–59,
168
Feminine Mystique, The (Friedan), 77
Feminist Anti-Censorship Task Force
(FACT), 57
Feminists
masturbation and, 14–15
pornographic films and, 37, 56–60,
76–80
Feminists For Free Expression (FFE),
37, 56–60, 76
Femme Productions, xv, 40, 42, 46, 47,
48, 49, 53, 63–67, 68, 69–70, 89–
90
Fetishes, in domination and submission,
145–46, 153, 161–62
FFE, *see* Feminists For Free Expression
Fiedler, Leslie, xiii, xiv, 153, 157
Finan, Chris, 78
Fitterman, Marilyn, 78
Fogelnest, Robert, 168
Foucault, Michel, 144, 146
Francoeur, Robert T., 21
Franklin Furnace, 60, 62–63, 64
Freaks (film), 276
*Freaks: Myths and Images of the Secret
Self* (Fiedler), xiii, xiv
Freeman decision, 43
Free Speech Coalition, 44
Freud, Anna, 72
Freud, Sigmund, 145
Friday, Nancy, 49, 78
Friedan, Betty, 57, 77
Futter, Ellen V., 58–59

Gaiety Theater, 100, 113–14, 115–16
Gardos, Peter Sandor, 117–18
Gatta, Gina, 98
Gay dance clubs, 95, 96, 98, 100, 105,
106, 109–10, 113–14
Gays
domination and submission and, 155
nude dancing and, 95, 96, 98, 100,
105, 106, 109–10, 113–14
Gender dysphoria, 203, 212
see also Transsexualism

Gerard (lover of Ava Taurel), 180–82, 199
Gillers, Stephen, 118, 119
Godard, Jean-Luc, 43
Government, pornographic films and, 31–39, 40, 43–44, 49, 57, 80, 88–89
Graham, Sylvester, 20–21
Green, Richard, 168, 210
Greenwald, Harold, 8
Greer, Germaine, 14–15
Gross, Amy, 13–14
Grove Press, 17
    Evergreen Review and, 17
    I Am Curious Yellow and, 43
Gynemimetophile, 216

Hard Soap, Hard Soap, 48, 49–50
Harkins, Deborah, 5
Hart, Veronica, 62
Hartley, Nina, 44
Harvey, Phil, 80–90
Headspace, 219
    see also Lovemaps
Hill, Kirk, xiv, 94–95, 96, 97, 98, 100–101, 102, 103–14, 117, 121, 131, 132–33, 138, 140–41
Hite, Shere, 25, 242
Hollander, Xaviera, 177–78, 179, 180
Holmes, John, 48, 50
Homosexuals
    behavioral deconditioning for, 73–74
    transsexuals and, 211, 213
    see also Lesbians
Hot and Saucy Pizza Girls, 50–51
Hot Rackets, 51–53
Human Sexuality (Masters and Johnson), 27, 83
Human Sexual Response (Masters and Johnson), 20, 22
Hunter, Nan, 57

I Am Curious Yellow, 16, 43
Idol, Billy, 255
Ihlenfeld, Charles, 209–10, 211, 227–29
Indiscretions, I through IV, 44
Institute for the Advanced Study of Human Sexuality, 227
Instructional sex videos, 81–89
International Commission for Prostitutes Rights, 262
International Escorts, 5, 168, 247

International Herald Tribune, ads for escort services in, 271
Ivans, Molly, 77

Jay (male escort), 251–54
Johnson, Virginia, 20, 22, 27, 83, 96
Jon (male escort), 259–62
Jong, Erica, 78
Jorgensen, Christine, 209, 210, 223
Joy (stripper), 122–23, 124, 127, 128, 131, 132–33, 138

Kaminer, Wendy, 78
Kaplan, Helen Singer, 20, 71–76, 104
Kaplan, Louise J., 59, 145, 153, 158–59, 168
Kara (transsexual), 205
Kate (transsexual), 203–5
Katz, Leanne, 76–77, 79
Kegel, 20
Kellogg, John Harvey, 21
Kellogg, William Keith, 21
Kelly (transsexual), 205
Kim (transsexual), 221–27, 239, 240
King, Dianah, xiv, 92–93, 94–95, 96–97, 98–99, 100, 101, 102–3, 104, 107–8, 109, 110–13, 114, 117, 120–24, 127–29, 130–40
Kinsey, Alfred, 211, 212
Klein, Marty, 182–86
Kollar, Michael, 82–84
Kosner, Ed, 5, 8, 163, 167, 169, 170, 193

Laqueur, Thomas, 21–22
Law, Sylvia, 57
Leah (booker for escorts), 254–59
Leanard, Gloria, 60, 62
LeBears, 98
Leigh, Vivien, 92
Leilani (pornography star), 48, 50
Leitenberg, Harold, 213, 222, 226
Lesbians, transsexuals as, 221–27
Levine, Ellen, 32, 79–80
Levine, Larry, 193, 194–96
Lewis, Anthony, 76
"Liberating Masturbation" (Dodson), 17–18
Liberating Masturbation (Dodson), 19, 58
Lilly, Bobby, 44
Linz, Daniel, 32
Lovelace-Marciano, Linda, 35

Lovemaps (Money), 188
Lovemaps, Money and, 154, 188, 219, 261
Lucky Stiff, The, 54
Lynne, Amber, 121, 122, 124–27, 129–30, 140

McAlary, Mike, 247–48
McCarthy, Barry, 242, 243
McCarthy, Emily, 242
MacKinnon, Catharine, xv, 41, 46, 56, 57, 60, 65, 66, 71, 72, 73, 76, 78, 79
Madonna, 147, 238, 251, 252
Maidenform, 76
Mailer, Norman, 43
Making Sex (Laqueur), 21–22
Malle, Louis, 270
Maltz, Wendy, 182–87, 189, 192
Mans, Geoff, 155
Maquire, Jennifer, 58
Margold, Bill, 44, 67
Marie Claire, Dodson in, 14–15
Mark's Showplace, 111–12, 117, 120–24
Masochism, 145, 151
    see also Domination and submission
Masters, William, 20, 22, 27, 83, 96
Masturbation
    facts on, 13, 20–22
    teaching, xiv, 13–29, *see also* Dodson, Betty
Mayflower Madam case, 8
Mayflower Madame, The (Barrows), 9, 253
Media Coalition, 78
Meese, Edwin, 88
Meese Commission, 31–39, 49, 73, 80
Miller, John, 248
Millet, Kate, 57
Moglia, Ron, 71, 168, 187
Money, John, 20–21, 32, 154, 168, 188, 210, 216, 219, 237, 261
Moore, Demi, 91, 92, 93, 94
Moser, Charles, 73, 217, 227
Moser, Donald, 99–100, 116
Ms. Magazine, Dodson in, 17

National Coalition Against Censorship (NCAC), 58, 76–78, 79
National Organization of Women (NOW), 19, 42
NCAC, *see* National Coalition Against Censorship

Nero, Susy, 62
New York Magazine
    ads for escort services in, 271–72
    article on escorts in, xi–xii, 3–11
    domination and submission article and, 149, 193–96
New York Psychiatric Association, 18
New York Times
    on adult videos, 87
    Dowd article on strippers in, 91, 92, 93, 94
    MacKinnon pornography article in, 76
Nichols, Kelly, 62, 63
Niemi, Lauren, 64, 65, 70
Nine Lives Hath My Love, 47
Norvind, Eva, *see* Taurel, Ava
NOW, *see* National Organization of Women
Noyes, Andrew, 127, 128
Nude dancing, *see* Strippers

O'Keefe, Georgia, 18
Onanism, *see* Dodson, Betty; Masturbation
Only Words (MacKinnon), 46, 76
Ordinary Couples, Extraordinary Sex, 82

Page, Betty, 36
Paglia, Camille, 92
Pally, Marcia, 37, 57, 59, 76
Pamela (stripper), 123, 131
Paraphilia, 154, 188
Pauly, Ira, 210
Pendergast, William, 192
Penn & Teller, 57
Perfume, 189–90
Per (husband of Candida Royalle), 45–46, 47, 56, 64, 70
Perry, Ann, 53
Perversion, therapists/sexologists on, 153–54, 158–59, 197
Petty, Rhonda Jo, 64
PHE, 88
Phillips, Mary, 17
Photographer, The, 64
Piano, The, 64
Pleasure and Danger: Exploring Female Sexuality (Vance), 58
Pomeroy, Wardell, 210
PONY, *see* Prostitutes of New York
Pornographic films, xv, 16, 31–90
    Adam & Eve and, 80–89

Pornographic films *(cont.)*
  antipornography activists and, xv, 40–41, 46, 49, 50, 57–59, 60, 65, 66, 69, 71, 72, 73, 76, 78, 79
  background of, 43
  child pornography and, 36
  Club 90 and, 32, 62–63
  courts on, 43, 49, 57, 58, 88, 89
  critiques of, 41, 44, 55–56, 60, 61, 67–69, 71–76
  Betty Dodson and, 56, 58
  feminists and, 37, 56–60, 76–80
  Feminists for Free Expression and, 37, 56–60, 76
  Femme Productions and, xv, 40, 42, 46, 47, 48, 49, 51, 53, 63–67, 68, 69–70, 89–90
  government and, 31–39, 40, 43–44, 49, 57, 80, 88–89
  Margold on, 44–45
  Meese Commission report on, 31–39, 49, 73, 80
  myth vs. reality of, 33–35
  rape fantasies and, 38–39, 49
  Candida Royalle and, xv, 40–43, 45–56, 58, 60–62, 63–67, 68, 69–70, 71, 74, 75, 89–90
  therapists/sexologists on, 32, 59–60, 67–69, 71–76, 77
  Veronica Vera on, xiii, 32–39, 62, 63
  videos and, 40, 59, 64, 73, 80–89, 95
Pornography Victims Compensation Act, 57
Portrait of a Sexual Evolutionary (Vera), 33
Power, *see* Domination and submission
Presidential Commission on Obscenity and Pornography, *see* Meese Commission
Pretty Woman, 250
Project Post Porn, 88
Prostitutes of New York (PONY), 10, 11, 262–63
Prostitution, 92, 210
  escort services busted for, 8, 246
  legalization of, 10
  rights groups for, 262–63
  transsexual, 215–21, 228, 229–38
  see also Escorts/escort services
PSI, 87–88
Psychologists, *see* Therapists/sexologists

Rakelle (stripper), 131, 132
Ramos, Norma, 66
Rape fantasies, pornographic films and, 38–39, 49
Raymond, Janice, 212, 222
Rechy, John, 155
Rehnquist, William A., 118, 119
Residents, The, xiii-xiv
Revelations, 70
Rich, Adrienne, 57
Rich, Frank, 91, 92
Richards, Renee, 210, 211
Robin (transsexual), 205–6, 208
Robin Byrd Show, The, 97, 100, 101–4, 140–41
Rosemary (transsexual), 204
Rosset, Barney, 17, 43
Royalle, Candida, xv, 40–43, 45–56, 58, 60–62, 63–67, 68, 69–70, 71, 74, 75, 89–90
Ruppell, Howard, 147, 160
Rush, Florence, 42

Sacher-Masoch, Leopold von, 143, 144–45, 146, 153
Sadomasochism, *see* Domination and submission
Sandstone retreat, 13, 21
Schad-Somers, Susanne, 154, 155, 159, 168
Schaefer, Leah Cahan, 209–10, 211, 212, 224
Schroeder, Marianne, 227, 228
Seicus, *see* Sex Education and Information Council of the United States
Seifer, Judith, 82–83, 85
Seiman, Catherine, 58
Seka (porn star), 34, 38
Sex (Madonna), 147, 251, 252
Sex and Sensibility (Pally), 57
Sex Education and Information Council of the United States (Seicus), 209
Sex For One, The Joy of Selfloving (Dodson), 15, 18, 19
Sex industry
  disavowal of, 104
  reason for existence of, xiv, 104, 275–76
  therapists/sexologists on, 188
Sex offenders
  Taurel and, 191–92, 197, 198
  therapists/sexologists on, 192

Sexologists, *see* Therapists/sexologists
Sex Over 40, 87
Sex roles
    response to pornographic films and,
        67
    response to strippers and, 99–100
    reversal of, *see* Domination and
        submission
    sexual performance and, 106, 241–43
    therapists/sexologists on, 59–60, 106,
        241–43
Sex therapy, 75, 241–43
    see also Therapists/sexologists
Sexual Attitude Reassessments, 202
Sexual Behavior of the Human Male
    (Kinsey), 211
Sexual boutique, Eve's Garden as, 58
Sexual dysfunction, sex roles and, 241–
    43
*Sexual Healing Journey, A Guide For
    Survivors of Sexual Abuse, The*
    (Maltz), 182
Sexual Outlaw, The (Rechy), 155
Sexual psychology, *see* Lovemaps
Sexual relationship, paid-for sex versus
    everyday, 241–43
Sheen, Charlie, 255
Sheinberg, Marsha, 156, 157
Sinclair, Lloyd, 81
Sinclair Institute, 86, 87
S&M, *see* Domination and submission
Snitow, Ann, 57
Society for the Scientific Study of Sex,
    117, 147, 188, 210
Sonya, Mistress, 150–52, 163–66
Souter, David H., 95–96, 119–20
Specter, Arlen, 35–39
Spitz, Rene A., 20
Sprinkle, Annie, 58, 60, 62, 63
Stanley, Alyssa, 92
Stoller, Robert J., 44, 67, 69, 146, 155,
    168, 197
Strippers, xiv, 91–141
    courts and, 95–96, 117–20
    critiques of, 99–100, 104
    Dowd and, 91, 92, 93, 94
    earnings of, 100, 110, 112, 120, 121,
        124, 126, 127
    Kirk Hill, xiv, 94–95, 96, 97, 98,
        100–101, 102, 103–14, 117, 121,
        131, 132–33, 138, 140–41
    Dianah King, xiv, 92–93, 94–95, 96–
        97, 98–99, 100, 101, 102–3, 104,
        107–8, 109, 110–13, 114, 117,
        120–24, 127–29, 130–40
    Amber Lynne, 121, 122, 124–27,
        129–30, 140
    men dancing for men, 95, 96, 98, 99–
        100, 104, 105, 106, 109–10, 113–
        14, 115–17
    men dancing for women, 98, 100,
        108–9, 114–15, 116–17
    Demi Moore and, 91, 92, 93, 94
    requirements for, 100, 101
    The Robin Byrd Show and, 97, 100,
        101–4, 140–41
    therapists/sexologists on, 99–100
    women dancing for men, 97, 98–99
    women dancing for women, 98
Striptease, 91
Strossen, Nadine, 78
Sue (transsexual), 202–3, 213–21, 224,
    226, 229, 239–40
Supreme Court
    I Am Curious Yellow and, 43
    on nude dancing, 95–96, 117–20
    on stripping, 95–96, 118–20
Susan
    dominatrix, 147, 148–53, 159, 160–
        68, 169, 170
    escort service madam, 4
Suzi, Mistress, 213–21
Szaz, Thomas, 154

Talese, Gay, 13, 14, 21, 245
Taurel, Ava, 58, 71, 72, 73, 146, 148,
    152, 161, 166–67, 171–83, 194,
    195–96, 197–99, 231
Therapists/sexologists
    on domination and submission, 145–
        46, 147, 153–57, 158–60, 174,
        182–86, 187, 197
    on escort services, 8
    on instructional sex videos, 81, 82–84,
        85
    on masturbation, 20–22
    on perversion, 153–54, 158–59, 197
    on pornographic films, 32, 59–60, 67–
        69, 71–76, 77
    on sex industry, 188
    on sex offenders, 192
    on sex roles, 59–60, 106, 241–43
    on strippers, 99–100
    on transsexualism, 212–13, 216, 217,
        222, 226, 227–29
Thorp, Isaac, 8

Three Daughters, 48, 64, 65
Thy Neighbor's Wife (Talese), 13, 14, 21, 245
Tiefer, Leonore, 27, 77
Tight Bondage, 36, 39
Time Magazine, Dodson in, 16
Tissot, Samuel August, 21
Tom (transsexual), 236–38
Topless dancing, *see* Strippers
Transition, transsexualism and, 204
Transsexual Empire: The Making of the She-Male, The (Raymond), 212, 222
Transsexualism, xv, 201–40
  Benjamin and, 209–12, 224, 227
  bisexual, 234–35, 236–38
  clubs (Edelweiss) for, 219, 221, 229–38
  doctors involved with, 209–12, 227–29
  fantasy business and, 213–21
  female-to-male, 227
  gender dysphoria and, 203, 212
  hormonal treatment of, 216–17, 224, 227, 233, 234
  Ihlenfeld and, 227–29
  lesbians and, 221–27
  male-to-female, 201–8, 227–28
  opposition to, 212–13
  political, 228
  prostitution and, 215–21, 228, 229–38
  Standards of Care of Harry Benjamin Society and, 212
  suicide and, 240
  support groups for, 203–8
  surgery for, 222, 224–26
  Mistress Suzi and, 213–21
  therapists/sexologists on, 212–13, 216, 217, 222, 226, 227–29
  transition and, 204
  transvestism and, 73, 204–5, 220–21, 238
Transsexuality: The Epitome of Sexism and Homosexual Denial (Leitenberg), 213
Transsexual Phenomenon, The (Benjamin), 210
Transvestism (cross-dressing), 73, 204–5, 220–21, 238
Tribe, Lawrence, 119

Urban Aboriginals (Mans), 155
Urban Heat, 64, 89

Vamps (Kim), 222
Vance, Carol, 58
Vanity Fair
  Dowd and, 92
  Demi Moore and, 91
Venus in Furs (Sacher-Masoch), 143, 144–45, 153
Vera, Veronica, xiii, 32–39, 62, 63
Videos
  of Dodson's workshops, 19–20
  instructional sex, 81–89
  of pornographic films, 40, 59, 64, 73, 95
Village Voice, ads for escort services and domination and submission in, 195, 271
Vincent, Chuck, 54–55
Viper (porn star), 45
Vogue, Dodson in, 13–14

Waitt, Don, 97–98
Washington Post, Harvey and, 88
Waterloo Bridge, 92
Wattleton, Fay, 78
Webb, Alice, 212, 227, 228
Wendy (house mom for strippers), 132
Westheimer, Ruth, 15, 18
Wheeler, Christine, 209, 211, 212
White, Byron R., 119
Wickersham Gallery, Dodson's exhibit at, 16, 17
Williams, Dell, 58
Williamson, Bruce, 65
Willis, Ellen, 57
Winchell, Alex, 92
Wolf, Diane, 262–63
Woman's Traveler, The, 98
Women Against Pornography, 42, 59, 66

Xavier (stripper), 131
X-rated films, *see* Pornographic films
X-Rated Video Guide, The, 45

Yellow Pages, ads for escort services in, 243
Your Sexual Secrets (Klein), 185

Zeus Shopper, The, 95
Zussman, Leon, 242
Zussman, Shirley, 242